D0679206

RONIN

PRAISE FOR MIKE TUCKER

"One of the top five books to have come out of the Iraq War
is Mike Tucker's *Among Warriors in Iraq*. Tucker has
more street cred than any other war author."
—Matt LaPlante, *Salt Lake Tribune*

"In *Hell Is Over* Mike Tucker has told a story we should
know, but would not except for his bravery."
—Former Senator Bob Kerrey

"*The Long Patrol* is a refreshing, overdue look at what is
sadly one of Asia's least-reported stories: the Burmese junta's
continuing oppression of its ethnic minorities. Mike Tucker
crafts a thoughtful, humane, no-nonsense story about
the plight of the Karen freedom fighters."
—Joe Cochrane, *Newsweek*

"A classic on deep reconnaissance, *The Long Patrol*
should be required reading at the John F. Kennedy
Special Warfare Center and School."
—Maj. Kirk Windmueller, U.S. Army Special Forces

RONIN

A MARINE

SCOUT/SNIPER

PLATOON IN IRAQ

MIKE TUCKER

STACKPOLE
BOOKS

ISBN-13: 978-0-8117-0318-5

This book is for Ronin scout/sniper platoon,
the Marine scout/snipers of 2nd Battalion, 6th Marine Regiment,
2nd Marine Division, who kindly allowed me to attach to their missions
in Fallujah and western Iraq, September 22, 2005, to April 11, 2006.

And it is dedicated to the memory of the Marines
and members of the U.S. Army and Iraqi Army killed in action
in Fallujah, Al Saqlawiyah, Karmah, and all of western Iraq during
our combat tour of duty, September 2005 to April 2006;
Staff Sergeant Patrick Lybert, twenty-eight years old, Ladysmith,
Wisconsin, 10th Mountain Division, killed in action in Afghanistan,
June 21, 2006; and Private Raban "Anthony" Kimungu,
Black Label Platoon, Weapons Company, Second Battalion,
Sixth Marine Regiment, killed in a car accident
in New Hampshire on October 28, 2006.

It is further dedicated to my mother and father;
to St. Jude Thaddeus, Catholic patron saint of lost causes;
and to the memory of Saigyo, Japanese poet and Zen Buddhist.

"The mosques in Fallujah and western Iraq are terrorist COCs? You're asking me, for the record, yes or no answer? Yes. That is a very accurate statement. The mosques in Fallujah and western Iraq are terrorist command-and-control centers."

> —MAJOR MICHAEL MULLER,
> Marine advisor to the Iraqi Army in Fallujah,
> 25th Marine Regiment, January 9, 2006

"The Marines appointed Sheikh Khalid Hamood Mahal Al-Jumaili to the Fallujah City Council in December 2004. Just after Second Fallujah— Al Fajr, second battle of Fallujah. Sheikh Khalid is a known terrorist, with deep connections to Zarqawi and Al Qaeda. He was one of the most-wanted terrorists in Fallujah and western Iraq prior to Al Fajr. This is madness. The Americans are their own worst enemy. Sheikh Khalid remains on the Fallujah City Council, as we speak. He continues to support Al Qaeda. The Americans appointed him. That is like inviting Osama Bin Laden to dinner at the White House and appointing him to the Joint Chiefs of Staff."

> —AHMED,
> Iraqi interpreter and native of Mosul,
> February 2, 2006

"The American people have to know the truth on the street here; they deserve that from us. We know the ground truth of the war here; we know just how dirty and corrupt the Fallujah Police are, and we will not lie to our people. We will not lie to the parents of all of us who are going in harm's way here."

> —CORPORAL DUDLEY KELSO,
> Ronin3 assistant team leader, January 13, 2006

CONTENTS

RONIN SCOUT/SNIPER TEAMS

PLATOON SERGEANT
Staff Sergeant Christopher Williams, age thirty-three,
California, Marine scout/sniper and former Marine
scout/sniper instructor

CHIEF SCOUT AND SCOUT/SNIPER
Sergeant John Matter, age twenty-six, Wisconsin

RONIN1
Team leader: Sergeant Efraim Parra, age twenty-five, Colorado
Assistant team leader: Corporal Bobby Parker, age twenty-two,
Tennessee
Scout/sniper/grenadier: Lance Corporal Jason Hillestad, age
twenty-two, Maryland
Scout/sniper/light machine gunner: Lance Corporal Billy
Getscher, age nineteen, Maryland.

RONIN2
Team leader: Corporal Brian Areballo, age twenty-two,
Georgia
Assistant team leader: Corporal Noah Fleming, age twenty-
three, Virginia
Scout/sniper, grenadier, and demolitions specialist: Corporal
David Hodulich, age nineteen, Virginia
(For most of the deployment, this was a three-man team.)

RONIN3
    Team leader: Corporal Derrick Boyer, age twenty-two,
      Maryland
    Assistant team leader: Corporal Dudley Kelso, age twenty-two,
      Mississippi
    Scout/sniper and grenadier: Corporal Danny Milstid, age
      twenty-two, Florida
    Scout/sniper and light machine gunner: Corporal Kyle
      Palmer, age twenty-two, Mississippi

RONIN4
    Team leader: Corporal Darren Smykowski, age twenty-two,
      Ohio
    Assistant team leader: Corporal Justin Novi, age twenty-two,
      Pennsylvania
    Scout/sniper and grenadier: Corporal Jay Elder, age twenty-
      three, Massachusetts
    Scout/sniper and light machine gunner: Corporal Stephen
      Lutze, age twenty-two, Florida

RONIN HEADQUARTERS ELEMENT:
    Communications chief: Lance Corporal Jon Zwirblia, age
      twenty, Massachusetts
    Computer and photo specialist: Lance Corporal Jim Owen,
      age twenty, North Carolina
    Corpsman: "Doc Gute," HM3 Joshua James Gutierrez, U.S.
      Navy, age twenty-six, Texas

SIGNIFICANT ACTIONS OF RONIN SCOUT/SNIPER TEAMS

September 22, 2005: Ronin arrives at Camp Bahria forward operating base in western Iraq, near Fallujah, formerly called Forward Operating Base Volturno when western Iraq was under U.S. Army command (April 2003–March 27, 2004).

Mid-September 2005–mid-November 2005: Golf 2/6 firebase in Al Saqlawiyah, western Iraq, is mortared and rocketed nearly daily, sometimes twice a day, by Ahmed Sirhan's Black Flags Brigades and also Al Qaeda.

September 28, 2005: Muhammad, Iraqi Arab translator with two and a half years in combat in western Iraq, warns that Al Qaeda as well as Black Flags Brigades led by Ahmed Sirhan are using the main mosque in Al Saqlawiyah as a house of war and will use the mosque to attack the Golf 2/6 firebase and the police station within one month.

September 29, 2005: Lance Corporal Watson, Lance Corporal Matthews, and all of 3rd Platoon Golf 2/6 survive a massive roadside bomb near a bridge over a canal, within two miles of the Golf 2/6 firebase in Al Saqlawiyah. Watson's and Matthews's firsthand accounts are in this book. Ahmed Sirhan's Black Flags Brigades planned the attack and planted the roadside bomb, two 155-millimeters artillery shells jury-rigged together ("daisy-chained," in grunt jargon). Ronin3 team leader Derrick Boyer has Sirhan, leader of Black Flags Brigades, forward observer for mortar and rocket attacks on Golf 2/6 firebase, and one of the most wanted terrorist/insurgent leaders in western Iraq, in his sights, but Captain Greg Wardman, Golf 2/6 company commander, orders him not to capture or kill Sirhan.

October 5, 2005: Ronin4 scout/snipers Corporal Noah Fleming and Corporal Justin Novi kill the first *erhabi* (Arabic for "terrorist") in the Golf 2/6 area of operations, on the sixth day of a reconnaissance and surveillance/sniping mission on the Euphrates River.

October 26, 2005: As Muhammad predicted in late September, Al Qaeda and Black Flags Brigades attack Golf 2/6 firebase and the police station in Al Saqlawiyah, using the mosque. In the heaviest ground fire in western Iraq since the second battle of Fallujah in November 2004, four Marines in the police station, led by Sergeant Mirza Fejzic of Golf 2/6, hold off more than thirty Al Qaeda terrorists and Black Flags Brigades, who were using the main mosque in Al Saqlawiyah as their base of fire, command post, and ammunition resupply station. The police chief left the station twenty minutes before the attack, and the Iraqi police dogpiled in a corner, cowering, during the entire attack and its aftermath.

October 27, 2005: Ahmed Sirhan plans and executes mortar and rocket attack by Black Flags Brigades on the Golf 2/6 firebase, killing Corporal Robert Eckfield and Corporal Jared Kremm of 1st Platoon, Golf 2/6.

November 6, 2005: Captain Wardman denies Ronin2 and Ronin3, on a combined scout/sniper operation to find Black Flags Brigades mortar and rocket firing sites across the Euphrates River, perfect reconnaissance and surveillance positions to target those exact sites. Wardman also denies Ronin key field intelligence on the Black Flags Brigades mortar and rocket sites—intelligence coming directly that night from a sheikh who had seen Black Flags Brigades fire mortars and rockets at Golf 2/6 countless times. Ronin2 and Ronin3 abort the mission and return to base. Wardman flies into a rage at their return, curses them out, and orders them off Golf 2/6. At 3:00 A.M. on November 7, Ronin scout/snipers roll to Camp Bahria; Marine infantrymen of Golf 2/6 now have no Marine scout/snipers to support them in combat.

November 15–December 1, 2005: Ronin carries out countersniper reconnaissance and surveillance missions in Fallujah. No intelligence on Al Qaeda terrorist snipers is given to Ronin by 2/6 S-2, battalion intelligence section, led by Captain Mason Harlow.

December 1, 2005, 3:00 A.M.: Ronin4 team leader Corporal Darren Smykowski is told by 1st Reconnaissance Battalion, along with all Ronin, that "we now own 2/6 Marine scout/snipers, for all December." Ronin is ordered to stand guard duty for December while 1st Recon Marines, with no previous experience in Fallujah on countersniper missions, run countersniper operations along with U.S. Navy SEALs and U.S. Army Special Forces. Later in the day, Ronin begins the "month of hell," standing guard in Fallujah, denied the chance to kill terrorist snipers there. Regimental Combat Team 8 (RCT-8) orders me not to attach to any Marine missions in Fallujah. Major Dan Sullivan attempts to find out who issued the order but is stonewalled. Meanwhile, I discover that the Iraqi Army is running its own countersniper missions in Fallujah. Bypassing RCT-8, I link up with the Iraqi Army for eighteen days, from late December to mid-January. The countersniper missions of the Iraqi Army result in the capture of numerous high-value terrorist and insurgent targets and end with the capture of a nine-terrorist sniper cell on January 16, 2006.

Mid-December 2005: U.S. Navy SEALs reach out to Ronin for their field intelligence on terrorist snipers in Fallujah, resulting in combined U.S. Navy SEAL/Ronin countersniper missions. On one of those missions, Fox company 2/6 Marine infantry nearly kill U.S. Navy SEALs and Ronin4, because of a failure of communication between the Fox 2/6 command-and-control center and the Fox 2/6 Marines on patrol. A firsthand account appears within these pages.

January 3, 2006: Fallujah Police fail to kidnap me while I am on patrol with the Iraqi Army.

January 6, 2006: Fallujah Police fail to kill me in a roadside bombing and ambush coordinated by the Fallujah Police with Black Flags Brigades insurgents. Later that night, Lieutenant Mohammed, Iraqi Army commander, warns that the Fallujah Police are letting insurgents and terrorists move plastic explosives through checkpoints manned by police along with Marines, and that they will launch a massive suicide bombing attack on the main checkpoint in Fallujah, Entry Checkpoint One (ECP-1).

January 13, 2006: Ronin continues on countersniper missions in Fallujah. I meet British and American clandestine field officers in Fallujah, who hand me Coalition intelligence reports on Al Qaeda and Black Flags Brigades sniper training camps in Iraq, Syria, and Jordan, as well as terrorist sniper methods, weapons, and financing in Iraq, all of which, according to the covert operators, have reached 2/6 battalion intelligence section. I confirm that the reports reached 2/6 S-2 and hand the reports to Ronin. The Marine scout/snipers state that 2/6 S-2 never gave them the intelligence. Interviews of the two covert operators appear within. Ronin3 scout/sniper Corporal Dudley Kelso and team leader Corporal Derrick Boyer inform Tucker that Wardman ordered them not to capture or kill Ahmed Sirhan on September 29, 2005. The scout/snipers tell me that Captain Harlow and 2/6 S-2, furthermore, never informed Ronin that Sirhan is the leader of Black Flags Brigades.

January 20–25, 2006: Then-1st Lieutenant Marty Keogh, Black Label gun truck platoon commander, Weapons 2/6, informs me that Al Qaeda and Black Flags Brigades have deeply penetrated the Fallujah Police. Ronin scout/snipers, Iraqi soldiers and commanders, and Marine advisors have also stated this based on their firsthand observations in Fallujah. After I accompany Keogh's men on five days of missions with Keogh's men against Al Qaeda in Fallujah, RCT-8 orders me off all missions in Fallujah. Again, RCT-8 stonewalls Major Dan Sullivan when he attempts to discover who gave the order.

January 24, 2006: Kurdish military intelligence, after investigating both Fallujah Police actions in early January, verifies that the Fallujah Police have a death threat on me because of my writing on Fallujah in *Among Warriors in Iraq*. I make Ronin, Keogh, and Major Dan Sullivan aware of the Kurdish military intelligence analysis. Sullivan sends an official report of the two Fallujah Police actions against me to RCT-8, Camp Fallujah.

February–March 2006: Ronin teams operate throughout Fallujah and Al Saqlawiyah, on reconnaissance and surveillance missions and in support of Marine infantry as designated marksmen, patrolling with the infantry.

March 10, 2006: Al Qaeda and Black Flags Brigades in Fallujah coordinate a suicide bomb attack on ECP-1, just as Lieutenant Mohammed had predicted in early January. Lance Corporal Long, Marine infantryman, is killed. Corporal David Soto, of O'Donnell, Texas, is badly wounded. Despite his wounds and being deafened by the blast, Soto kills an insurgent in the immediate aftermath of the suicide bombing attack. Soto's firsthand account appears within.

Early April 2006: 25th Marine Regiment scout/snipers rotate in-country, and Ronin begins to rotate back to Camp Bahria.

April 15, 2006: En route to America, Ronin celebrates with whiskey and beer at Shannon International Airport, Republic of Ireland.

AUTHOR'S NOTE

The real names of Coalition interpreters attached to Marine units on missions in western Iraq, Iraqi Army commanders and soldiers in Fallujah, and Iraq civilians are revealed nowhere in this book, to protect them from the Iraqi Police in Fallujah, Al Qaeda, and other terrorists and insurgents in the Near East. Likewise, in keeping with my long-standing agreement with Delta Force commandos and members of the U.S. Army Special Forces, their real names and ranks are kept in strict confidence. Finally, to safeguard Western clandestine field officers in Europe, the Near East, and Far East, their real names are not revealed in this book or any other of my writings.

A Marine Scout/Sniper's Journey

CORPORAL JUSTIN NOVI,
RONIN4 ASSISTANT TEAM LEADER
AND SCOUT/SNIPER

grew up in a middle-class family in the suburbs of Pittsburgh. Western Pennsylvania is home. My parents worked hard to provide a great childhood for my sister and me. My people on both sides have been in the union. I joined the Marine Corps in August 2002, when I was eighteen and just out of high school. My name is Justin Novi, and I'm twenty-two years old.

Everyone, including me, thought that I would go to school or join the union and become a sprinkler fitter like everyone else. My cousins Chad and Matt were in the Army, as well as both of my grandpas. My uncle John was in the Navy.

But up until my senior year in high school, I never saw myself being a Marine. I never saw myself doing anything involving a rifle, for that matter. In fact, I still haven't lived down the time I shot at several squirrels during my first hunting season and missed all of them because I was shooting with the wrong eye.

I completed boot camp in December 2002, moved on to the school of infantry, and began my journey in the corps with Fox Company, 2nd Battalion, 6th Marine Regiment, in Marine infantry. Shortly after my arrival to the fleet, we deployed to Iraq for the invasion in February 2003.

We pulled security for the 1st Marine Expeditionary Force as a part of the headquarters element. Frequently on the move pushing north, we convoyed everywhere in gun trucks and humvees.

The sandstorms were a nightmare, and so was the sun. But surprisingly, morale was good. There was not too much excitement except for the occasional Scud missile threats and shootouts between farmers and chicken thieves. We humped our rucks, carried our assault rifles and grenade launchers and machine guns, wore our flaks until they felt like a second skin—albeit, a very thick and heavy second skin—and thank God, survived.

Babylon was our final stop in Iraq in April 2003. Three months later, we were home before we knew it. Okinawa, Japan, was our next stop, on regular unit deployment in September 2003.

In Okinawa, we learned riot control tactics, completed close-quarter shooting training, and ran. A lot. We ran like marathoners, it seemed. That was a seven-month tour and I hated every minute of it.

Next on the agenda was Afghanistan.

Attached to the Fourth Marine Expeditionary Brigade on antiterrorist duty, we guarded the U.S. Embassy in Kabul, Afghanistan. It was then I went to my first shooting school, the Designated Marksman course, which is a great school.

Short- to mid-range shooting was mastered, and that was the hardest rifle qualification I ever did in my four years in the Marines. You've got to put it in the black on that course, no exceptions.

Little did I know this would be nothing compared to what lay ahead. In Kabul, I'd sat on top of the embassy on the Sniper Post Six.

Every day was scripted: Six hours on duty, six hours off duty. Then six hours on duty, and twelve hours off duty.

No one penetrated the American Embassy in Kabul, on our watch.

Every other day was a day off where we would go to ranges and practice team and squad movements to contact.

In Kabul, I decided that I wanted to go to the sniper platoon.

My friends Corporal Darren Smykowski and Sergeant Efraim Parra were in the snipers already. Smykowski is a great sniper and good friend. Parra is one of the toughest and most clever Marine snipers alive. In Kabul, Smykowski would spend his off time studying with me. Parra also helped me at every opportunity.

Smykowski was very instrumental in getting me over to the platoon. My partner on Sniper Post Six was Corporal Donnelly from Fox Company, 2/6, and I've been with him since my first deployment in Iraq. Donnelly is one of my best friends. He helped me out too, tossing me pop quizzes and preparing me with note cards to get ready for Smykowski's tests.

I wouldn't have made it past the knowledge portion without Donnelly's help. Up until then, I was labeled as having a bad attitude, but in 3rd Platoon, Fox Company, I became a fire team leader. Gunnery Sergeant Briar, 3rd Platoon sergeant, was the first platoon sergeant to give me a chance. It was the first real opportunity I'd had in the corps, and I was fortunate to make the most of it.

We did many patrols outside the wire in Kabul, and our team shined. I knew that I had to show that I was good enough to get a shot to go to the sniper platoon and to Marine Sniper School. With a lot of hard work from everyone in the team, we were the best, and with a lot of help from my friends, I got my chance to join the 2/6 scout/sniper platoon upon returning stateside from Afghanistan.

The screening consisted of an interview the day after my twenty-first birthday. I almost blew it. I looked like I was hit by a train, to make a long story short. But my experience and billet as a fire team leader in the grunts really paid off in the end, and I made it in. The next few months were to see how bad we wanted to be there.

Going from a fire team leader in a Marine infantry squad to a "PIG" (Professionally Instructed Gunman) in sniper platoon was a big adjustment. Snipers have a very different mindset than grunts, no question.

The senior snipers and team leaders in sniper platoon beat some very basic things into our heads, to ensure that we understood that life in sniper platoon was a different kettle of fish than our days in the grunts:

1. New guys are PIGs and will listen to HOGs (hunters of gun-
   men, experienced Marine snipers) like their lives depend on
   it, because they do.
       When in doubt about anything in a sniper platoon, refer to
   the First Law of PIGs, as stated above.
2. PIGs want to someday be HOGs. Nobody will give it to you;
   you have to earn it.
3. PIGs run everywhere. Walking is unacceptable. You will not
   walk, unless you enjoy push-ups without end.
4. PIGs hate weekends. Large amounts of homework will be
   given on weekends. The weekends of PIGs revolve around
   homework, memorizing small-arms manuals and cleaning
   sniper rifles. There are many beautiful women in America,
   and rest assured, PIGs, one day you will meet them. But not
   on your weekends of PIG existence!
5. PIGs hate sleep. Do not plan on sleeping if you go to the field.
6. PIGs hate food. One MRE will be split between all PIGs . . . if
   you *do* eat. Food is a privilege, not a right. Like all the other
   privileges taken away from you once you're a PIG, one by one
   they are given back.
7. PIGs love the mud. Don't ever plan on staying clean in the
   field or in garrison. Do not fear the rain, mud, sleet, or cold.
   The mud is your friend.
8. PIGs love push-ups. Push-ups remind PIGs that they must one
   day become HOGs, if only to never again do push-ups as
   PIGs! If you get a question wrong, it's 25 and 5 (25 regular
   pushups, 5 diamond push-ups).
9. PIGs stick together. If one PIG screws up, you all screw up.
   You play together, you pay together. You understand real
   quick that when you take care of your brother sniper, he'll
   take care of you.
       Needless to say, I got over being away from my old friends real
quick. It was high time for us PIGs to heed the wisdom of a Marine
proverb—"improvise, adapt, and overcome"—and we did just that.
       Jason Hillestad, James Owen, Danny Milstid, Dave Hodulich,
Billy Getscher, Stephen Lutze, and myself were the PIGs, and we

were well aware of it. I simply didn't have any time to dwell on no longer being a grunt, because learning how to be an effective sniper became foremost in my waking existence.

The PIGs became real close real quick and developed a strong hatred for the HOGs. In Iraq, however, I gained real perspective on just why the HOGs hammered us as young novice snipers. In truth, in Fallujah, I became more than a little grateful that we'd been challenged so frequently and trained so hard.

It was the HOGs, who are now the best friends and comrades I know, and who led us through the winter of terrorist snipers in Fallujah, who were the same ones taking us on rucksack runs with forty-pound sandbags in our rucks, and weapons, and gear.

The HOGs, to whom all Ronin owes our thanks: Parra, Smykowski, Areballo, and Boyer. I doubt I would have said that on a rucksack run or at the end of another set of push-ups with my face in the mud and pine needles in North Carolina. But once in-country, I understood how wise the HOGs were to be so tough on us, so demanding. They forced us to think outside the box, they made us reflect on the Marine infantry proverb "easy to be hard, hard to be smart," and they taught us the wisdom of never letting your ego command your judgment. We are far better scout/snipers, and better young men, for their leadership.

They were the same ones who had me do record-breaking amounts of push-ups, and made you feel like you didn't have a friend in the world. It didn't make sense at the time, but I would soon find out it made the physical and mental part of sniper school so much easier. And it definitely made combat in Iraq easier to deal with, because we'd already pulled together as snipers and as young men.

After only a little over a month in sniper platoon, I got my shot to go to Sniper School in Quantico, Virginia.

As professional as any school in the Marine Corps, it is as tiring as it is demanding. I was both nervous and excited. Never before had I worked so hard at something. I qualified with the M40A3 7.62x51-millimeter caliber bolt-action sniper rifle, passed the written and observation tests, and was looking forward to graduating.

But as fate had it, I watched my dream slip away as I was busted on my final stalk. Stalking is arguably the most difficult part of the final testing of a Marine sniper, and there is no margin for error.

It haunted me for a long time, but I turned my failed goal into an obsession. I made it my mission in life to be the best damn Marine scout/sniper that I could be. To that end, my whole world, as it were, became tracking and stalking.

I worked harder after school than I did before it. But due to the crammed schedule as the battalion was leaving to train in California, I didn't have time to jump into another class to redo stalking, so I would have to learn to master it on my own, and from help within the platoon.

Regardless, the platoon that I'd left, split down the middle between the PIGs and HOGs, was now a tight-knit group. After all, we were about to go in harm's way together. The combined-arms exercise we came through in the Mojave Desert in California in the summer of 2005 was essential to this. Our personalities showed through as we started getting to know each other, learned how to deal with one another, accept each other's faults and lean on each other's strengths.

This is what I learned about each of the guys I was in combat with in Iraq from September 2005 to April 2006:

Sergeant Efraim Parra, Ronin1 team leader, is the consummate quiet professional. Soft-spoken, a powerfully built Mexican-American, who would do anything for his friends. True man of action, and a man of few words. Intimidating when you first meet him, but he is one of the best friends you can have. Don't take his kindness for weakness, though. Outstanding sniper team leader.

Corporal Darren Smykowski, Ronin4 team leader (everyone calls him "Ski"), is loud, obnoxious, dramatic, and hilarious. By far the funniest person I've ever met. He doesn't eat Skittles, he inhales them. A real no bullshit guy, too. When he sets his mind to something, it will be done no matter what it takes. Ski really looked up to his older brother, Sergeant Mark Smykowski, a Reconnaissance Marine killed in action in western Iraq just weeks after we'd returned to America in April 2006. Ski is a great friend and an exceptional sniper team leader.

Sergeant John Matter, chief scout of our platoon is the guy you want on your side when live rounds rock. A bar fighter, an excellent leader, with a great sense of humor—he could turn anything into a joke—but hard-core serious on missions. He definitely knew how to distinguish work from play. Brilliant mind for covert work.

Corporal Bobby Parker, Ronin1 assistant team leader, is Parra's right-hand man, with a sharp sense of attention to detail. At times quiet, he can also be extremely sarcastic and hilarious. Fine knowledge of small arms. Parker highly values his friends and family.

Corporal Daniel Milstid, Ronin3 scout/sniper, is an excellent musician, impulsive buyer (as are most musicians), with a great sense of humor, and is a great assault man as well. Milstid plays a mean guitar and sings pretty good, too. Without our music—we wrote songs and recorded them, when not on missions in Fallujah and western Iraq—it would've been a much tougher tour of duty.

Corporal Jason Hillestad, Ronin1 scout/sniper, is very professional for his short time in the Marine Corps. Performs well above his pay grade, fun person to hang out with, not afraid to throw the bullshit flag. Analytical mind, shrewd and savvy.

Corporal David Hodulich, Ronin2 scout/sniper and demolitions specialist, is motivated, dedicated, and really takes pride in his job. Master of sniper rifles, pistols, and all small arms. Witnessed the 9/11 attacks by Al Qaeda on the Pentagon. Always wanting to go to the next level, loves hunting, surfing, and punk rock.

Corporal James Owen, headquarters element scout/sniper, loves to throw the bullshit flag, usually can't win an argument if his life depended on it, brunt of the platoon's jokes, good sport, good friend to have. Articulate, well read, and reliable to a fault.

Corporal Brian Areballo, Ronin2 team leader, is known as "Hollywood" because he looks like a movie star. Ladies man, always looking good, laid-back, strong leader. Stands for his team at all times. Outstanding knowledge of covert skills, tracking, and all aspects of sniping. Never hesitates to pass on his experience to his younger snipers, like Hodulich.

Corporal Dudley Kelso, Ronin3 scout/sniper, is very smart, with exceptional computer-hacking skills, an accomplished locksmith, very intelligent young man. Integrity is his middle name. Sees right to the heart of things and will let the world know when he's upset about something. If Kelso's upset about something, moreover, there is a damn good reason for it. Excellent Arabic, also.

Corporal Stephen Lutze, Ronin4 scout/sniper, is an ex-gang-banger who found God. Very well read, one of the platoon's intellectuals. Great trash talker, even though he doesn't ever swear—hard to believe, but there is one Marine in history who never curses, and that's Lutze. He loves spreading the word of God. He likes to pick our brains on other religions also—inquisitive guy. Very respectable Marine, solid in martial arts, top-notch close-quarter combat skills. The platoon's caffeine fiend, he can drink coffee anytime and does.

Corporal Jay Elder, Ronin4 scout/sniper, is heavily tattooed, loves Boston, is passionate about integrity, excites easily, cools down quickly too. Very insightful—like Kelso, Elder has a gift for getting right to the core of things. Elder was the only one of us who could look Fleming in the eye. Elder and Lutze made for some interesting conversations, behind the wire.

Corporal Noah Fleming, Ronin2 scout/sniper, missed his girlfriend the whole time. His woman was always on his mind at war in Iraq. Great conversationalist. Good to talk to, good sense of humor, good friend, missing a few fingers due to a wood-chopping accident. Amazing that he can still fire a pistol, for instance, despite his accident. Big, tall guy like Elder.

Lance Corporal Billy Getscher, Ronin1 scout/sniper, is quiet, keeps quiet until he gets to know you. Nice guy, likes to surf and recently began playing guitar. Excellent attitude in the field. Inquisitive, eager to learn and apply new knowledge. Listened well and closely to Parra and Parker. Solid young Marine.

Corporal Derrick Boyer, Ronin3 team leader, is an honest man. Short in height with a shorter temper. Irish to the core. Brilliant team leader. Hilarious guy, he alone matched Ski in the platoon for all-out natural humor. Good friend, loves to fish, big music lover.

On the whole, we were a very professional platoon who built a tight bond around our sense of humor. That's one thing we all had in common. Predeployment leave, before our mid-September flight to Iraq, ended as quick as it began. I spent a majority of it in and out of the emergency room for poison oak and poison ivy. Everyone said good-bye to our friends and family like we've done so many times before.

But this time it was different. We all knew that this deployment was the real thing. Our expectations were sky-high, and we had a lot of weight on our shoulders. But we were all more than ready for the task at hand.

When we arrived at our firm bases in western Iraq, we immediately began patrolling with our sister battalion, 1st Battalion, 6th Marine Regiment (1/6). They showed us the ins and outs of the city.

My first patrol, I remember going into a large abandoned building, on point. I couldn't see a damn thing, and I remember saying to myself there is no way I'm coming home.

And it crossed everyone's mind one time or another, but you learn to live with it, and you push on. Each day is one day closer to coming home. As we started getting into a groove, with more missions under our belts, we heard that an author wanted to attach to us.

To say we were apprehensive would have been generous. We weren't sure, actually, about how it would work out. We were all kind of edgy about the idea. Tactically and operationally, we were not exactly keen, on first take. It's bad enough going out with four people in Fallujah. Another would just be extra baggage, or so we thought.

But after we met Mike Tucker, and he told us about himself and what he was all about, we let him join us on missions.

That was a damned good decision, all the way around.

We discovered that Mike has worked with Special Forces teams in Northern and western Iraq and been on missions with Delta Force. He's seen more of the country than us. He has significant clandestine experience behind Burmese Army lines, in 1992 and 2002. So he was more than qualified, and not to mention, he was a Marine infantryman in the late 1980s.

He is a man of his word. Mike Tucker's undying passion for his profession in counterterrorism and writing made him a valuable asset to our scout/sniper platoon.

And as he explained what the book would be about—how he wanted us to tell it straight, no chaser—we liked him even more. When I've come back to the States after both tours in Iraq, I've noticed a household trend. The only thing that people know is what the news is telling them. People base their opinions on the war in Iraq from that. And it's not their fault.

What they need to realize is that there are people out there, in guard posts and reconnaissance missions and patrols and raids, going out on the wire night and day, guys at the tip of the spear who know the truth and want it to be heard. But nobody wants to look for it. It's easier to turn on CNN and hear about a couple of roadside bombs and attacks in Iraq.

Unlike most authors, Mike Tucker realized this and has put your search to an end by providing an accurate account of the war from the heart of the beast. He joined my brother scout/snipers and me on countless missions. Mike Tucker went where no one else dared to go to bring you the truth.

Welcome to the streets of Fallujah as seen through the eyes of Ronin scout/snipers, Marine infantrymen, Iraqi soldiers and officers, Marine advisors, and Western intelligence services clandestine officers.

This is how it was for us, when we came to understand just how deeply Al Qaeda and other terrorists and insurgents have penetrated the Fallujah Police—and I respect the hell out of the Marine officers in this book, like Captain Marty Keogh, Major Michael Muller, and Major Tim Murphy, for having the backbone to state the truth about the Fallujah Police.

We speak in this book from firsthand experience and observation, at all times—these are the missions and these are the men. Like Corporal Derrick Boyer, Ronin3 team leader, says, "This is our generation that is bleeding here."

Looking back on my tour in Fallujah and western Iraq, I finally started to realize how lucky I am to be sitting here today. Our platoon made it back in one piece, and I thank God every day for our survival. As many of us, and our brother Marine infantrymen, state in this book, there were times when we didn't expect to leave Iraq alive. We are grateful to see each sunrise, for sure.

And as we've neared the end of our tours of duty, we're starting to go our separate ways. We've been back a few months now and are moving on with our lives. We have a chance to achieve our dreams and are well aware that many of our brothers will never get that chance.

Like Corporal Brian Areballo, Ronin2 team leader, says, "We are Ronin and we are one." And that will always be true.

Now, some of us are getting out and some are staying in. We are young and damn glad to be alive with all our roads open before us. Regardless, we are all adjusting to the huge change of pace since getting back to America, preparing for our new lives and new battles that lie ahead.

But no matter what path we may follow in life, one thing will hold true: We will never forget Ronin, Fallujah, and western Iraq.

We will never forget the people, the noises, the smells, the heat, the rain, the mud, the gray skies and blue skies, and the cold. Sun that seemed to melt the bones off you, in September and October. The heavy, drenching, constant flood of rain that winter—a blue sky in Fallujah that winter was as common as a scarecrow at sea.

Desert missions, the sand as far as your eyes could see in places. Camels, donkeys, cows, and the inevitable dogs, the wild dogs that would come from out of nowhere in farming villages and out of alleys in Fallujah. High walls of reeds along the Euphrates River, when silence was our only friend, waiting for insurgents and terrorists to smuggle mortars, RPGs [rocket-propelled grenades], plastic explosives, machine guns, and rifles.

The Iraqi Police in Fallujah, smiling their diabolical smiles, flashing their high beams to signal terrorists and insurgents that we were stepping out on the wire. There was no difference between the Iraqi Police and terrorists and insurgents in Fallujah, for real.

And the winter of the terrorist snipers in Fallujah, when we'd move out in four-man teams, hustling from street corner to street corner in Fallujah, staying in the shadows. Doing everything possible to keep from being seen, which in our trade means death.

Low-crawling on broken glass on rooftops in the dead of night. Tracking Al Qaeda in the mud and cold. Sweating buckets in the western Iraq sun. The good times and bad times. The friendships we made in Fallujah and western Iraq are a bond that will never be broken.

We will never forget the ones who didn't make it home, like Ski's brother, Mark.

We will never forget that goddamned city, Fallujah.

Take good care,

Semper Fi,   .
Corporal Justin Novi
Marine scout/sniper
Ronin4 assistant team leader

Pittsburgh, Pennsylvania
July 27, 2006

PART ONE

"We had Ahmed Sirhan in our sights."

"We named ourselves Ronin, samurais without masters, before we got in country. In the guerrilla war here, we discovered that we truly are samurais without masters: shafted, stonewalled, and ignored. But we survived, brother. We are Ronin and we are one. We left America together and we're going home together."

—CORPORAL BRIAN AREBALLO, RONIN2 TEAM LEADER, APRIL 11, 2006

The Marine scout/snipers of 2nd Battalion, 6th Marines, named their platoon Ronin in homage to the samurais without masters of ancient Japan. Their four-man scout/sniper teams, Ronin1, Ronin2, Ronin3, and Ronin4, carried out reconnaissance and surveillance and sniper missions throughout Fallujah and northwest of Fallujah. Ronin took on that call sign, for identifying itself on all combat radio transmissions and for its platoon name, in July 2005, before setting foot in Iraq.

Ronin scout/snipers stalked fields and desert, lay silent in covert hides in thick reeds along the Euphrates River, and low-crawled on rooftops over broken glass in the cold winter rains in Fallujah, as Corporal Justin Novi noted in the Introduction. Ronin scoped for enemy west to the wide brown waters of the Euphrates and northwest to the village of Abu Shiezel in Al Saqlawiyah, the northern border of 2/6's area of operations. It was the "winter of the sniper," as we called it, when Al Qaeda snipers roamed Fallujah at will while Marine commanders on Camp Fallujah refused to employ Marine scout/snipers to track and kill Al Qaeda for weeks on end.

To a man, Ronin scout/snipers were the equal of anyone I have ever been in combat with and carried out clandestine actions with—stalwart and savvy; fiercely loyal to one another, their teams, and their platoon; brilliant in the field; and completely fearless when it came to their field intelligence analyses of just how badly the Fallujah Police had been penetrated by Al Qaeda, Black Flags Brigades, and other terrorists and insurgents in western Iraq. The Kurdish democracy activist and former underground leader Fawsi Muhammad Bawrmarni said in Dahuk, Iraqi Kurdistan, on August 5, 2003, that "Hemingway had both kinds of courage, moral and physical. . . . One without the other is no good."

Without question, the Marine scout/snipers of Ronin, like Hemingway, exhibited both moral and physical courage time and again in Fallujah and western Iraq; it was a great honor and privilege to join them. I'd vowed on September 11 to chronicle a Marine unit at war. As a Marine infantry veteran, I owed this generation of Marines a book on their sacrifice and struggle—their honor, courage, and commitment. Headquarters Marine Corps Public Affairs Office at the Pentagon turned the key in the lock for me in late July 2005, approving my embed request for western Iraq. Ronin opened that door on September 22, 2005, in Fallujah. Semper Fi, brothers.

The truth about any of us who ever humped a ruck and carried a rifle in the Corps is that the Marines didn't have to take us. Volunteering for Marine infantry does not mean the recruiting sergeant says, "Very good, thank you, sign here and you're on Parris Island next week." But the Marine Corps gave me a chance, which I never got anywhere else in America: an opportunity to serve my country and to earn a master's degree on the GI Bill. Thanks to the Marines, I had the great good fortune to listen to the wisdom of Shakespeare, Coleridge, Yeats, Homer, and Frost, which professors at James Madison University like Dr. Marina Favila, Dr. Bruce Johnson, Dr. Tony Eksterowicz, and the late Dr. Geoffrey Morley-Mower imparted to me in Harrisonburg, in the heart of the Shenandoah Valley. Those professors constantly challenged me to be a better poet and writer, and I often reflected, on this last tour for me in Iraq, on the life lessons I was fortunate to gain from them on fortitude, will, desire, and perseverance.

But it was, as many of the scout/snipers express within, a grueling combat tour, perhaps even more psychologically demanding than anything else. I have never seen a special operations unit—and Marine scout/snipers are just that, a special operations unit—not listened to in combat before. As a Marine infantry veteran, I am ashamed to say that I saw Ronin ignored in Fallujah and western Iraq, time after time. I was likewise amazed that they were able to hold it together, stay focused, and remain professional, vigilant and hard-core, night and day. They just got tougher, harder, and smarter with every week.

Ronin, denied their core mission of killing the enemy with accurate, long-range, lethal fire, made survival their mission in life. Why did Marine scout/snipers, some of the most highly trained, physically fit, street-smart, savvy, and intelligent warriors in the U.S. military, decide they should look out strictly for themselves? The best answer to that came from one of their own, a Marine scout/sniper of whom the battalion executive officer, Major Dan Sullivan, from Huntington, Long Island, New York, said, "Kelso is hard-wired not to lie, an outstanding Marine and one of the most thoughtful men in the battalion, of any rank."

Corporal Dudley Kelso stated on January 13, 2006: "Ronin scout/snipers know for a fact that we've been refused key intelligence on the enemy here and denied kill shots on known high-value terrorist and insurgent targets. We are tired of getting jacked over. Our mission has come down to one word: survival."

That same day, Kelso told me of Golf 2/6 company commander Captain Greg Wardman's failure on September 29, 2005, to capture or kill Ahmed Sirhan, leader of Black Flags Brigades, son of the infamous insurgent leader Khamis Sirhan, and on the most-wanted list of terrorists and insurgent leaders in western Iraq for more than three and a half years at the time of this writing.

On February 16, 2006, a month after Kelso's revelation, Wardman's failure to kill or capture Ahmed Sirhan again came to light.

Staff Sergeant Travis Twiggs, age thirty-three and a native of New Orleans, Golf Company 1st Platoon sergeant, pointed to a pond in Abu Shiezel bordered by wild grass, and then to a tree line, saying, "That's the pond Ahmed Sirhan was fishing in. That's the tree line Boyer had his team set in, covertly. Boyer had him in his sights. Battalion S-2 [2/6 battalion intelligence section, led by Captain Mason Harlow] never told Boyer's team exactly who Ahmed Sirhan was. Harlow only gave the scout/snipers physical intelligence on him—photo, height, weight, and so on. *Nobody told Ronin that Ahmed Sirhan was one of the most wanted terrorist/insurgent leaders in Iraq.* Nobody told Boyer's team that Ahmed Sirhan leads Black Flags Brigades and has strong, strong connections to Al Qaeda. Well, Wardman refused to order Boyer to kill or even capture him." Twiggs glanced around, his M16A-4 5.56 assault rifle jutting out from his right shoulder, a clip jacked in, his face red in the sun.

Twiggs, a graduate of the highly respected Australian Special Air Service combat tracking school and regarded in the U.S. military as one of the best combat trackers alive, left the Marines in 1999 and returned two years later, explaining, "I am a warrior, this is what I was born for, and it's the only thing I'm really good at." He shook his head by the pond, unsmiling, going on: "Even had Boyer simply been ordered to capture him, he could've done so easily. His team had plenty of tools. Trust your man on the ground. Listen to your scouts. If you're a Marine company commander, and especially a Marine battalion commander, with Marine scout/snipers on a mission to take down a known high-value target, a terrorist/insurgent leader the Coalition has been on the hunt for since May 2003, why do you refuse to allow your scout/snipers to take down the terrorist? Why do you not only refuse to order us to kill the enemy, but also even to capture the enemy? It was a goatfuck that day. Captain Wardman let a known terrorist walk. That is exactly what it was, and it was Marine command's goatfuck."

———

Tactics are strategy in guerrilla war. And deception is the mother of stealth.

If you cannot order your scout/snipers to kill the enemy, and when you refuse to let them operate in the field with independence and daring, using deception at every opportunity, you prove that in guerrilla war, you have no business being in combat. Effective reconnaissance and surveillance, and sniping, are central to victory in guerrilla war, historically. Without effective reconnaissance and surveillance—"eyes on recon," in special ops parlance—you cannot take down the enemy.

The U.S. Army, unlike the Marines in western Iraq, did not fail to capture or kill a known high-value terrorist target when they fought guerrilla war in Fallujah. Delta Force, along with U.S. Navy SEALs, captured Ahmed Sirhan's father, Khamis Sirhan, who had led Black Flags Brigades *erhabi* since April 2003, on a daring raid in Fallujah on January 13, 2004.

Likewise, the U.S. Army 82nd Airborne Task Force 1Panther, helmed by Lieutenant Colonel Brian Drinkwine, took down 80 percent of their main terrorist and insurgent targets, killed or captured, in its seven-month deployment in Fallujah between September 2003 and late March 2004.

In counterterrorist raiding, that's an 80 percent hit rate—you've taken down 80 percent of the terrorists that you've tracked and targeted. The 2nd Marine Division's Task Force Spartan, commanded by Lieutenant Colonel Scott Aiken, had a less than 5 percent hit rate on its seven-month deployment in Fallujah two years later, from September 2005 to April 2006.

A colossal human intelligence failure lies at the heart of the Marine counterterrorist failure in Iraq: Doctrinally, the Marines are completely opposed to using U.S. Army Special Forces A teams to gather field intelligence. The Army, however, uses Special Forces A teams to gather field intelligence in combat all the time, night and day, twenty-four/seven.

The Marines, furthermore, refuse to listen to and act on U.S. Army battlefield successes in counterterrorism, which began with the Army's more than fifty years of employing Special Forces teams in clandestine human intelligence missions.

Delta Force in January 2004 masterfully leaned on its deep, broad human intelligence network in Fallujah, one that extended to mosques, markets, schools and banks, to take down Khamis Sirhan, then terrorist commander of Black Flags Brigades in Iraq. Next to Zarqawi, Khamis Sirhan was the most-wanted terrorist leader in western Iraq since April 2003.

We whooped with joy in Fallujah on January 14, 2004, hearing of Khamis Sirhan's capture. But his sons took over the family trade: Chaos, Havoc & Terror, Inc., courtesy of Black Flags Brigades. We stayed on the hunt for his three sons: Ahmed, Muthar, and Mohammed.

Wardman's failure to strike and kill Ahmed Sirhan haunted the Marines in western Iraq like nothing else. Ahmed Sirhan, insurgent leader of Black Flags Brigades, financed, planned, and executed mortar and rocket attacks on American Marines, Iraqi Army, U.S. Army, and other Coalition forces in Iraq.

Throughout September, October, and going into early November 2005, Golf Company 2/6's outpost in Al Saqlawiyah was rocketed, mortared, and regularly attacked by Black Flags Brigades and Al Qaeda. Two Marine infantrymen of 1st Platoon Golf Company, Corporal Robert J. Eckfield Jr. and Corporal Jared J. Kremm, were killed by Black Flags Brigades mortar fire on the base on October 27.

The day before, Al Qaeda terrorists had taken over a mosque in Al Saqlawiyah with the support of the imam, who was a notorious terrorist financier and cell leader, and attacked the Al Saqlawiyah Police Station, aided by Ahmed Sirhan's Black Flags Brigades.

A little over a week later, on November 4, Twiggs laid his hands on the helmets of Eckfield and Kremm at their funeral service, bowing his head. Twiggs, their platoon sergeant, had befriended each of them, and he and his wife, Kellee, had welcomed the two men to their home in North Carolina on many occasions.

Two Marines from 1st Platoon, who'd known Eckfield and Kremm for all their time in Marine infantry, Sergeant Brian Sebastian of Lynchburg, Virginia, and Corporal Jared Underwood of Wise County, southwestern Virginia, gave personal reflections about their fallen comrades, Marines nodding their heads in quiet agreement as they spoke.

The street fight in Al Saqlawiyah nine days earlier, on October 26—the day before the Black Flags Brigades mortar attack that killed Eckfield and Kremm—had seen the heaviest ground fire in the Fallujah area of operations since Al Fajr, the second battle of Fallujah, in November 2004.

Thanks to the leadership of Sergeant Mirza Fejzic of New Jersey and 3rd Platoon, Golf Company, the Marines held in a fierce action, taking heavy machine-gun fire and RPGs from Al Qaeda terrorists on the minaret of the main mosque in Al Saqlawiyah. With four Marines, Fejzic denied more than thirty terrorists and insurgents the police station in the heart of Al Saqlawiyah. Fejzic, a naturalized American citizen who hails from Bosnia, low-crawled under fire to carry ammunition to his Marine comrades and killed Al Qaeda and Black Flags Brigades *erhabi* with his M16A4 assault rifle.

Days later, Coalition Iraqi Arab interpreters, through sources in western Iraq, confirmed that Ahmed Sirhan coordinated the attack on the police station with Al Qaeda, as well as the mortar attack the next day. The Marines had known since March 2004 that Ahmed Sirhan led mortar and rocket attacks on Coalition forces. Before the Marines took command of western Iraq on March 27, 2004, Delta Force commandos and U.S. Navy SEALs had specifically targeted Ahmed Sirhan.

Only thanks to the integrity and professionalism of Novi, Boyer, Kelso, Elder, Lutze, Staff Sergeant Twiggs, and Ronin scout/snipers was I finally made aware, beginning in mid-January 2006, of how Wardman failed to kill or capture Ahmed Sirhan. I didn't get an opportunity to interview Boyer directly until April 2 of that year in Fallujah.

Boyer was bitter about Wardman's failure, and that bitterness extended to Lt. Col. Scott Aiken, who treated Ronin with scorn and contempt after the Ahmed Sirhan incident, blaming the scout/snipers for not being aggressive. Yet it was not Ronin's decision to let a known insurgent leader with deep connections to Al Qaeda walk. Boyer did not reenlist in the Marines, as a result of Aiken's failure to respect Ronin and treat the scout/snipers with professionalism and dignity.

The Ronin3 team leader returned to his home just west of the Chesapeake Bay's wide, dark waters. He is a Marylander, of the breed that carried out orders to stand to the last man at Brooklyn Heights in the battle of Long Island on August 27, 1776, and that alone will serve him well. He is a witty, gregarious young man, ebullient and jovial, and his brother scout/snipers think highly of him.

"We had Ahmed Sirhan in our sights."

CORPORAL DERRICK BOYER,
RONIN3 SCOUT/SNIPER TEAM LEADER,
APRIL 2, 2006

Corporal Derrick Boyer was born in Baltimore and grew up in Odenton, Anne Arundel County, Maryland. Odenton is roughly twenty miles northeast of the state capital, Annapolis. The sparkling blue-green waters of the Severn River reach from Boyer's hometown to the Chesapeake Bay. Like Justin Novi, Stephen Lutze, Jay Elder, and all of his generation of Marine scout/snipers, Boyer knew when he volunteered for the Marines in 2002 that he would be going to war.

Arundel High School, from which Boyer graduated in 2002, has a long tradition of academic excellence and athletic accomplishments. Its football team is still, just as it was when I was at Annapolis High School in the late 1970s, known for its aggressiveness and toughness.

Five-four, redheaded, and straight-talking, the stocky former high school wrestler and lacrosse defenseman was outstanding on clandestine missions in Iraq. Some people have a gift for covert missions, and Boyer is one of them. Moreover, he treated his team with respect, courtesy, and professionalism. He moved fast, listened closely to his men, and never lost one of his team in combat. He carried an M40A3 7.62x51-caliber long-barreled bolt-action sniper rifle, an M9 9-millimeter Beretta sidearm, and also on occasion an M203, M4, and M16A4.

Tall, keen-eyed scout/sniper Corporal Jay Elder praised Boyer's leadership highly on March 27, 2006, in Fallujah, speaking for all Ronin: "Boyer is one savvy Ninja Turtle, man, amazing that he can get around like he can. Excellent on-the-spot thinker, no hesitation. Sharp mind. A tough, saavy operator. Clever and a damn good team leader."

A Marine infantryman who volunteered for Marine scout/snipers in 2nd Battalion 6th Marines, like all Marine scout/snipers, Boyer was the real McCoy: school-trained, having earned an 8541 military occupational specialty (MOS). Being an 8541 as a Marine scout/sniper means that you have graduated from Quantico Scout/Sniper School in Quantico, Virginia; Stone Bay Sniper School at Camp Lejeune, North Carolina; or Pendleton Scout/Sniper School at Camp Pendleton, California. The USMC Quantico Scout/Sniper School is demanding, exacting, rigorous, and so well regarded within the U.S. military that the Navy SEALs send their snipers there to be trained, as do U.S. Army Special Forces and the FBI.

Boyer, like all the Ronin team leaders, was highly skilled on the M40A3 7.62x51-caliber (NATO round) sniper rifle, a long-barreled bolt-action rifle with a massive scope on it, accurate out to 1,000 yards in combat. Fluent in many sniper systems, he was also familiar with the SR-25 7.62x51-caliber sniper rifle, favored by U.S. Navy SEALS, and the Dragonov, a Soviet-era 7.62x54-caliber sniper rifle that Al Qaeda snipers are carrying in Iraq, the Near East, Africa, Central Asia, and the Far East.

Boyer, like all the team leaders and many of the scout/snipers in the platoon, sought excellence in all aspects of being a Marine scout/sniper: photography and computers, lock-picking, spider-climbing walls, covert entry and forced entry, stalking, reconnaissance and surveillance, scoping, sniping, covert infiltration and exfiltration, and the most important: *Don't get seen, caught, or killed.*

In a tent in Fallujah on April 2, 2006, with his scout/sniper team—Corporal Dudley Kelso, Corporal Kyle Palmer, and Corporal

Daniel Milstid—kicking back around him, tuned in to iPods, drinking Gatorade and coffee out of metal canteen cups, waiting for the word on our exit date, Boyer spoke of his seven months in Fallujah and western Iraq, his four years in the Marines, and Wardman's failure to order the kill on Ahmed Sirhan.

The Ahmed Sirhan goatfuck was on September 29, 2005. In the Pocket, Abu Shiezel, Al Saqlawiyah. We set in at about 1 A.M., just doing a hold and security on a family. We took a house.

The house was across a field from Ahmed Sirhan's house. We were on the roof, on over watch, surveilling his house. My team's mission was to capture or kill Ahmed Sirhan.

I had a lot of intelligence on Ahmed Sirhan. I had a photo of his face. I had his car. And his general description. We also knew where his brother lived, who was also a target. All intelligence was physical.

S-2 [2/6 intelligence section, led by Captain Mason Harlow] did not tell us that he was Khamis Sirhan's son. Did you know that it was not until you told us, after you found out about all this in mid-January, that *we* found out he was Khamis Sirhan's son? Failure to communicate, Jesus.

Captain Wardman never told me just how high a target Ahmed Sirhan was. It wasn't until we talked with you in January 2006 about this mission that we understood that he was Khamis Sirhan's son, and who exactly Khamis Sirhan was, and that Delta and Navy SEALs took down Khamis Sirhan.

Had we known that prior to the mission on September 29, we would've killed Ahmed Sirhan straightaway. This is the kind of mission that you think of, when you're a scout/sniper: taking down Ahmed Sirhan. This is a bad guy, this is what you signed up to become a sniper for. We're supposed to take down terrorists and insurgents. He was battalion target 58, and now we're into the 1,100 zone. Roger that, it means that we have over 1,100 high-value terrorist and insurgent targets that we have not killed or captured. The hit rate is abysmal.

The 2/6 counterterrorist hit rate is less than 5 percent.
That is an intelligence failure, at the heart of that, and that is
2/6 S-2 intelligence failure. What's so bad about it is that S-2
just hears a name, and they slap a target on him. But they
won't give us a description, they don't give us a picture of
him, and then they expect us to track him and take him
down. That's crazy. That's happened to us before.

It goes down like this:

S-2: "OK, this is a battalion target's house."

"Sure, what's he look like?" I'll say.

S-2: "Medium height, 180 pounds, dark hair, with a Saddam
mustache."

"Well, that's about every adult male in Al Anbar," I'll say.

S-2: "OK, just give us a call if you see any military age males
enter or leave the house."

S-2 is just shitty. I mean, you're talking godawful intelligence. Captain Harlow, the 2/6 intelligence officer, never
goes out the wire. If you're not in the field, you can't analyze
what comes from the field.

Really shitty intelligence. And then it just gets to the point
where you realize, I'll do this mission and get it out of the way
because we, in actuality, have no hard human intelligence on
our targets here.

Do the mission, get it done, and call for extraction when it's
done.

It was our first mission on September 29, the Ahmed Sirhan
goatfuck. About eight o'clock Kelso and me were up on the
roof. Milstid and Jay were downstairs. It was eight o'clock A.M.,
and I was looking through the spotting scope. About 800
meters out, and I saw this guy. He was 800 meters from us, at
this point. Well within range of our 40s. Now, we had a lot of
physical intel on Ahmed Sirhan—photo, height, weight, and
so on.

It pretty much matched to a tee: "180 centimeters tall, and
he's about 200 pounds." I knew right away it was Ahmed
Sirhan.

I was sure it was him, and he looked to be about 210. He walked away, and about an hour later, I saw the same guy.

He was wearing the same clothes, a blue shirt and blue sweatpants. He was walking right toward us. We were on the west side of him. There's a little canal that runs north and south. We were in the house, on the other side of the muddy canal.

We had Ahmed Sirhan in our sights.

He kept walking right toward us.

It was incredible. I had his picture between my legs, and I was glancing down at his picture and matching it to his face as I looked at him in my spotting scope. I knew it was Ahmed Sirhan. There's a bald patch that he has on the right side of his head, near his ear.

When he got about 400 meters out, I could see that very small bald patch through my scope. I called it in and said, "We've got 100 percent ID on this guy. Do you want me to shoot him?"

Captain Wardman asked me, "Is he armed?" And I said, "No, he's not armed." Then the captain told me, "We're coming out with a squad to get him. Just hold on and we'll be right out there."

You've gotta be kidding me. I mean, it's Ahmed Sirhan. That's like asking if Osama Bin Laden is armed. You don't ask if Osama Bin Laden or Zarqawi is armed; you kill them. But it's heavy, now, knowing that Wardman, Aiken, and Harlow, all of them, never told us that he was Khamis Sirhan's son, and how important he is to Black Flags Brigades.

Well, I said, "You'd better hurry up," and I could see that Ahmed Sirhan was fishing in a canal. He'd keep going into the weeds, and then come out of the weeds, however. At first I thought he was checking cache sites, for hiding enemy weapons and explosives, mortar rounds, and rockets. But the pole in his hands was a fishing pole.

He was fishing. I was thinking, at this point, we're denied the kill but we can still capture him.

But Wardman wanted the glory. We could've easily walked up to him with perfect cover, the whole time—there were weeds between our position and the canal. You can only see that if you're in the field.

All of us agreed that we, and we alone, should take him down. Snatch and grab, flex cuff and gag, put a hood on him, call it in and throw him in the back of a humvee.

I only found out later that day how important Ahmed Sirhan is to the terrorists and insurgents—Ahmed Sirhan is the mortar FO, the forward observer, for the terrorists and insurgents. I now know, because you told us since mid-January, that he is the commander of Black Flags Brigades. The Marines didn't tell us that, either. Ahmed Sirhan was behind Kremm and Eckfield's deaths a month later, after Wardman refused to order the kill on Ahmed Sirhan. He planned the mortar and rocket attacks on Golf Company.

Golf was getting mortared and rocketed every day. Kremm and Eckfield died because of Sirhan's mortar systems. We could've stopped it on September 29, 2005. I would've shot him, if I had ever just known that he was Khamis Sirhan's son, first, and leader of Black Flags Brigades, second.

My team could've stopped the mortars from being shot at Golf.

I never would've called it in; with that much intelligence on him, I would've made the call on the spot. I would've taken him down. That's my duty, as a scout/sniper team leader.

But Captain Wardman wanted the glory. He wanted to be the guy who captured a very high-level battalion target. It's a shame we never got the order to kill Ahmed Sirhan. It's criminal that S-2 never told us before the mission that Ahmed Sirhan is the leader of Black Flags Brigades.

Well, Ahmed Sirhan was closer to the gun trucks and seventon massive trucks than we were, so he probably heard them coming way before we did. But that was the thing, REACT was taking so long to get out there, and Ahmed Sirhan was starting to walk away.

I kept calling Captain Wardman and asking him, "How far are you out? How far are you out? He's walking away; he'll be gone in maybe two minutes." And the captain replied, "We're still five more minutes away."

Half the time I called Captain Wardman, he'd just say, "We're loading up now." The Golf REACT was incredibly slow.

Ahmed Sirhan walked out and cleaned the mud off his sandals in the grass. He slowly started walking away from the pond, walking back to the houses he'd come out of.

When he started walking away, and I noticed REACT wasn't going to make it in time, I reiterated to Captain Wardman, "Just let me shoot him, he's getting away." But the captain said again, "No, no, no." He was all hyper and anxious, freaking out, talking all fast over the radio. Really freaking out.

Meanwhile, Ahmed Sirhan was walking east, toward Lobster, toward the road. The road was his immediate escape route, of course, leading to the highway we called Mobile, that runs to Syria. And now we know, of course, that he has a safe house in Damascus.

Here's the kicker: REACT turned down Grouper [a hard dogleg left that veers away from Abu Shiezel and leads directly to the Euphrates River] to get behind the village. They should have stayed on Lobster, but they didn't stay on Lobster. They took the fork left onto Grouper, which takes you deep into the Pocket.

What I was thinking was the common-sense thing: They had two squads. I would've sent a squad straight onto Lobster and sent a second squad into the village to push him out into view. Leave him no option, seal off his escape routes. Chop his flanks up, corner him, leave him no option.

Close off Ahmed Sirhan's main avenue of escape, Lobster first. That's just classic tactics. Shut down his main avenue of escape. Then force him back toward the village. But no one asked us, of course, and even if we'd ventured our opinion, you've got to remember, you're dealing with Captain Wardman, who thinks he's God's gift to the Marine Corps.

If Captain Wardman had ever asked us, "Can you go out there and grab him?" Hell, yes. Everybody in our team would've had no problem with that. But he didn't ask us. The 1/6 scout/snipers told us that they had no problems leaving a hide, to go secure a site or capture a terrorist, until REACT showed up. Simply, 1/6 Marine scout/snipers had done just that—captured terrorists and secured them, then flex-cuffed them, put hoods on them, and put them on the back of a humvee.

A good REACT shouldn't take more than ten minutes from Golf firm base to Ahmed Sirhan's village. That's a very short distance, from Al Saqlawiyah to Abu Shiezel. The drive itself is five minutes, max.

The high almighty captain that Wardman claims to be, you would think he would know how to do land navigation. He got the REACT lost; he fucked it all up, at that point.

He took that turn onto Grouper, to sneak up on the flank. He was trying to be way too slick. That turn onto Grouper, as it turned out, was no mistake. He wanted to do that. Well, I was constantly on the radio: "Hurry up, he's getting away, hurry up." Ahmed Sirhan could hear those trucks, the seven-ton and the humvees, and he'd been on his cell phone.

I thought that Wardman would make a beeline for Ahmed Sirhan—we were losing valuable time. I finally got eyes on the Golf Company Marines, on the patrol on foot. And I told them, "I lost sight of him behind these weeds. So most likely, he's still in those weeds or somewhere around those weeds."

I showed Wardman and the Marines exactly where the weeds were, where I last saw Ahmed Sirhan. But they refused to search the weeds, and went immediately into houses about 50 meters away.

I told Corporal Moore, who was Captain Wardman's radioman on the patrol, "tell him to search the weeds." And Moore said, "Roger, copy, search the weeds." But Wardman only kept walking toward the houses, and he never searched the weeds. I say again: Wardman never searched the weeds.

Wardman's Marines never even looked in those weeds. They went into the houses and talked to the neighbors. The villagers denied that they'd ever seen Ahmed Sirhan. Of course, the *erhabi* is very tight; they're not often going to dime out their neighbors and relatives.

Captain Wardman stayed in that village about an hour. No one used Lobster to get to the village. Ronin3, my team, was about 100 meters west of Lobster. Ahmed Sirhan was about 150 meters west of Lobster as he was fishing. The perfect approach to capture Ahmed Sirhan was on Lobster; anyone 10,000 miles outside of Iraq, just reading a map of that area, can see that easily.

If Captain Wardman and Golf Marines had taken the pragmatic approach to the village, straight on Lobster, they would've come up right on him. They would have seen him from the road, very easily. They searched for about an hour. My team was ordered to stay in place.

Right when it got dark, about nine P.M., I saw four guys digging on the edge of a field. You don't plant at night. All four had shovels. So that's likely digging for a cache to hide mortar rounds, rockets, and other munitions in. I called it in. There was no response to kill, just "Roger." Here's the thing about Golf Company: Their radio watch is lame.

They just don't give a fuck. The only thing that the Golf Company radio watch is concerned about is "Man, I get off radio watch in about two hours, then I can chill and watch a DVD." It has happened to us on numerous times, out at Golf. The Golf Company Marines on radio watch just don't care.

We've had many occasions where we've called in, "Hey, we've got guys doing something very fishy. We could use some enlightenment from someone higher. One guy just handed a bag to another guy, and the other guy just sped off. Do you want us to shoot him or what?"

And the radio watch would just say, "Roger." Just "Roger."

With me, when I hear something over the radio, even if it's just one squad getting a radio check with another one—

anything that comes over the radio—I respond, and if I can't
fix it, I get someone who can fix it, someone who knows more
than I do.

But with Golf 2/6, we kept getting no response from their
radio watches on missions, and we knew that Golf didn't care.
We started feeling useless in Al Saqlawiyah. So we just stopped
calling in.

I could go on all day about 2/6 failing to employ us as
scout/snipers.

December was the worst. Just god-awful. The countersniper
operations in December were a complete waste of time. That's
when we knew—our battalion just does not give a fuck about
us.

December was living proof of just how much Aiken didn't
give a fuck about us. That's what really pissed us off—that 2/6,
RCT-8, Regimental Combat Team-8 at Camp Fallujah, and
Naval Special Warfare used us Marine scout/snipers as glori-
fied gate guards, completely wasting our time at static positions in the so-called countersniper operations in December.

That's a core mission for us, countersniper ops, one we are
specifically trained for by the Marine Corps to execute in combat.

But Aiken had no faith in us, and he flat out refused to
stand for us in December—he rolled over big-time for regimental command. And all we could do, since RCT-8 ordered
us to stand guard, was stand guard.

We are Marine scout/snipers, and we were pulling guard
duty in Fallujah while our brothers were getting killed by terrorist snipers in Fallujah. I say again: Terrorist snipers were
killing our guys in Fallujah, and we are Marine scout/snipers,
but we were relegated to guard duty all of December. I want the
parents of every Marine killed by terrorist snipers in the Winter
of the Sniper to know that; that is the damned sad truth.

That's insane, but that's Aiken. It happened, you witnessed
it, and I know for a fact that 2/6 screwed the pooch by refus-
ing to listen to you also, just like they refused to listen to us.
You were the only one in this battalion who'd been here

before, and you were in deep, night and day. You were on missions with Delta, for Chrissakes, and on desert reconnaissance. No one in 2/6 can say that. But not listening is a prerequisite for combat command if you're under Aiken.

The battalion commander just rolled over and played dead for RCT-8. And Recon [1st Reconnaissance Battalion], those stellar fuckers, they just fucked that all up. This is what we did for the month of December 2005: We did radio watch in Fallujah, at observation post Shocker [OP Shocker]. Because Recon owned us, and Recon owned us because Aiken let them.

We all said, "This is the biggest pile of bullshit. Let's make them think that we're working. We'll just call in our hourly radio checks." And at night, we'd go up on the roof. OP Shocker was mad haunted—you can hear bodies being dragged on the floor at like three in the morning.

That place is haunted. You'll pop fifty chem lites, and all you can see is a little bit of light—you can't see shit in that place.

It is for real crazy mad haunted, it is spooky. So at night, we'd get up on the roof. We waited out the month of December like that—that's how we wasted a month in combat in Fallujah in December 2005.

That's when the whole platoon just did not give a shit anymore.

We stopped fighting for missions that we should've been doing, stopped trying to sell ourselves to Captain Grube, the Fox Company commander. He didn't listen to us either; he just didn't care.

"Hey sir, you guys are doing this. We can help you by doing this, and this and this . . ." we stopped doing that, entirely.

We realized that the battalion really didn't care about us. We knew you understood how we felt when we talked with you in January. You were the only one who gave us the intelligence on terrorist snipers being trained in Syria and western Iraq, also.

We all talked about that, how our own Marine Corps refused to give us intelligence on Al Qaeda and other terrorist and insurgent snipers, but Mike Tucker did not fail to give us the intelligence. You cared more about us than our own command.

We were all on the same page with you at that point. Let's just survive, survival is victory, because all we can count on is Ronin—all we could count on is ourselves.

January was pretty much the same. February was more bullshit. Granted, we were going out on more missions. Al Qaeda and Black Flags Brigades saw the gutless decisions being made and acted accordingly, got more aggressive. We got hit with suicide bombs not long after. And more terrorist snipers. The enemy here is not stupid.

I hit my two-year mark in August 2004, and I seriously thought about reenlisting. I mean, becoming a scout/sniper, that's been my life goal. I wanted to be a scout/sniper in the Marines, all my life. But no more.

This combat deployment has not totally made me regret volunteering for the Marines, but one notch below regret. I've lost all respect for the Marine Corps. The only thing I'm worried about right now is getting out and what happens after I get out.

That's my new life goal, but after that, I really don't care. It's been a rough, rough deployment for us. Our rules of engagement [ROE], too, fucked us.

We are not under combat ROE. We're in a guerrilla war, and we're not under combat ROE. That's mad. But it's real. There's way too much politics now.

Now I'm getting the hell out. I hate this place. And everybody in it. I really feel like this now: Fuck the Corps, I need to get out.

This is my third deployment. My first deployment was in 2003, with Golf Company. I had to stay at Camp Commando in Kuwait on guard duty. Then we ran supplies north toward Baghdad. I have no idea where we were; they never told us.

I want to tell the American people that I love my brother scout/snipers to death. We came here together and we are leaving together. That's the one thing that I'm going to miss when I get out: pretty much everybody in the platoon.

We are a band of brothers. We are Ronin. We are samurais without masters, 8541, scout/snipers, the real deal. I will never forget my brothers.

Novi and Lutze, Elder and Ski, Sergeant Parra and Hodulich, all of us. We lived side by side in the same rooms for seven months. Every day you have to hear Lutze's war cries, Lutze the cagefighter, a wild man and a helluva good Marine. Roger that, we all hear Lutze's war cries and listen to Novi's and Milstid's songs, watch Novi's videos, feed Ski Skittles and candy. We all bitch about the same things, and we all have sacrificed together.

We are Marylanders, Virginians, Texans, and New Yorkers— we are Marines. This is our generation that is bleeding here. And that means men in the ranks my age and commanders your age.

"Six days without a cigarette, no joy on that frequency."

CORPORAL DARREN SMYKOWSKI, RONIN4 TEAM LEADER;
CORPORAL JUSTIN NOVI, RONIN4 ASSISTANT TEAM LEADER;
CORPORAL STEPHEN LUTZE, RONIN4 SCOUT/SNIPER AND
LIGHT MACHINE GUNNER; AND CORPORAL NOAH FLEMING,
RONIN2 ASSISTANT TEAM LEADER; OCTOBER 5, 2005

After six days without a cigarette, Ronin4 scout/snipers, led by Corporal Darren Smykowski, killed an Iraqi *erhabi* moving munitions by boat on the Euphrates River, just after dawn on October 5, 2005.

Golf 2/6 was still being hammered by Black Flags Brigades enemy mortars and rockets, like clockwork, every day at roughly two in the afternoon on the firm base in Al Saqlawiyah, after Captain Wardman's failure to order Boyer's team to kill or capture Ahmed Sirhan. Occasionally we'd get hit at dusk, too, mortars and rockets thudding inside our compound, Marines rushing to get flak jackets and helmets on, fire team leaders and squad leaders and platoon sergeants screaming, "Get a fuckin' head count! Make sure everybody is up! Get fuckin' accountability!"

Ronin4's mission was to carry out reconnaissance and surveillance from a hide site on the Euphrates, in the ruins of one of the late Uday Hussein's former palaces, and kill any *erhabi* on the river. The enemy mortar and rocket points of origin, where we believed Ahmed Sirhan was planning and executing the attacks on Golf Company's base, were in the Shark's Fin, across the Euphrates.

Human intelligence from Iraqi interpreters led Ronin4 to believe that mortars and rockets were being moved from caches in the Shark's Fin, across the Euphrates in small boats, carried into the Pocket—to villages such as Abu Shiezel, for instance—and then fired from farmland near heavily reeded shorelines of canals, directly north of Golf Company's base in Al Saqlawiyah.

Smykowski, a whip-smart and jovial twenty-one-year-old Marine from Mentor, Ohio, with two brothers in the Marines, set Ronin4 in a hide site in the ruined palace, wrecked by J-Dam bombs in March 2003, a palace I later entered with Travis Twiggs and 1st Platoon Golf Company Marine infantrymen.

Climbing through the ruins of Uday's palace with Twiggs in early November 2005, we reached Smykowski's former hide site. Dust swirled in the stinking palace, stench like dead animal smell throughout the mounds of rubble and concrete slabs jutting up at all angles. Rusted red steel rebars were exposed in the walls, like looking at the skeleton of a whale.

You could see the Euphrates less than fifty meters away—on the opposite side of the Euphrates, the infamous Shark's Fin. Renowned for deep and broad support of Al Qaeda in Iraq and Black Flags Brigades, many retired Ba'athist *Mukhabarat* and many of Saddam's Army officers call the farming villages of the Shark's Fin home.

Walls of reeds climbed both shores of the Euphrates. Wide groves of date palm trees poled the sky, across the river. You could not see the river from the ground. The only way you could carry out reconnaissance and surveillance on enemy activity on the western banks of the Euphrates, in the Shark's Fin, was from a rooftop of a house or the ruins of that Ba'athist palace.

On October 5, 2005, from the hide site within the ruins of the former Ba'athist palace, Corporal Noah Fleming and Corporal Justin Novi were the first of anyone in 2/6 to kill an Iraqi *erhabi*.

After Ronin4 extracted, being picked up from the mission and returning to Golf Company's base in Al Saqlawiyah, I interviewed Smykowski's team. Smykowksi is referred to by his nickname Ski throughout the interview.

Smykowski was a stocky, burly team leader who carried the M40A-3 like a toothpick across his broad shoulders. Brown-haired, about five-eleven and built like an outside linebacker, he loved to talk about the Great Lakes and Ohio and his girl back home. He planned scout/sniper missions with exceptional attention to detail and was well respected by his comrades.

His brother Sergeant Mark Smykowski, Reconnaissance Marine, was in 2nd Reconnaissance Battalion. The Smykowski brothers reunited at the end of Ronin's combat tour, in April 2006, in Fallujah. Mark's death in combat in western Iraq, just after his brother returned to America, hit Ski hard. Sergeant Mark Smykowski's funeral, with full military honors, was attended by many of Ronin's scout/snipers, and more than 3,000 mourners.

Corporal Justin Novi of Pittsburgh, Pennsylvania, a great good friend of Ski's, was Ronin4's grenadier in October and later Smykowski's assistant team leader, aiding Ronin4 in pre-mission planning, land navigation, and using his conversational proficiency in Arabic at all times necessary.

Five-nine and lean, dark haired, and dark eyed, Novi was always first to spider-climb a wall and enter target houses on Ronin4's missions in Fallujah. A huge fan of the Pittsburgh Penguins ice hockey team, Novi is a brilliant young filmmaker. His documentaries, which ranged from the comical to the poignant to the absurd, kept us all on an even keel—without Novi, it would have been a much tougher combat tour. Novi kept it light. He also wrote songs and played guitar.

With Corporal Daniel Milstid of Ronin3, he recorded original songs on his computer when not on missions in western Iraq, some stomp-down hilarious and many very moving and well crafted. Novi is a born songwriter; he has the gift. He is a natural creative soul and long may he thrive. Novi's primary weapon was an M203 grenade launcher/assault rifle. He was qualified on all sniper systems and superb on reconnaissance and surveillance. He also carried an M9 Beretta 9-millimeter pistol on his right hip, a clip jacked in and two extra clips on the side.

Corporal Stephen Lutze of Ronin4 is the best tail-end Charlie I've ever seen in combat, and an outstanding Marine. He grew up in Interlachan, Florida, roughly an hour and a half west of the Atlantic, and claimed to "rassle gators" with his bare hands, "sharks on both sides of us and gators in the middle—makes life interesting." Lutze quoted from the Bible at the drop of a hat and inquired about Zen Buddhism at every opportunity. He carried a light machine gun and also, on occasion, the SAM-R, an M16A4 with a free-floating barrel in it for greater accuracy, similar to a Remington .308 hunting rifle, and unlike the regular M16A4s, with a setting for full automatic fire.

A generous soul, he was a master of hand-to-hand combat, an articulate and reflective man, and a great light machine gunner. He studied combat tracking and martial arts under Staff Sergeant Travis Twiggs. "I will not rest until my generation does what we must do to take down Osama Bin Laden and all Al Qaeda," Lutze said. "We must destroy the evil of radical Islamic terrorism; there is no choice." There was always a stack of books beneath his bunk. A gangbanger from Florida in his youth, Lutze straightened out his life in the Marines. You could always find him reading the Bible, texts concerning Christianity, Islam, and Buddhism, and other religious works when he was not on missions.

Corporal Noah Fleming of Ronin4 never failed to surprise us in Fallujah and western Iraq with his keen eye for detail and sixth sense for enemy activity. Fleming hailed from Windsor, Virginia, and was twenty-three years old in the spring of 2006. He had great reconnaissance mojo. He had a mysterious ability to point out exactly the right reconnaissance and surveillance positions on a rooftop or in a tree line near the Euphrates, for instance, and his instincts were always dead-solid perfect.

Fleming was forever writing letters to his girlfriend, and like any Marine with a woman stateside, he thought of her night and day. The Kurdish general and *peshmerga* veteran General Jamil Besefsky told me on September 26, 2003, in Dahuk, Iraqi Kurdistan, "War is always a far voyage, like a journey into the unknown. This was true of all the years I fought Saddam. And what has kept me alive is knowing my woman has never forgotten me, as I have never forgotten her—she is always on my mind, always in my heart. With death on our backs, we carried on, fought in the mountains for many years against Saddam. And now we have prevailed, brother, now we have prevailed. With death on our backs and women on our mind, after so many long journeys into the unknown, after losing so many of our comrades, now we have prevailed." Fleming reminded me of Besefsky, in his way.

Broad-shouldered and genial, Fleming was the tallest of Ronin, at six five, and only Corporal Jay Elder could look him in the eye. The scout/snipers called him by his first name, Noah, and Lutze never hesitated to ask him where the ark had really touched ashore. "Don't give us that song and dance about Mount Ararat in Turkey. No, that's not where you left it for real, Noah, be for real, now."

Like Lutze, Fleming loved to read and was a great sniper. Fleming carried the M40A3 sniper rifle, a scoped-out SAM-R, an M9 9-millimeter Beretta pistol, and a few fighting knives. Like his brothers in Ronin, he was clutch on all small arms.

Following is my interview with the men of Ronin4 after their mission.

Ski: Monday morning at 3:17 A.M. we inserted. Thirtieth September. Zero dark thirty. Six days ago. It was very bright out.

A lot of moon. We had two attachments from Golf. It was one of Uday's palaces. It was almost daylight; it had been bombed. There was nothing there at the top of the stairs. The only two rooms were facing east and west along the river.

There was a crawl space under one of the rooms. We put three on the eastern side and three on the west. Set up our hides. We had to hoist up our packs with parachute cord. 5:30 A.M., we had everyone up. Me and Novi set up on eastern side. Fleming and Lutze were on the western side.

Mission was to find the origin of the mortar attacks. Kill the enemy before he can kill us again. What I could see on my side was the sharp bend in the river. We had two klicks [kilometers] covered down the river. Mainly we watched the northern side of the river—northern side was our area of operations, southern side of the river was U.S. Army area of operations.

Fleming: We set up two-man rotation for two hours on, four hours off. Golf Marines did what we told them to: good infantrymen. Solid.

Ski: It was next to impossible to remain quiet because there was so much rubble.

Fleming: Took us about an hour to realize it was Rat Central. Rats everywhere, knocking around pebbles and stones.

Ski: There were bats everywhere and pigeons. We realized no one could sneak up on us without the rats and pigeons and owls serving as our early warning system. Heard about eight explosions. We had solid communications, solid comm. The explosions crashed out at about five in the morning on October 3rd. At 6:15 A.M., a huge explosion shook the palace ruins.

Fleming: Right at the time of the huge explosion, I saw a small blue skiff, wooden boat with oars, coming down the river, and there were fish everywhere now on the surface of the river. On the bank of the river was a ten-foot wall. Reeds fifteen feet high. He was in the dead space. I could see him, but Ski could not, because of the angle I had.

Ski: You could see the dead space we were missing. The explosion shook the entire house. Called it in. It seemed that on that day, and the fourth, that someone may have known, or suspected, that we were there. That night, on the third, I reported a boat on the river with a mortar tube at 9:30 A.M. The rules were nobody can cross the river. But rules of engagement were that you have to identify a weapon in hand. We didn't shoot. From the Army side, to our side, at late dusk, we saw two males. They'd pull into the reeds and vanish. We maintained surveillance. Notified Golf Company. Sent 60-millimeter illum [illumination]. Eleven rounds. Then there were a couple more explosions. .50-cal rattled for a good hour on the Army side. More impacts. Every night we were out there, there were impacts. Sounded like mortar rounds.

Lutze: Now, October 4th. Still on the Euphrates, brother. The fourth river God made, says the Good Book. Mad shady, now the shady stuff hit us. Made us for sure think that the

enemy knew we were there, for real. Mad shady. Got dicey, on
October 4th. We had Novi the Ice Hockey King, so we knew
we were cool. Rock on, King Novi. Mad shady, baby.

Fleming: Lutze is dead-on. Roger that, it was mad shady.
Way too quiet. It was, honest to God—the wind wasn't even
blowing. You could hear a pin drop—oh no, you could hear a
pin falling through the damn air. I took my M40A3 and I was
in the dead zone, posted myself there so we could see the
dead space. In the rubble. Dust and rubble, and rats crawling
everywhere.

Ski: Me and Novi, all that day, we were looking at each
other, same look: It's too fuckin' quiet.

Novi: Only thing going in the logbook was radio checks.
Fleming said the same thing. No sighting of any enemy. No
one on the water. We were on the case, professional, taking
care of business.

Ski: Roger that. On the Euphrates, dusk came on quick, but
right before dusk, there was one boat out on the water. Green
boat, two males, same wooden skiffs. Talking to each other
and pointing to us. Talking and looking at each other. Their
hands were motioning up toward us.

The only thing I could think of was that the bird feathers
were catching on the outside of the screens. And they were
noticing that, likely. There were no hanging screens on the
balcony, on any of the windows in the ruins, before we set up
our reconnaissance. Without the screens, however—there was
no other way to set up our hide.

Fleming: We were supposed to pull out, and we got a radio
call, "What do you need for resupply? You'll stay out for two
more days."

Novi: We were still good on water. We came very well pre-
pared.

Lutze: The first day, I was sick to my stomach. O Lord! Doc
Gutierrez, the great Doc Gute from Texas, came out to help
me. Cool Papa Doc, the righteous Navy Corpsman. Lone Star
State, hell yes. You're talking Doc Gute, baby. There is only one
Doc Gute, and he is bad. God is a friend of Doc Gute! Long live

Doc Gute. People will one day write songs and make movies about Doc Gute. I kid you not, brother. The Doc from Texas.

Novi: There was activity on our position, with that linkup, at about three in the morning. That day was wild, come dusk. October 4th. The drive-by hit us at 1830. A screech right after, and we figured it was a drive-by. There was muzzle flash. Enemy fire. We realized they were testing us. And our resupply came. Humvees, blacked out.

And we found a powerboat on the palace grounds. Very expensive and totally stripped. No doubt, Uday's powerboat. You can see where the money went in this country: powerboats, palaces, gold-plated toilets, Saddam flying in the whores every month and flying in new ones when he'd fly out the old ones after a month, and these people we see in western Iraq, dirt poor. No plumbing, no electricity, no schools, no health clinics, no hospitals, no roads. You can see where the money never touched.

Fleming: As soon as we got back in the house, our resupply came. Threw it over the house. But it wasn't enough.

Ski: I said to Fleming, "We need more water. And we only found one bag of chow, but there was supposed to be three." Fleming and Novi came back with two more chows and we started praying.

Fleming: Justin saw the owl inside the palace.

Novi: I heard something hit the roof. And I saw the owl. And I remembered my mom telling me, "Every time I see an owl, someone in the family dies." And she was right, too. And we'd get a phone call, like a day later.

Lutze: And it's true, somebody did die, but luckily it wasn't one of us.

Ski: You know, we had to dump all our piss and poured it all down a toilet drain. Now our whole building smelled like piss, and right then our call for resupply came. We put an IR chem light on all our trash and left it for the pickup. Now it was today, October 5th, at five in the morning.

Fleming: I set up my perch in the rubble. It was absolutely beautiful. I saw a blue boat come out of the reeds, paddling

against the current, from the Army side. He got all the way,
right past me. I jumped up and ran so I could see him come
up on our shore bank. He was using the current now, no pad-
dles or oars. I had the 40. And he was drifting slowly into a
group of reeds and reaches down and grabs a huge grenade.
He threw it and got behind the reeds, and it blasted us. He
went behind the reeds, and I lost visual. He got dead-smack
center in the dead zone. Couldn't see him anymore.

Ski: I got on comm and told my guys, "If you see him, shoot
him."

Fleming: I switched out with a Golf Marine, got an M16A4,
and Novi and Ski ran with me to the river wall. On the river
wall, we climbed through a fence and broke through the
reeds, about forty feet of reeds. I could see the bow of the
skiff.

Novi: I yelled at him in Arabic, "Come out! Come out
now!"

Fleming: Right then, I heard him insert a magazine. An
AK-47 makes a loud noise, if you slap a clip up in it real quick.
I could hear that metallic hard slap of the clip going in, slam.
I opened up on him.

Novi: He stood up and I had him in my crosshairs. We lit
him up.

Fleming: I wanted to get that damn boat too. For evidence.
He fell right over into the river. I didn't realize how strong the
current was.

Lutze: Noah and Novi fired, almost together.

Fleming: I got the boat, and Ski and Novi were looking for
the body.

Ski: We reckoned that he might have explosives on him.

Lutze: Fleming gave that Golf guy the 40, and he handed it
to me. I saw through my scope what happened. Clear as day.
God is good, he made me a Marine and I scoped out everything at that point.

Fleming: In the boat, I found a case for an arty round, for a
155. We pulled the boat up, ran upstairs, and our platoon sergeant, Staff Sergeant Christopher Williams, began searching

for the body. I jumped back in the river, and his body was all twisted but he wasn't dead. He had one arm under him, like he was holding something.

Ski: Staff Sergeant Williams screamed at him in Arabic, and he put his hands up.

Fleming: Both his knees were gone. One shoulder was gone. There was blood all over his face, his mouth was mush.

Lutze: When I was observing, I thought we fired five rounds into him.

Ski: I thought his legs would come off in my hands. If we'd hit him with five rounds of 7.62, he'd be done.

Novi: When you have to take down enemy in combat, as a Marine scout/sniper, training takes over. You do exactly what you are trained to do, you are professional. But we need bullets with real stopping power.

Ski: This was our first combat action as a team of Marine scout/snipers. It was 7:30 when we got out of there this morning. No cigarettes for Fleming: It was a real trial for the big fella from Virginia. We almost cried for him.

Fleming: Six days without a cigarette, no joy on that frequency. I really enjoyed that cigarette this morning. Lutze even applauded!

Lutze: It was good to see Noah smiling, lighting up that smoke. We all did our job out there—Novi's right, we need heavier rounds, more stopping power. 5.56-caliber is for varmint hunting, not combat.

Ski: Right. If we were firing .308 or 7.62, any true combat round, we would have killed that insurgent today. 5.56-caliber is bullshit. It's not a combat round. It has no stopping power. You have to shoot five, six rounds to stop someone.

One 7.62 will drop a man. Two well-placed 7.62s will drop and kill the enemy. Stopping power is the main thing—and our enemy fires heavier, combat-effective rounds. The vital question on anything related to war, as far as weapons and munitions, what we take to war: Is this rifle, bullet, grenade *combat effective?* Will it help me *in war?* Will it help me destroy my enemy?

Any 6.8-caliber round, 7.62, .303, .308 round—yes. These
are all combat effective. More to the point, they are designed
for war, not for varmint hunting. 5.56-caliber is not designed
at all for combat. It was created for varmint hunting: rabbits,
squirrels, etc. You can look it up. The official designation for
the original 5.56 round is "for varmints."

Novi: You don't use a penknife to cut through steel. You
use a welding torch. But the majority of our combat weapons
are like penknives going up against forged steel. Wrong
answer.

This is not rocket science, this is war; in war, you must kill
your enemy. Our assault rifles, for instance—they are not built
on the philosophy of "kill the enemy." You can shoot to
wound with the M16A2 and M16A4, or M4. Any of the Stoner
5.56-caliber systems shoot to wound very well. I'm not at war
to shoot to wound. None of us go to war to shoot to wound.

We're Marines. We fight to win and we shoot to kill. Give us
a weapon we can win with, because in this war, here and in
Afghanistan, it's all about stopping power, speed, deception,
surprise, and swift, violent actions.

Quit sending Marines and the Army to war with rifles that
are combat ineffective. Send us to war with rifles designed for
war.

"There's no for-sure place you are going to land when you are free-falling in the air."

LANCE CORPORAL ROBERT WATSON,
MARINE INFANTRYMAN, 3RD SQUAD,
3RD PLATOON, GOLF COMPANY 2/6,
MARCH 8, 2006

Lance Corporal Robert Watson, who was born in Florida and now calls Rockford, Illinois, home, survived a roadside bomb attack on September 29, 2006, an attack planned and executed by Ahmed Sirhan's Black Flags Brigades, on a bridge crossing a canal near Golf's firm base in Al Saqlawiyah. I was fifty meters behind when the two 155-millimeter artillery rounds, set deep in dirt and gravel, shot shrapnel right by all of 3/3, 3rd Squad, 3rd Platoon.

Fist-size shards of steel blasted by us. Marines raced to the sides of the road, setting up firing positions. Fire team leaders ran from Marine to Marine, getting accountability.

I thought Watson was dead, along with many Marines from 3rd Platoon on the patrol. The blast was concussive and massive, and a huge black smoke cloud rose from the northern side of the canal bridge.

By some miracle, Watson survived. What was even more incredible, as Watson explains, is that the point man Lance Corporal DiLoretto survived. Watson was less than ten feet from the IED went it went off, and DiLoretto was basically right next to it. But quite fortunately, the *erhabi* who planted the IED dug it in next to a heavy concrete stanchion on the northern side of the bridge. Most of the blast went away from the road, back-blasted by the concrete into high reeds and saw grass west of the bridge.

Watson is an easy-going young infantryman with a generous spirit. Redheaded and freckle-faced, he endured many guerrilla war actions, like all of 3rd Platoon.

Combat changes people—that was true when Xenophon fought in Cunaxa, Mesopotamia, in 401 B.C., just a stone's throw from where Watson survived the roadside blast, and is equally true in our time.

By the time Watson spoke to me in March 2006, he'd changed too, like all of us. Hardened, happier than ever to be alive, like his brother Marine infantryman from 2nd Platoon, the irrepressible American of Irish blood, Lance Corporal Kellen Burke of Boston, who stated matter-of-factly, "We are Marines, and it is our duty to face death," Watson similarly accepted the rigors, challenges, and sacrifices that are part of being a Marine infantryman.

Well, let me start by saying that I'm from Florida. But I went from the sunshine to the snow. We moved to Illinois when I was seventeen. My first day of boot camp was August 12, 2004. I graduated from boot camp on November 5, 2004. Very close to the Marine Corps birthday on November 10. It was hell in boot camp. I had the Confederate flag tattooed on my left shoulder, and all my drill instructors were black.

This is my first deployment to Iraq. I'm a .203 gunner. I carry six grenades at all times, on missions. I carry eight magazines.

There were only three of us on the fire team: Lance Corporal DiLoretto, Corporal Williamson, and me. Only a three-man fire team that day.

We had just crossed over the bridge, over the canal. Right near the bridge, I looked over at Corporal Williamson and smiled. And it went off. There was smoke everywhere.

I could hear shrapnel flying everywhere. As I was going through the air, I felt my sling going off from around my neck, and I saw myself going toward the ground.

All I could see was dust and stuff, so I closed my eyes. And at that moment, my Kevlar hit me in the back of the head and knocked me out. I woke up and my weapon was gone.

I got up. And I ran behind a building and took a knee. Then I found my weapon, caked full of dirt. And I slung it again. My ears were ringing, but I could hear a faded echo of people calling my name. The echo in my ears was so loud.

I ran up to our Marines on the road. I took a knee. There was smoke everywhere, and I was alive. Dust and smoke, a haze.

People were telling me it's amazing that I was alive. It blew the whole stanchion up. Thank God the IED was pointed away from the road.

I carried on, like nothing ever happened. After that, I kind of became the IED magnet. Now, every time I'm close to an IED, I'll get an upset stomach.

And I tell people, "There's an IED." And damn sure, after Staff Sergeant William Klinger, my platoon sergeant, said, "We better check it out," it turned out to be an IED and we set up a cordon. That was in early October. Any time since, if I feel the IED in my gut and get an upset stomach, there it is.

I remember, from when that first IED went off, there was a guy that Corporal Williamson said looked suspicious. And that's the moment when Williamson smiled. He saw that guy in a white *dishtasha*.

Then the IED went off. And Doc Guzman said he saw two guys running through the field.

I'll never forget flying through the air; it was unreal. I was looking up at the sky. I thought for sure that I was going into the water. There's no for-sure place you are going to land when you are free-falling in the air. And the water was right there, right there beside me. I was right on the bank when it hit.

I landed about three feet from the side of the water, but my weapon landed at least ten feet away from me, on the other side of the small house.

Watson paused here and looked down for quite a spell. He looked up and sipped from a cup of coffee, and then began talk-

ing about Sergeant Adams, late of Weapons Company, a Marine
killed by a roadside bomb on October 15, 2005. The IED attack
occurred just east of where Watson had been blown into the air on
September 29, 2005. Sergeant Adams had volunteered for the
combat tour. He could have remained stateside, but he volunteered to go in harm's way with Weapons Company 2/6 and was
one of the most respected Marines in the battalion. Adams died on
the date of the constitutional referendum elections in Iraq. Watson
was one of the last Marines to see him alive. What follows are his
reflections on the death of Sergeant Adams.

You know, when Sergeant Adams died, we all kind of lost it.
He was one of my good friends. Me, Sergeant Fejzic, and so
many of us hung out with him in Wilmington, North Carolina.

Right before Sergeant Adams died, there was a car. Right at
the road.

Four Iraqis, standing outside the car. They smiled and
waved to us as we went down the road. The IED went off. And
they ran into their car and hauled ass. We chased that car
down and shot the hell out of it.

And the cease-fire went around. I was out of rounds. And I
grabbed my M203, but Sergeant Fejzic told me, "That's a no-
go."

And Doc Guzman was still trying to help Sergeant Adams. I
was holding his head in the truck. His head was in my hands.
My hands were full of blood. We were all talking to him, trying
to comfort him. Hoping he would stay alive.

He died right there in the truck with us. We said a prayer
for Sergeant Adams—we prayed for him right there, for his
soul. We prayed. O Lord. Then the Golf Company REACT
came and took him.

Now let me tell you about the Iraqi Police and the IEDs.
The Iraqi Police are crooked sonsobitches. There's plenty of
IEDs that the IPs could have stopped here. But I am certain
that the IPs are behind many IEDs.

The IPs are worthless. They are in with the *erhabi*. I don't
trust them. They say don't trust the Iraqis in Al Saqlawiyah.

But I will trust the Iraqis here before I trust the IPs. The IPs will come around you and act like they are your friends. But as soon as you've got your back turned, that's when they'll stab you in the back.

Yet we're working with the IPs, teaching them everything that we know. Arming them. Training them. Giving them all kinds of weapons and equipment to help them out! For what? For them to turn the weapons against us. The Iraqi Army, on the other hand, is badass.

I have no issues with the Iraqi Army; they are badass. They go after the terrorists. And they know that the police are just as bad *erhabi* as Diya Shakur Farhan himself. [After Ahmed Sirhan, leader of Black Flags Brigades, Diya Shakur Farhan was the most-wanted Iraqi Sunni Arab insurgent/terrorist leader in western Iraq—and like Ahmed Sirhan, at the time of this writing, the Marines have failed to kill or capture him]. The IPs are real cowards and support terrorists here. Diya Shakur Farhan is one stone-cold evil terrorist leader, and the IPs are his friends.

I want the American people to know that we did our damnedest to help the people of Al Saqlawiyah to stop the *erhabi* from hurting them, kidnapping them, and stealing their property. But there is only so much you can do to help the Iraqis, without them at some point realizing they need to help themselves.

We stood tall for every mission and helped one another to stay alive. We're the main squad that does raids. We put on our cammie paint and bust in like a SWAT team. Make the raid—do what we've gotta do and get the fuck out of there. Now that we've been here, we feel like the Marine Saqlawiyah Police Department, not like Marine infantrymen. I'm so glad to be done here. I'm ready to go home and get married.

"Miles shot two insurgents
in the mosque. He was on the rooftop.
Right, he didn't hesitate to engage. He
killed them in the mosque."

LANCE CORPORAL JAMES MATTHEWS,
MARINE INFANTRYMAN, 3RD SQUAD,
3RD PLATOON, GOLF COMPANY 2/6,
MARCH 8, 2006

Lance Corporal Jimmy Matthews, twenty-three years old and a comrade of Watson's, was just steps behind him when the Black Flags Brigades roadside bomb went off on the northern side of the canal bridge on September 29, 2005. A native of Harden County, Kentucky, he'd served in Marine infantry for three years and three months by the time he kindly allowed me to interview him.

Matthews stood about five-nine and was lean and soft-spoken and very quiet, and hard—a good man to have next to you on patrol. With his brothers of 3/3, 3rd Squad, 3rd Platoon, he'd seen more action than anyone else in Golf. It was 3/3 that was hit by the first roadside bomb in Al Saqlawiyah on September 29, 2005, and 3/3 came under fire again in the heaviest action in the Fallujah area since Al Fajr, on October 26, 2005, when their machine-gun posts at the Al Saqlawiyah Police Station were riddled with Al Qaeda 7.62-caliber bullets fired from rooftops and alleys southwest of them.

Rocket-propelled grenades (RPGs) slammed into them on the rooftop and against the walls of the police station on that late October day also. Heavy fire came from the mosque some 200 meters north of the Al Saqlawiyah Police Station. With Sergeant Mark Buchman and the REACT squad, from Twiggs's 1st Platoon of Golf Company, I entered the mosque later that day and again with Iraqi Army elements on March 17, 2006, in search of *erhabi.*

With an Iraqi Army lieutenant and an interpreter, I climbed the minaret tower on March 17. Marines and Iraqi interpreters had seen *erhabi* firing RPGs and machine guns at them from the parapet of that same minaret on October 26. Iraqi interpreters and Iraqi soldiers later confirmed, through Iraqi Arab sources in Al Saqlawiyah and Fallujah, that thirty Saudi, Jordanian, and Syrian Al Qaeda terrorists had launched the joint assault on the Al Saqlawiyah Police Station from the mosque and surrounding neighborhoods.

A narrow stairwell wound up the center of the minaret. It was a very tight fit for all of us on March 17, even our interpreter, who was about five-six and slim.

For Al Qaeda and Ahmed Sirhan's Black Flags Brigades to have stored the tremendous amounts of small-arms ammunition and RPGs that they fired out of the minaret on October 26, 2005, they had to have stored that ammunition in large quantities for many days, right on the parapet of the minaret in the mosque.

You can carry only a small backpack within the one-man-wide winding staircase of the minaret. You can't even drag anything up with a rope; there's not enough room. You could maybe carry up small wooden crates or small bags of loose ammunition; you could not carry up the large wooden crates that 7.62x39-millimeter ammunition, for AK-47s, and 7.62x54-millimeter, for Iraqi machine guns, are commonly stored in.

The mosque, like all mosques in Fallujah and western Iraq, is a perfect military outpost, with lines of sight extending twenty miles in each direction on a clear day. Moreover, it easily overlooks the Marine outpost in Al Saqlawiyah—commands the high ground, in military terms—and you can see from the minaret all the way out to the canal on which we were attacked with the roadside bomb on September 29, 2005.

Matthews drank from a can of orange soda on March 8, 2006, in Al Saqlawiyah as he spoke in his quiet, reflective way of that day

and days since under fire in Iraq. His squad leader, Sergeant Mirza
Fejzic, received the Bronze Star with Combat V for Valor, for his
actions on October 26, 2005. An interview with Fejzic and Corporal Jack Smith, who also kept the police station from being overrun
by Al Qaeda and Ahmed Sirhan's Black Flags Brigades, follows that
with Matthews.

Crossing the bridge, Watson's fire team was right in front of
me. I was right behind, on second fire team. We were getting
ready to come on the bridge when it blew up. Corporal Jack
Smith was my fire team leader. We came on the bridge and
the blast knocked me down. I didn't see what happened to
Watson. My ears were ringing a little bit. After that, Corporal
Smith, Sellars, and Spittler and me went down to the left, trying to find enemy set in there. Near the reeds.

After that, we got called back onto the bridge. And we
pushed forward to our objective, the houses that we searched.

Watson was right next to the IED when it went off. God
only knows how he survived. Yes, man, it was a miracle. Roger
that.

The Iraqi people know who put the *erhabi* ammunition and
munitions in the mosque, and the grenade launchers. The
machine guns. They just don't want to tell us. They say they
are looking after their kids. But if they were looking after
their kids, they would let us know so that we could take care
of the situation.

I want to say this before I forget to: My squad is awesome.
We are 3/3 and we are one. Sergeant Fejzic. Corporal Smith.
3/3.

I want Americans to know that my squad has worked
together for seven months, and we have been in quite a few
incidents, we've seen a lot of action. Corporal Smith is healing
now from the IED attack a couple days ago. He went to Germany, and he's stateside now. [Corporal Jack Smith has now
recovered from his wounds.]

The day of the attack on the IP station, October 26, 2005,
was the most fire in this AO [area of operations] since the sec-

ond battle of Fallujah. I know for a fact that it was not reported to the American people in that way. But the truth is, it was.

First, I was sitting at Post One, on the ground floor of the IP [Iraqi Police] station. Sellars was at Post Two, up on the roof. In a machine gun outpost, he had two machine guns: an M249 5.56 SAW and an M240 Golf 7.62-caliber medium machine gun.

I heard some small-arms fire. I didn't think much of it, right, I thought it might have been Iraqi Army or even IPs. Then I started hearing what seemed to be rockets, RPGs. And they started suppressing fire. It was pretty loud. Sellars was being pinned down pretty good, as was I. I could hear rounds going right above my head.

Then it all came down, like a flood. Heavy fire, all around. I could hear many, many rounds thudding into the sandbags. When the fire fell off a little bit, I saw what seemed to be an Iraqi that was wearing civilian attire. He ran right in front of my post. I didn't know who he was, so I drew my weapon on him. He saw me and he quickly announced himself as Iraqi Army. I told him, "Let me see your badge."

What turns out is that he was an Iraqi soldier coming off leave. He heard the fire, and he wanted to help us. And he quickly went inside to get his uniform on. He got in the fight. But before that even happened, the Iraqi Police hauled ass. You know, I thought that the IP's initial job was to help me lay down suppressing fire if we were attacked. Well, we were attacked. And not one Iraqi policemen at that station helped lay down suppressing fire.

We were attacked, and the IPs didn't help at all. When I looked over my left shoulder, I saw an IP running into a building. And he stood in one room with all the other Iraqi policemen, every one of them. That IP near me, at Post One, abandoned his post.

Then Sergeant Fejzic kicked in the door because the Iraqi Army had run out of ammo. Sergeant Fejzic grabbed all the magazines off the Iraqi Police and ran up to the rooftop and

spread-loaded it. He was low-crawling everywhere, Sergeant
Fejzic, low-crawling and firing on the roof.

Sergeant Fejzic started engaging the insurgents. Spittler
started engaging the insurgents at that time too. Sergeant
Fejzic and Spittler both got confirmed kills. Sergeant Meyers
got a confirmed kill too. [Sergeant Meyers was a Marine
reservist from North Carolina, a sheriff stateside, activated to
train Iraqi Police in Fallujah and Al Saqlawiyah, who said to
me in the police station that day, "Brother, we are in the eye
of the hurricane."]

Then, when all the fire was dying down, we started checking to make sure that each of us was all right.

Miles, our interpreter, shot two insurgents in the mosque.
He was on the rooftop. I heard him firing. Right, he didn't
hesitate to engage. He killed the insurgents in the mosque, firing from the parapet. Corporal Jack Smith, we call him
"Blue," he was hard-core too, brother. I will never forget Blue
and Sergeant Fejzic on that day, October 26, 2005.

Post Two, now, where Sellars was, you can still see bullet
holes through the wood. We still stand guard at the IP station.
Sellars still goes up on the roof, and so do I.

3/3 has done a lot since then, a helluva lot. We've been in
four IED attacks, three firefights, three mortar attacks on us,
and of course, the IED attack that killed Sergeant Adams.

Sergeant Adams was a good man. We miss the hell out of
him, and I want to talk about him. We were going to do security missions for the October 15, 2005, constitutional referendum elections. And we drove by this same area at least five
times, along the canal. We had sectors we had to cover.

It just so happened that the last time that we drove by, there
was a black car sitting in view along the canal. The first, second, and third gun trucks all said that they had seen the car.

And the driver looked like he was smiling. We rode over it,
and it blew, hitting Sergeant Adams in the back of the neck
and head.

All I remember seeing, when we were in the vehicle, was a
lot of dust.

And the vehicle had caught fire.

Sergeant Adams collapsed in the vehicle. He landed in the passenger's lap. He wasn't moving. Everyone was asking, "Is everybody okay?" Marines said, "No, Sergeant Adams is not moving."

His head was in Watson's lap. We were all praying. Before this happened, Sergeant Adams knew that I was nervous about the mission, but he told me, "Don't worry, we've been hit before. This thing is like a tank." He was one of the greatest NCOs that I've ever met and talked to, because he cared about his men like nobody else.

He'd volunteered to go up in the turret for that mission. He told the Marine in the turret, "I've got this one." Right after he got up in the turret, that's when it happened. The driver did one heck of a job, keeping the vehicle from going into the canal. That's a deep, swiftly moving canal. If we'd gone into the canal, there would've been a lot more dead.

We called REACT and started taking fire on that little road. We returned fire while Doc Guzman and a Marine were tending to Sergeant Adams.

Everybody else was engaging the target. After that, they rigged up the truck to a seven-ton and started dragging it back. They got Sergeant Adams out.

The most frustrating thing for me is that we haven't caught more insurgents. You can never catch enough before they wind up hurting you or someone else. And also, the IPs—the Iraqi Police—how cowardly they really are. They don't do their job the way they are supposed to and they don't seem to care. The Iraqi Police refuse to fight against the *erhabi*.

I want the American people to know that 3/3 did our job. We didn't do it for ribbons or medals or anything like that. We did it because it was the right thing to do. Because we care about the man on our left and on our right. We're trying to get home.

"So I got the Iraqi soldier
to engage his PKC machine gun on
the mosque. He was hitting everything,
really throwing down on the mosque."

SERGEANT MIRZA FEJZIC AND
CORPORAL JACK SMITH, FIRE TEAM LEADER,
3RD SQUAD, 3RD PLATOON, GOLF COMPANY 2/6

Sergeant Mirza Fejzic of New Jersey and Corporal Jack Smith of Florida coordinated accurate counterfire on Al Qaeda on October 26, 2005, denying Al Qaeda key terrain, and turned back the heaviest attack any Marine or Coalition unit in the Fallujah area of operations had seen, at that time, since the second battle of Fallujah.

Fejzic, born in Brcko, Bosnia, is a naturalized American citizen who now calls Hackettstown, New Jersey, home. Twenty-two years old, a Marine sergeant by combat meritorious promotion, Fejzic came to the United States when he was eleven, with his mother, father, and two brothers. About six-one and lean, he is a calm man under fire and a great combat leader. Astute, very combat savvy, and possessed of a crafty, creative mind, Fejzic never hesitated to praise Corporal Jack Smith, one of his fire team leaders in 3/3 who was also an accomplished Marine infantryman.

Smith is an easy-going guy with a big heart. Like Fejzic, he is a master of all Marine small arms and a brilliant leader in combat. Smith calls the Land of Lakes, Florida, a suburb of Tampa, home, not far from U.S. Special Operations Command (SOCOM) at MacDill Air Force Base. Thirty years old in the spring of 2006, he was wounded by a roadside bomb in early March on his second combat deployment in Iraq and evacuated first to Germany, then on to the United States. He has since recovered from his wounds.

On October 26, 2006, Smith could see the mosque from a ground-level position, just outside the entrance to the Al Saqlawiyah Police Station. When I later said to him, "The war is in the mosques," he nodded and replied softly, "No question about it."

He knew for a fact, as we all did, the truth of an Iraqi interpreter's prophetic warning on September 28, 2005, almost a month to the day we were attacked by the terrorists in the mosque: "That mosque is dirty, like nearly every Sunni Arab mosque in Fallujah and western Iraq. The imam is a radical Islamic imam, and he supports, finances, and arms terrorists. He is a terrorist himself. We will be attacked from that mosque, and it is not a question of if, merely when."

Smith: I saw fire coming from the mosque about halfway through the firefight. At first we thought a lot of fire was coming from the south, especially the massive fire that hit Sellars' post. For a fact, heavy gunfire came from that mosque.

I saw the muzzle flashes from the mosque. I engaged. So did Fejzic.

When it all went down, I was on the radio giving sit reps [situation reports], and I didn't want to be on the radio. Fejzic and Spittler were on the roof.

I was by the front door. I could see two Iraqis on the minaret, firing AK-47s at Sellars and Fejzic and Spittler. Thank God, they were inaccurate, but the fire from the mosque was heavy. The terrorists had a lot of ammunition stored on the parapet of that minaret in the mosque, for sure.

Three Marines were on the roof, and I kept radio contact, giving sit reps. I was out at the front door, on the wall, engaging.

Perfect view of the minaret. I went through at least two magazines, engaging on the mosque.

They started aiming at me, and 7.62 rounds started impacting on the lights and the parking lot around the lights.

The terrorists on the minaret were wearing Adidas black sweatpants and sweatshirts. They did not have on masks. I was looking through my ACOG and I saw them clearly, firing on us.

It all started when me and Fejzic, Spittler, and Sergeant Meyers were sitting at the police station command and control center.

Rounds started impacting on us. At first I thought it was our own IA on the roof. But then the volume of fire increased tremendously, and the impact was sudden.

Then the RPGs hit us, a shit ton of RPGs, one after the other. What worried me is that the IP station was under renovation, definitely open to being overrun because one wall had just been torn down.

The construction workers left a door open too. Fejzic and me both thought insurgents would run through one of the open areas and kill us. Fejzic ran out and closed the hatch— no flak, no helmet, under fire.

Fejzic cared more about saving our lives than he did about his own life—he knew how much time it would take to throw on his gear, and he took care of his Marines first. Low-crawling under fire without a flak or helmet on. Getting ammunition to our Marines on the rooftop. Incredible.

I couldn't get Sellars on the horn, but Matthews was good. I finally got Sellars, and he told me, "I'm doing all I can do."

I looked out the front door, and all I could see was dust from all the rounds and RPGs hitting his post. It was an avalanche of enemy fire, pouring down on Sellars. If he had popped his head up at any time, he would not be alive today, no way. He did the right thing, the only thing he could do.

Fejzic immediately started bitching at the Iraqi Police, because the IPs were all huddled in a corner, all dogpiled in the corner.

Twenty of them, and none of them fired their weapons that day. All twenty dogpiled in the corner. And one of the Iraqi Army soldiers came, said, "We need ammo," and told us, "There are terrorists everywhere, driving in cars and trucks and dump trucks, and firing from the dump truck, picking up their wounded, and continuing to attack us."

Fejzic went to the IPs' armory, and it was locked.

Fejzic: I asked the Iraqi Police where the key was to the armory, and one IP told me, "The guy with the keys left for the day."

Four IPs, including all the higher-ups, Major Ali among them, left about twenty minutes before the attack went down. Check that out: The highest-ranking IP officer, the chief of police for Al Saqlawiyah, bolts twenty minutes before the attack, with the three other highest-ranking officers. Buddy, you don't have to be Albert Einstein to understand that Al Qaeda has a strong connection to the Iraqi Police here, no question.

Once they told me the door was locked, I kicked it down.

I handed the PKC machine gun to the Iraqi Army soldiers, and all the ammo in the room. That gave us fire superiority from the roof, and Corporal Smith was talking to me, and I ran back up to the roof and talked with Sellars. Make sure he was still all right. And he said, "I'm OK." Then I saw an Iraqi Army soldier with a jammed weapon on the south end, suppressed by machine gun fire from a building. I low-crawled over to him and started shooting. There were insurgents all over the place. He got his weapon unjammed.

Not long after that, the quick reaction force showed up. That's when we saw you, with the QRF. After I came back, our interpreter, our terp, said, "They're shooting from the mosque," and I popped the corner, and 7.62 fire came down heavy near me from the mosque.

So I got the Iraqi soldier to engage his PKC machine gun on the mosque. He was hitting everything, really throwing down on the mosque. And then they fled. The fire from the mosque ceased at that point. We killed at least six insurgents. We took zero Marine casualties and zero Iraqi Army casualties.

Smith: Hawk [the author's nickname], I thought the *erhabi* were going to ambush you as you were coming out of Post Six. Our Iraqi Army soldier on the roof was telling me they could see a lot of *erhabi* moving toward you and Sergeant Buchman. [Buchman led 1st Platoon's QRF to aid 3/3 at the police station. He was a corporal at that time, but shortly afterward, he received a combat meritorious promotion to sergeant for his actions under fire that day.]

He could see you and he could see Sergeant Buchman. He could see all of you moving toward us. The *erhabi* were moving on you and firing heavy on you. There were rounds flying everywhere. You guys were taking a lot of rounds everywhere, and so were we.

Fejzic: Right, I popped back in and got cover behind a wall, when the fire from the mosque came down on me. That's when I got pissed off and ordered our Iraqi Army machine gun to throw down on the mosque.

I'm sure the terrorist lookouts decided to get the hell out of Dodge. We were putting a lot of rounds downrange at them at that point, and it was accurate fire.

Smith: If they let us go in mosques, we'd find a lot of shit, a lot of terrorist weapons and munitions. But command refuses to let us enter mosques.

When you've got terrorists storing weapons and munitions in mosques all the time in Iraq—look, the terrorists know Marines are forbidden from entering mosques. What better place to hide weapons and munitions? Look at Karmah. The terrorists put a satchel charge on that police station. 2/2 got hit hard. [During an Al Qaeda attack on the Karmah Police Station, fifteen miles north of Fallujah, in early December 2005, Marines from 2nd Battalion, 2nd Marine Regiment, kept the police station from being overrun and took heavy casualties.]

Know this: We only had a fire team in the Al Saqlawiyah Police Station, in an unsecured IP station under renovation.

Fejzic: The terrorists had intelligence from inside the IPs, no question.

You could see that it was under renovation. The walls were out, and they knew we only had a fire team there.

The chief of police and his higher-ups flew the coop just before the attack, and that was the final signal for the terrorist attack to go down—all the terrorists had to look for was vehicles leaving the station.

Smith: As soon as we cut down from a squad to a fire team, on duty at the IP station, then the attack came. We'd had a squad on security at that IP station before, and we were never attacked.

We cut down to a fire team, and boom—we got hit.

Fejzic: The terrorists knew that if they had any chance of overrunning and taking over the IP station in Al Saqlawiyah, that it was on that day. That was no accident, that Al Qaeda attacked us on that specific day. They had the inside scoop from the IPs, no question.

Over thirty heavily armed terrorists, with RPGs, medium machine guns, light machine guns, and grenades—against one Marine fire team and a handful of Iraqi Army soldiers. That's seven-to-one odds, and they had high ground, fire superiority, mobility—it's a bitch defending a fixed, fortified position with only one fire team, but we did it—and basically, they had everything on their side. But we held. My men held, and they were magnificent, as was Sergeant Mcyers.

I have no doubt that is why the attack came on that day— look at the timing. Look at what Corporal Smith is saying. Exactly.

Smith: IPs in Saqlawiyah, same as in Fallujah. We have a saying: the Iraqi Police are the Mob in town. The IPs are the Mafia in Iraq. Everything that goes down in Saqlawiyah goes through the Iraqi Police first.

We had a rocket fired from behind the IP station—an IED was planted right behind the IP station, and they even had time to spray paint on the wall after they planted the IED.

Roger that on the Iraqi Police in Fallujah, also, I concur with Major Tim Murphy, absolutely: At least 70 percent of the Fallujah IPs are directly supporting terrorists and insurgents in Fallujah. And Murphy is there every day, he sees it even more than we do—plus, he's tight with the Iraqi Army, so he gets better intelligence off the street, from Iraqi sources, than 2/6 S-2, which doesn't give us shit. 2/6 S-2 is worthless.

Someone is watching our firm base all the time. Easiest place to eyeball our firm base is from the minaret of the mosque.

All indirect fire happens when someone is outside. Every time we get hit with mortars and rockets, there's someone outside in our compound—the *erhabi* sees people outside in our firm base and launches the mortar rounds. There are enemy eyes on the firm base, maybe from someone across the street. Mortars land on us only when there's a Marine outside.

I sure in hell don't trust any of the Iraqi Police. They are worse than the terrorists, in my eyes, because they won't even come out and straight-up fight us.

I'm very proud of my fire team—they were taking heavy fire, and they did everything they could do. Lance Corporal Spittler, without any hesitation, ran on the roof under fire to engage the enemy.

Fejzic was everywhere, without his flak and helmet. And I kept having to calm him down—he was under fire without any gear on, without hesitation, running through the building to shut the door. Like I said, he cared more about us than he did about himself. He'd come hauling ass back, bitching at the IPs, kicking down doors to get ammo, and with just a fire team there and our squad leader.

No one froze under pressure. Everything clicked, people knew what to do—you didn't even have to tell them.

Hesitation would've killed us, and no one hesitated.

We took the fight to the insurgents, instead of them taking the fight to us, at that point. They scattered to the wind.

Fejzic: That was Al Qaeda that attacked us. Right, we heard the same thing, a little over thirty foreign fighters. You can definitely tell the difference between Al Qaeda and local *erhabi*. It was coordinated, well thought out. Al Qaeda is always well trained and well financed.

Al Qaeda never hesitates to use mosques as terrorist command-and-control centers, terrorist operations centers, roger that. No question.

Smith: The view they had from the mosque, and from the rooftop of a construction site, was ideal for a coordinated attack on the police station. The mosque gave them perfect firing position, perfect fields of fire to attack us with. They were firing from that mosque.

They fired from inside a doorway on the parapet. I saw the muzzle flashes, steady and constant, from the parapet.

Two posts took direct RPG hits. I went up to Sellars' post after the firefight and there were holes everywhere. Thank God he survived. Sellars is really lucky, I'm sure he is grateful to be alive.

Fejzic: It sounds crazy, but this is true: Every grunt dreams of a gunfight like that, where your men come through under fire. I know it sounds crazy, but it is true.

Smith: Every time we walk by that mosque, we look for the parapet. We patrol by the mosque every day. We keep eyes on that mosque all the time. It is terrorist country, that mosque. We don't trust that mosque at all.

Definitely penetrated by Al Qaeda.

"Every mosque in Fallujah
is penetrated by Al Qaeda."

MUHAMMAD, IRAQI ARAB TRANSLATOR,
NATIVE OF BAGHDAD, SEPTEMBER 25, 2005

A prayer call echoed in the blue of the evening from the mosque Smith and Fejzic spoke of, the dark-blue-and-tan-tiled minaret of Al Saqlawiyah's oldest mosque, at dusk on September 28, 2005. It was some 300 meters northwest of the firm base, our mortar and machine gun cratered five-story concrete base in the heart of the Euphrates River Valley.

I'd earlier scoped the minaret from the rooftop. The minaret, a round tower shaped from thick blocks of stone and white mortar, had a massive red-painted steel door, which faced south toward the police station. The door opened onto a parapet, around which there were small, square windows sealed with steel latches. From the minaret, you could see the entire town. Strategically placed, the mosque was perched on a low rise on the northeastern edge of Al Saqlawiyah.

I talked with our interpreter, Muhammad, about Kurdish counterterrorists penetrating Al Qaeda cells in Northern Iraqi mosques and stopping suicide bomber attacks. He kept glancing at the mosque in Al Saqlawiyah, and he praised Kurdish counterterrorism. I asked him if the prayer call was being used to alert *erhabi* to our patrol. He nodded.

"That mosque is dirty," he said, glancing at the minaret.

"Zarqawi terrorists and Al Qaeda are in the mosque now. Yes, they are marking us," Muhammad said, motioning toward the minaret. "This prayer call, out of time, as you say, lets the terrorists in Al Saqlawiyah know that Marines are leaving the base. We will be attacked from that mosque, and it is not a question of if, merely when."

Muhammad was a native of Baghdad and had been in western Iraq for more than two years now, translating for the U.S. Army Special Forces, 82nd Airborne Division, 1st Marine Division, and now 2nd Marine Division in autumn 2005. A Sunni Arab Muslim, he was to prove invaluable to me with Marines and the Iraqi Army in western Iraq. Easy-going and levelheaded, he was a wealth of intelligence on the sheikhs and imams who support Al Qaeda in western Iraq.

Muhammad had lived in Baghdad, Central Iraq, and western Iraq all his life. He spoke classical Arabic, western Iraqi dialects, and English fluently. He possessed a conversational proficiency in German and French. His woman, Layla, was in Baghdad, and he missed her dearly: "Oh, my Layla! She is the flower of Iraq. I miss her like a garden misses the cool shade of cypress trees, brother. Layla is the queen of Iraq."

He owned an encyclopedic knowledge of Zarqawi's terrorists in western Iraq, *Fedayeen* Saddam terrorists, and radical Islamic terrorists in Fallujah, Al Karmah, Al Saqlawiyah, Ramadi, Al Habbiniyah, and other towns and villages in western Iraq. Muhammad was slim like a long-distance runner.

Dark eyes fierce, nodding his head slowly, he pointed a finger at the mosque and spoke as a gust of wind kicked up dust around us.

That mosque is a terrorist mosque. The mosque is the terrorists' operations center, for Al Saqlawiyah. Many Sunni mosques, of course, in western Iraq are the same: Salafi Islamic and Wahabi Sunni Arab mosques that are terrorist operations centers.

Every mosque in Fallujah, for instance, is penetrated by Al Qaeda, and each imam, of every mosque, supports Al Qaeda.

Marines fought very hard to clear Fallujah of terrorists.

But the terrorist operation centers, what you call command-and-control centers [COCs] remain firmly under Al Qaeda's control, with Al Qaeda operating out of Fallujah mosques—planning, tracking our movements, storing weapons in mosques, and so on.

I think the Americans have the phrase, yes, that you can win a battle but lose a war. We won in Al Fajr [second battle of Fallujah, November 2004], of course, but we lost everything in Fallujah after Al Fajr, back to Al Qaeda. Al Qaeda is just as strong now in Fallujah, because it controls the mosques, as it was in summer 2004.

The mosques in Fallujah, like the mosques throughout western Iraq, are terrorist COCs. The Fallujah imams are Wahabi and Salafi imams, and Sunni Muslim imams sympathetic to Wahabi and Salafi Islam. These imams are funded by Saudi Islamic charities and other Islamic charities.

The Saudi imams issue *fatwas*, which Sunni Arab Muslims in western Iraq are well aware of, that are death warrants against anyone supporting the new Iraq and helping the Coalition here—me, for instance.

Due to Saudi Arabia's strong support of Al Qaeda in Iraq and the Near East, particularly in Saudi mosques—Osama Bin Laden is Saudi and Salafi—our troubles here reach far beyond western Iraq. Remember, Osama Bin Laden is Salafi, that cannot be overstated, and Al Qaeda has very strong ties to Salafi Islam.

Saudi Al Qaeda infiltrate into Iraq; we share a very long border with Saudi Arabia. Alpha 1/6 detained the imam in Al Saqlawiyah for his ties to Zarqawi. The imam has been at Abu Ghraib for four months now, but word is he is returning.

It is a mistake to release this imam, a grave mistake. You will see—attacks will come from this mosque now, as before.

Within a month, I suspect. The Kurdish counterterrorist colonels said it, exactly: "The war is in the mosques." This mosque is the center for Zarqawi and Al Qaeda in Al Saqlawiyah.

"We had the enemy mortar sites right in our hands at dawn, provided that we hold position and simply let the sheikh point them out to us."

CORPORAL BRIAN AREBALLO, RONIN2 TEAM LEADER;
CORPORAL DERRICK BOYER, RONIN3 TEAM LEADER;
SERGEANT JOHN MATTER, RONIN CHIEF SCOUT AND SCOUT/SNIPER;
CORPORAL DUDLEY KELSO, RONIN3 ASSISTANT TEAM LEADER;
CORPORAL DANNY MILSTID, RONIN3 SCOUT/SNIPER AND GRENADIER;
AND CORPORAL JAY ELDER, RONIN4 SCOUT/SNIPER AND GRENADER

On the night of November 6, 2005, Wardman again failed to take advantage of a perfect opportunity to take down Ahmed Sirhan and Black Flags Brigades *erhabi*, denied Ronin2 and Ronin3 a perfect over watch position, and annihilated Coalition chances to develop an ideal human intelligence source in Al Saqlawiyah, one of the very few Sunni Arab sheikhs in western Iraq willing to give up intelligence on Ahmed Sirhan, Black Flags Brigades, and Al Qaeda in Iraq.

It was the worst decision in combat I have ever seen in my life. Never in Spain, Burma, or Iraq have I seen such reckless disregard for field intelligence, such refusal to listen to one's scouts, and such lost opportunity to take down the enemy. Earlier that day, Wardman had bitterly complained that a recon team in the Pocket had been standing right next to Ahmed Sirhan, but their interpreter, new to Iraq and on his first mission in the Pocket with recon, had refused to listen to a local source, who kept telling the recon Marines in English in a low voice, "This is a bad guy, this is a really, really bad guy—you need to capture him."

The interpreter, a Somali on contract to the U.S. military, rebuffed the source, saying to the recon Marines, "Don't listen to this motherfucker, he doesn't know shit." The recon Marines had Ahmed Sirhan right in their pocket, but their own interpreter denied them a key opportunity to take Ahmed Sirhan down.

Strangely, on the very same day, Wardman did the same thing to Ronin2 and Ronin3.

The scout/snipers did exactly what they had briefed Captain Wardman on earlier—clandestine movement to a house on the Euphrates to carry out reconnaissance and surveillance on enemy mortar sites across the river—to accomplish the mission.

Late in the evening on November 6, with Areballo's team on point, we moved slowly through orange groves and fields of date palm trees in Al Saqlawiyah.

Elder was a few steps behind Areballo, carrying an M.203 and his 9-millimeter Beretta sidearm, staying in shadows cast by high date palms and orange groves, acacia trees, and reeds clustered along mud walls. No lights blinked from nearby houses and huts. We'd infiltrated clean, in special ops parlance: undetected covert insertion and movement. From that point forward, we were clandestine, exactly as planned. We headed toward the Euphrates.

Corporal Brian Areballo led Ronin2, and Corporal Derrick Boyer led Ronin3. Areballo, a very bright young man and graduate of Quantico Scout/Sniper School, dodged from palm to palm, staying low in the night. Sergeant John Matter, the chief scout for Ronin, crept behind Ronin2, loam and green camouflage paint streaked across his face like tiger stripes. You could hear the wind on the river, rushing through the reeds. No dogs barked as we moved for our target house, the same house on which Areballo had briefed Wardman earlier.

Our mission was to make successful covert movement to the Euphrates, gain covert entry, stay undetected, carry out reconnaissance and surveillance for enemy mortar sites across the Euphrates, in the Shark's Fin, and kill any *erhabi* carrying weapons, munitions, or mortar tubes. Additionally, if the opportunity presented itself, both teams were to gather human intelligence on Ahmed Sirhan, Black Flags Brigades, and Al Qaeda.

The opportunity presented itself, but Wardman did not let his men act on that opportunity, much less exploit it.

For the first time in Iraq with Coalition Forces, I got on the radio myself, to explain to Golf Company—without giving the sheikh's name, as that would have violated operational security—that the sheikh wanted us to stay three days and nights; was overjoyed with our presence; had real-time human intelligence on Ahmed Sirhan's location; had human intelligence on Black Flags Brigades cells; knew exactly where Black Flags Brigades were firing mortars and rockets from, in the Shark's Fin, at the Golf 2/6 firm base; and also was a personal friend of Sheikh Gazi Al Awal of Mosul, who is one of the very few influential Sunni Arab sheikhs in Iraq not in bed with Al Qaeda. Sheikh Gazi Al Awal was on the Iraqi Interim Governing Council in 2003–04. The sheikh on the Euphrates had photos of himself with Sheikh Gazi Al Awal at various meetings over the past two years, which he'd shown to both scout/sniper teams and me over a sumptuous meal he'd provided for us on the spot: strong dark sweet Ceylon tea, orange soda, water, fresh hot bread, and chicken with rice.

Wardman refused, however, to listen to Ronin2 and Ronin3. A classic mistake, one Custer paid for at Little Bighorn. Always listen to your scouts.

The scout/snipers were devastated. Ronin went from flying sky-high to hell on a shutter, in the blink of an eye.

Boyer and Areballo's scout/snipers had entered the house undetected. We knew for a fact that our clandestine movement to the house had been unseen by villagers and farmers. We'd immediately gained the trust and confidence of the sheikh, who knew exactly where Black Flags Brigades were firing mortars and rockets from, at Golf 2/6. The intent of Ronin's mission, as written in Areballo's operations order, had been accomplished in full, to the letter.

There are few times in war when things go exactly as planned. But up to that point, thank God, this was one of those times.

Come dawn, the sheikh was going to point out exactly where Black Flags Brigades had been firing from, in the Shark's Fin— and all within range of our M40A3 sniper rifles; all the enemy mortar and rocket sites were less than 700 meters from us.

We had a clear line of sight, we had a perfect clandestine position, and we had, by pure luck, chanced into a marvelous human intelligence source. The sheikh was on our side and wanted us to kill *erhabi*, take down Ahmed Sirhan, and silence Black Flags Brigades mortar sites.

A heartbeat later, we only knew that a great, incredibly fortunate opportunity to gain invaluable human intelligence on Al Qaeda in Iraq and Black Flags Brigades and to take down Ahmed Sirhan was all dust in the wind, thanks to Wardman, who after ordering us out of the perfect reconnaissance and surveillance position on the Euphrates, demanded that we stay along the river—even though he knew at that point that we'd been compromised.

Once we left the sheikh's house—and I have never seen anyone so confused in my life as that sheikh, who was clueless as to why we could not stay and kill the enemy across the river—lights started flashing and blinking in the village.

Hodulich scouted along the river and confirmed that there was no other place to see over the reeds and high grasses on the Shark's Fin side of the Euphrates. We'd had that position, but Wardman's contempt for Ronin again got in the way of taking down Ahmed Sirhan.

Lights were flashing madly in the villages near the Euphrates; informants knew we were there now, and it was only a matter of time until we'd get ambushed. Meanwhile, our sole purpose for carrying out the mission had been compromised by Wardman himself.

Areballo, to his credit, refused to continue listening to Wardman. Areballo's logic made good sense to me then, and it makes great sense to me now: "Save my team and save Boyer's team, because it is very obvious that Wardman does not care about killing the enemy, taking down Al Qaeda and Black Flags Brigades, taking down Ahmed Sirhan, and gaining a key human intelligence source with deep connections in both Western and Northern Iraq. We abort now and return to Golf 2/6 on foot."

As a former guerrilla commander on contract to the Sultan of Oman's Army, Major Peter Hudson, a retired British Royal Marine commander and native of Northumberland, England, told me in Al Ain, United Arab Emirates, on September 13, 2001: "When a commander proves that he does not care about killing the enemy, commandos take care of only one thing: themselves. You cannot fight for a man who has no fight in him. If he's not willing to take down the enemy, you can only do this: look after yourself and your comrades. And trust me on this: *Always* listen to your scouts. That worked in Alexander's time, and it is exactly the same in our time, mate."

Areballo: That was a clean covert movement to the house. No lights flashed on or off in nearby houses—the signal that Al Qaeda and Black Flags Brigades like to use at night to let each other know Americans are around is the blinking lights signal, on their front door and kitchen lights. In daylight, of course, they release pigeons. Well, we got in clean. Unseen. We were supposed to head toward the house which we'd chosen to take. We'd told Wardman exactly which house we'd be in—we'd shown him that on the map. He'd approved.

Matter: Areballo is very good at prepping a brief. Areballo had briefed the captain on our mission. The captain not only knew the area we'd be in, he knew the house we'd be in. We'd given Staff Sergeant Williams our position and told him that there was a house in the area.

Kelso: Right. We're supposed to have an SCC, sniper control center. We relay to them, and they filter the information and then either push it to the S-2 or to the company. We didn't have an SCC on this mission, however.

Matter: We shouldn't have to go over the radio and tell what we're doing, in the first place. It goes from a scout/sniper mindset to an infantry mindset. With an SCC, we can focus on our core mission: covert or greenside reconnaissance and surveillance and taking down bad guys.

Boyer: An SCC makes our job much easier. They can filter the information and make things much clearer to the companies, to S-2. Before missions, I'd brief Captain Wardman and tell him what we were planning to do, and he'd just say, "All right, do it." But even stateside, on maneuvers in California, he'd get hinky on us: He told me in the Mojave Desert, "I

don't know how to employ scout/snipers, so I'd rather not
employ you at all—that way, there's no way I can make a mistake." Bizarre, but when I look back at that now, he proved he
doesn't know how to use Marine scout/snipers on this mission.

Kelso: Roger that. When we were in the Mojave, he
wouldn't employ us, and he'd tell us, "I'd rather not employ
you, because I don't want to make a mistake employing you."
So he didn't employ us at all.

Boyer: He'd always been supportive of us, but he'd often
say, "I'm afraid of employing you wrong." Then I'd say, "Sir,
just tell us what you want eyes on constantly, and we'll work
out the mission." And that's how it would work out: he'd point
to a couple places on the map, and we'd work out the missions.

Kelso: We knocked on the door, and the sheikh appeared.
Immediately he invited us in. You and I were talking to him
immediately. You talked to him about food and tea and
Sheikh Gazi Al Awal in Mosul. He lit up. That's when I got up
and found an AK next to his bed.

I asked him if he had any weapons, and he said yes, he had
two AK-47s. Normally, of course, Iraqis can have one, but
sheikhs are routinely allowed two, because they are sheikhs.

We were going to start a rudimentary search, but since he
was a sheikh, we glanced around. Right away, he was giving us
intel on *erhabi*. It was beautiful. He really opened up. We were
getting good intel on our enemy here, on Black Flags
Brigades and Al Qaeda.

Right off the bat, they asked us if we wanted chicken or fish,
and his wife brought out four liters of Coke and orange soda.

Boyer: He was dropping dimes on everyone. We were there
less than an hour and he told us the enemy mortar sites, intel
on Ahmed Sirhan. That's when I knew we had a great opportunity to take down insurgents, when he gave us the intel on
the enemy mortar sites across the river and on Ahmed Sirhan.

Matter: We communicated. Two teams together, in that
house, and we immediately began working the intel. I was on
the roof by now. I had a map, and on the roof, based on his

intel, I was working out where I could get the biggest amount
of illumination over the suspected enemy mortar sites.

Boyer: At first we were trying to get a terp [interpreter] out
there. And we called back and tried to get a terp on line. Golf
wouldn't put a terp on the horn. They wouldn't listen to us.
That never happened, so we asked if we could have a terp out
there. They said, "Go ahead and make a linkup site, so we can
drop off the terp and one other person with him, and take
them back to the house." That's when I got off the radio and
started planning the linkup site. Elder got on the radio.

Elder: Basically, on the same linkup site that Derrick
planned, Golf wanted us to move the sheikh to the linkup site.
Big change. So Golf could flex-cuff him, take him back to the
firm base, and interrogate him. But the sheikh had done
nothing wrong.

You can't flex-cuff him if he's a good guy. Golf didn't understand at all, also, that walking him out in the middle of the
night denies us covert position, and denies us the mission to
carry out reconnaissance and surveillance for enemy mortar
sites.

We had the enemy mortar sites right in our hands at dawn,
provided that we hold position and simply let the sheikh point
them out to us. But Golf denied that happening. Wardman
denied that happening. And those mortar sites were aimed at
his men. Wardman never missed an opportunity to miss an
opportunity to take down Ahmed Sirhan.

Golf wanted Golf Marines in flaks and helmets, rolling in
on a humvee or a seven-ton, or both, to flex-cuff the sheikh
and put a hood over him. That would have broadcast to his
entire village that the Americans were going to interrogate
him. You're treating him like enemy, not a source. He'd done
nothing wrong. So when he gets back to the village, who is
going to pay a visit to him and likely kidnap him and murder
him? *Erhabi.*

Negative, we're not going to move a sixty-year-old friendly
noncombatant a klick on foot at two in the morning. That
itself would've compromised us, too—it would've given away

our position to Al Qaeda and Black Flags Brigades informants
in that village.

That showed the common sense level in Golf. They came
back on the radio, we argued back and forth, and they
ordered us to leave the house so Golf would bring in the QRF
[quick reaction force]. Bad history with Golf and QRF on missions when Ahmed Sirhan's name pops up, bad juju.

Boyer: I tried to negotiate with Golf, from our radio on the
rooftop, that we're risking compromise by bringing the sheikh
out of the house. I told them that we had perfect observation
on the river and the enemy mortar sites. But Golf wouldn't listen.

All we had to do was wait until dawn, when the sheikh was
going to point out the Black Flags Brigades mortar sites in the
Shark's Fin.

Elder: It got to the point where we were yelling. There was
hostility on the radio.

Matter: We had the perfect spot. The sheikh knew where
the insurgents were firing their mortars. He kept gesturing to
me, mimicking the insurgents dropping mortar rounds in
tubes, and the mortars being fired at Golf Company's firm
base in Al Saqlawiyah. You came up on the roof, I remember.
You saw this yourself. And Boyer.

Boyer: Roger that. I witnessed that. The sheikh came up on
the roof and pointed right across the river and mimicked the
mortars going off. He told us in Arabic exactly where they
were.

Elder: Then we got into the pissing contest with Golf about
the sheikh, the terp, and the movement. I told them, "If we
leave the house, we lose optimal observation on the enemy
mortars. The informant has given us direction and distance
on the enemy mortars. The informant knows exact location of
enemy mortar firing sites."

First Lieutenant Drake was trying to be very helpful; he was
relaying it to Golf. But Golf wouldn't listen. First Lieutenant
Maas, Golf company executive officer, said, "This is a direct

order from the CO [commanding officer, Captain Wardman]. You must leave the house."

I told him, "Again, if we leave, we lose all observation and we will be compromised." Captain Wardman refused to listen to us and wanted the QRF ordered out to flex-cuff the sheikh.

Kelso: That really pissed us off about the QRF. The QRF was completely unnecessary. They would've torn that house apart.

We lost the perfect opportunity to nail the enemy mortar sites. The sheikh wanted us to stay so he could point out the exact positions of the enemy mortar sites. He wanted us to stay at least three days. It was perfect. Perfect opportunity for us to complete our mission.

It would've been a clean shot for us as snipers. We marked the sites on our maps—550 meters, no farther. We had a clear line of sight. We could see over the reeds, and we could see over the water. Completely unobstructed line of sight.

We had the perfect opportunity to kill the enemy, an enemy that was daily firing mortars and rockets at Golf.

But Captain Wardman refused to listen to us and ordered us out of that house. And as you pointed out to us that night, we also lost a perfect opportunity to gain an invaluable human intelligence source: the sheikh.

Elder: They kept calling back and saying, "Move to a different site." I kept telling them, "This is the only place where we can see over the reeds and the water."

They just didn't care, and they just didn't understand: We had the perfect position, we'd got in clean, covert, and the sheikh was giving us the enemy mortar sites at dawn.

But Wardman freaked out. Like Sergeant Matter said, Areballo had briefed him on exactly where we'd be.

It was like Captain Wardman was thinking, "Throw away your ghillie suits, get your jet packs on, ignition, blastoff, fly over the river and observe the insurgents from the air! Pop Superman Marine ninja smoke, demonstrate your black belt karate moves in midair, stay in hover mode, in invisible suits, and complete the mission. And don't lose those invisible suits!"

Kelso: We got the hell out of Dodge. We made a quick security stop and did a map recon, and tried to figure out if there was any other possible observation post along the river.

There wasn't. Lights started flashing on and off in village huts, and lights outside the huts blinked too—*erhabi* informers signaling, "The Americans are here."

Areballo told Golf, "We're coming back in. Abort mission."

Golf said, "Negative, you will not abort mission."

We were obviously compromised. We wanted to extract but couldn't. There was no place to get eyes on the enemy mortar sites now.

Matter: At that point, we were just talking to the Golf RTO [radioman]. No one else at Golf would talk to us. We told him, "We're coming in."

Boyer: I was thinking, why hasn't Golf communicated to us about our return? It was about two hours before Golf watch officer said, "Why are you guys coming back?" Golf had forgotten that we were out there.

Kelso: You'd think the watch officer would know where we're at, but he didn't.

Boyer: Moving through the village, after being ordered out of the perfect position to kill the enemy, like Kelso said, we saw the houses switching their lights on and off—clear sign insurgents were signaling about our presence. We'd had a perfect clandestine position in that house, also.

Milstid: Staff Sergeant Williams took the brunt of it from Captain Wardman when we got back. I could hear Captain Wardman cursing at him, just vilifying him, with the door closed. Treating him like a boot at Parris Island. Typical Wardman, freaking out and melting down.

The whole mission was a wasted opportunity.

The main objective of our mission was to get the mortars and kill the insurgents firing the mortars. We had perfect position to do exactly that. Our missions for Golf have revolved around the enemy mortar sites. Captain Wardman wasted that opportunity on November 6th. He was in charge of pulling us out. It was the perfect opportunity to kill the enemy.

Elder: He didn't play his cards the way they were dealt. You can't fight guerrilla warfare out of a book.

Kelso: He could've brought out the terp, Muhammad, which we suggested. And let Muhammad question the sheikh in his house, and of course, develop him as a valuable source. Muhammad, after all, has the best human intelligence network in Al Saqlawiyah.

Captain Wardman lost the opportunity to put a foundation stone in the Coalition human intel network in western Iraq.

Elder: We're supposed to be the eyes and ears of the battalion, and they're not using us for that core mission. We're up there, we're seeing it, we know what's going on, and they're telling us what to do, based on no field eyes-on of their own, no real-time vision, no eyeballs on-site—simply based on their presence in a room full of radios.

At this point, we're more worried about Golf command than the insurgency.

Matter: With Echo Company, it's very different. The first sergeant from Echo is a sniper, one of the most decorated Marine scout/snipers in the history of the Marine Corps, First Sergeant Zickenfoose. He received a Silver Star for his actions as a Marine scout/sniper in the Persian Gulf War.

First Sergeant Zickenfoose just got selected for sergeant major. He went from gunny to sergeant major in two years. He rates it, he warrants it: He treats Marines with respect and professionalism, and he knows how to fight. Echo treats us with a lot of respect, and they really listen to us.

The first sergeant from Golf Company was never a sniper and has no respect for us as scout/snipers. Plus, he doesn't understand how scout/snipers are employed.

Kelso: First Sergeant Zickenfoose is pretty much the baddest man alive. Not many Marine scout/snipers ever received the Silver Star. He called in fire on Iraqi Army tanks, and he was pretty much all alone. A very brave man. Humble as hell, too, helluva nice guy.

Boyer: Roger that on First Sergeant Z. He is the man. I'll tell you what: When you've got a command that's backing you

up 100 percent, you actually look forward to going out on missions. You don't mind going out on missions.

Milstid: Because you know they are listening to you. When
you know they are listening to you, you know they respect you.
Respect is a two-way street.

Boyer: Right now, Golf Company has lost that with us. Golf
Company keeps fucking with us, and they are fucking in the
wrong direction. We are not the enemy. We are not Black Flags
Brigades. We are not Al Qaeda. But they just treat us like shit.

Kelso: We're at the point now where they've fucked us so
many times that it's hard for us to get hyped up to do a mission for Captain Wardman.

Elder: We've had platoon sergeants, on platoon ops, not
even knowing that we were even out there. And that can lead
directly to friendly fire, to blue on blue.

Kelso: Two days ago, on November 12, 2005, we had a mission where we were supposed to watch for IEDs on a road, in
an area where they'd gotten hit. Golf was supposed to have a
squad do a raid in the area, as well as drive vehicles up and
down the road that we were watching. The whole purpose was
to let the insurgents know that Golf Company was in the area.
Then order Golf Marines out, and hopefully the insurgents
would lay IEDs, move caches, etc. Bait-and-trap mission.

Failure to communicate on Golf's part on this mission
nearly got us killed in blue on blue, like Jay is saying. Unfortunately, word never got down that we were in the area. Golf
never passed on to Weapons Company, which had gun trucks
mounted with .50-caliber machine guns, that we were in the
area.

Meanwhile, we never saw a squad from Golf. They never
drove a humvee down the road. Captain Wardman wasted
twenty-four hours of our lives in combat. And nearly got us
killed. It was crazy.

Golf asked us if we could watch the bridge that keeps getting hit with IEDs. Same one you'd been hit on with 3rd Platoon. They didn't tell us that they already had a squad
watching the bridge. We were sprinting across the bridge later,

after we'd come out of the weeds, and I was staring at five chem lites and a .50-cal. By the grace of God, I did not get killed.

Golf did not tell us that a Weapons Company gun truck was in the area. They didn't tell us that they had a vehicle checkpoint set up on that bridge. The likelihood that there was an IED actually there was huge, but Golf gave us no idea. We should always know where friendly units are on any route of patrol we're on, but Captain Wardman fails to give that basic essential information to us.

Failure to communicate in combat leads to dead Marines.

PART TWO

"The Fallujah Police is the largest insurgent cell in Fallujah."

"Past error is no excuse for its own perpetuation. Tragedy is a tool for the living to gain wisdom, not a guide by which to live. Now as ever, we do ourselves best justice when we measure ourselves against ancient tests, as in the Antigone *of Sophocles: 'All men make mistakes, but a good man yields when he knows his course is wrong, and repairs the evil. The only sin is pride.'"*

—U.S. SENATOR ROBERT F. KENNEDY,
MARCH 18, 1968

An ambulance guarded by two Fallujah Police cars and one Fallujah police pickup truck rolled slowly in the rain at two in the morning on January 25, 2006, near the Blackwater Bridge, turning a corner toward First Lieutenant Marty Keogh and his men in the pouring rain. Keogh held over watch for a convoy coming into Fallujah; the convoy route ran right near the bridge.

"What's an ambulance doing at two in the morning? And it's moving awful slowly for a medical emergency," the lieutenant said, his driver Private Kimungu grunting in agreement. Corporal Wilson of Louisiana, who was wounded in November and had returned to combat in Fallujah, stood on our .50-cal in the pouring rain and said, "Roger that, sir, that's no medical emergency. Police guarding an ambulance moving weapons or terrorists, most likely." Corporal Higney of Colorado, who listened to Tupac Shakur in his downtime and said he only wanted "to get the fuck out of this shithole—the police in Fallujah are terrorist motherfuckers, and don't you ever forget it," affirmed Wilson's observation, adding, "They are driving directly away from, not in the direction of, the nearest hospital."

Near East clandestine field officers from Western intelligence services had informed me on January 13 in Fallujah that Al Qaeda, Black Flags Brigades, and other Iraqi *erhabi* had been moving weapons, munitions, plastic explosives, detonation cord, grenades, artillery rounds, rifles and machine guns, ammunition, and terrorists in ambulances throughout Fallujah since July 2005, guarded by Fallujah Police vehicles driven by policemen. All uniforms, vehicles, weapons, and ammunition on those Fallujah Police convoys guarding Al Qaeda in Fallujah were paid for by the Bush administration.

Moreover, the same officers told me that Coalition intelligence had sent analyses on Al Qaeda sniper training sites to all U.S. combat commands in Iraq. The intelligence reports spotlighted Al Qaeda using cars and vans for mobile sniper hides, allowing them to shoot in urban areas with little chance of being detected. The intelligence reports also stated that there was deep collusion between the Syrian Ba'athist dictatorship and Al Qaeda. Syria was, and is, training Al Qaeda snipers in remote desert sites, in cooperation with Zarqawi and Osama Bin Laden. Other Iraqi *erhabi*, including Black Flags Brigades, train snipers at the same sites.

A clandestine officer handed me the analyses and said, "This is intelligence on Al Qaeda snipers. The Marines and Army here have taken many dead from *erhabi* snipers in Fallujah since mid-November. The Marines are taking far too many casualties from *erhabi* snipers, and we know that your scout/snipers are being ignored. Tell Ronin to be especially aware of all activity by the Fallujah Police: At least 70 percent of the Fallujah Police are either *erhabi* themselves or supporting Al Qaeda and other *erhabi*. You were damn lucky yourself ten days ago."

He referred to the first of two incidents in which Fallujah Police had tried to kill me. The first time, on January 3, 2006, I was on patrol with Iraqi Army on Route Henry, having turned off Fran, when the patrol leader, Sergeant Saif, stopped a car. The tags and the vehicle matched a car we were on the lookout for, believed to be smuggling AK-47s, ammunition, and plastic explosives for Al Qaeda in Fallujah.

A policeman jumped in between the Iraqi sergeant and the car and swore at the sergeant in Arabic. Another behind us shuffled left and chambered a round in his AK-47, the bolt slamming home, aiming the rifle at us. Saif, his own AK-47 slung over his shoulder, grabbed his Walther PP9 9-millimeter sidearm from a shoulder holster.

Police swarmed over our patrol, driving up in Fallujah Police pickup trucks manned with machine gunners and surrounding us. I grabbed Saif's Walther and got him to holster it. One round from his pistol, and we would have been ventilated by Iraqi police machine guns, rifles and pistols.

A Fallujah police lieutenant came out of nowhere, grabbed my left arm, and screamed, "You are not Iraqi, you are American! We are taking you!" He had handcuffs in his other hand. A cop behind him raised his pistol toward me, leveling at my chest.

Saif had given me a 9-millimeter pistol before the patrol, a Browning. I threw off the police lieutenant's grasp, reached under my vest, and set a hand on my Browning. The lieutenant looked confused. He glared at me and started to move forward again.

Three Iraqi Army soldiers jumped in between us, barrels of their AKs just inches away from the police lieutenant's chest, and the lieutenant cursed at them and ran away. Around us, Iraqi soldiers and Iraqi policemen squared off in a Mexican standoff, rifles, pistols, and machine guns drawn, many of them just a few feet from one another.

The Fallujah Police heavily outgunned us—their machine guns outnumbered ours four to one, for instance. Police machine gunners, linked rounds slung bandolero-style across their chests, roamed the intersection, cursing in Arabic and daring the Iraqi Army to fire on them.

Three more Iraqi Police trucks manned by machine gunners showed up, none of the police wearing helmets or flak jackets. The Fallujah Police never wore helmets and rarely flaks. When your best friends are Al Qaeda in Fallujah, or you are Al Qaeda yourself, what do you have to fear?

We had two Iraqi Army pickups, mounted with machine guns, supporting us, but Fallujah Police now surrounded them.

Two more Iraqi Army gun trucks raced up, soldiers leaping out and scrambling up cinder-block walls, taking aim at Iraqi policemen.

We now held the high ground, with an outer circle of Iraqi Army on rooftops and cinder-block walls all around the intersection of Cathy and Henry. Iraqi soldiers took aim at Iraqi Police machine gunners and Iraqi Police officers.

Our Marine advisors—Staff Sergeant Sumner of Revere, Massachusetts, and First Sergeant Colby of Dorchester, Massachusetts—did not fail us, thank God. Marine advisors to the Iraqi Army, they rolled up in a humvee mounted with a medium machine gun, aided two Iraqi Army lieutenants on the scene, and shortly thereafter, the Fallujah Police drove away at the same time the Iraqi Army did. As the rusted, rap scrabble Iraqi Army pickup trucks rolled north down Route Henry, toward a small IA compound near the Fallujah train station, bursts of small-arms fire came our way from Fallujah Police gun trucks headed south on Henry toward Fran.

Both Colby and Sumner were convinced that the Fallujah Police wanted to kidnap me, hold me for ransom, put me center stage in a snuff video—"show your face and then slit your throat," as Colby, a strapping, red-haired American of Irish blood, a no-nonsense, compassionate, and street-wise Boston cop, told me that evening. "Hawk, you are the luckiest man in the world. That wasn't an arrest, it was a kidnapping attempt! If they'd grabbed you, forget about it, you'd be floating facedown in the Euphrates right now, brother," he said, toasting me over coffee later in the evening.

Both Colby and Sumner were Marine reservists called to active duty in the Iraq War, and along with Major Michael Muller of Arizona and Major Tim Murphy of Brooklyn, they were true professionals.

Without the Iraqi Army in Fallujah, no doubt the Iraqi Police would've killed me on January 3. On January 6, with a roadside bomb, the Iraqi Police made a second attempt, and again either I was lucky or the Almighty decided I needed another sunrise, or perhaps both.

On foot patrol again with the Iraqi Army, we passed the same intersection of Cathy and Henry. Five Iraqi policemen, all traffic policemen, drifted away, not even looking over their shoulders at us, as we neared the intersection. I greeted them in passing in Arabic, "As salaam Ah Laekkum." They said nothing and glared hate stares, a straight-up insult in Arab culture and a very bad sign in Fallujah.

Some twenty-five meters north, past the intersection, I looked back, scanning the rear of our patrol, and saw a Fallujah Police truck with a policeman sitting down in its bed, aiming an AK-47 at us. The red and blue police lights were flashing, the taillights were flashing, and as the truck turned the corner south on Henry, its siren went off. The police truck was moving very slowly, in no hurry as it rolled south.

The police are marking us for an attack by *erhabi*, I thought, and that was my last thought before the world went black. I got up, groggy, in smoke and dust, Lieutenant Keane bleeding behind me, badly wounded by shrapnel in both legs. He'd been right next to a roadside bomb, a 130-millimeter mortar shell jury-rigged with det cord and an explosive charge, when it went off. The blast had slammed me to the ground, roughly ten feet in front of him.

Keane was brave. Blood streaming down both legs, his face nicked and bleeding by shrapnel, he held down a corner, looking south down Route Henry, rifle stock in his shoulder, scoping our rear, providing us security as Iraqi Army soldiers tended to our wounded and gunfire rocked down on us from rooftops and alleys. It was the lieutenant's second day in Fallujah, and his last for that combat tour. Colby rushed up, treated his wounds, packed them with gauze, and wrapped Ace bandages tight around his legs. Keane later recovered from his wounds in Germany and America.

I had no doubt that the IED attack on us was perpetrated by the Fallujah Police, a coordinated ambush planned by the IPs and carried out by Iraqi policemen out of uniform—Fallujah *erhabi*.

The slow-moving IP pickup truck, coupled with the disappearing policemen just moments before the IED attack, coordinated with the *erhabi* small-arms attack on us, all occurred just three days after the Fallujah Police wanted to kidnap me. Major Dan Sullivan told me on January 13 on Camp Bahria in Fallujah, "The Fallujah Police had you marked to die. They wanted you dead on January 3rd. They saw another opportunity on January 6. By the grace of God, you are alive."

Sullivan, who had received the Marines' prestigious Leftwich Award in 1997 for outstanding leadership, gave me his word that he would send an intelligence report on the January 3 and January 6 actions, spotlighting the Fallujah Police attempts to kill me, "all the way up the chain." He kept his word, and to him, Semper Fi and thank you. He is now a lieutenant colonel on the staff of the Joint Chiefs of Staff at the Pentagon.

After another week of patrols with the Iraqi Army in Fallujah, I returned to Camp Bahria and handed the intelligence reports on Al Qaeda snipers to Kelso and Boyer, who briefed all Ronin scout/sniper teams on the Al Qaeda sniper threat, at that point, on January 13. You never want to see Americans going in harm's way without intelligence on Al Qaeda. To the Near East clandestine field officers who went out of their way to help us in Fallujah, a hearty thank you from Ronin.

Kelso had witnessed so many "shady, strange, and dirty" actions perpetrated by the Fallujah Police that he'd come to accept Al Qaeda's penetration of the Fallujah Police in a matter-of-fact way. "Make no mistake about it," he told me that day, "the Fallujah Police is the largest insurgent cell in Fallujah."

"The Fallujah Police is the
largest insurgent cell in Fallujah."

CORPORAL DUDLEY KELSO,
RONIN3 ASSISTANT TEAM LEADER,
JANUARY 2006

Born in Tupelo, Mississippi, the hometown of Elvis Presley, Dudley Kelso has lived in Memphis, Tennessee, for a few years now, enough for him to smile and proclaim, "Tupelo to Memphis, I'm still chasing Elvis." Five-eleven, lean as a sapling, hard-eyed, and with reddish brown hair, Kelso carried the M40A3 sniper rifle wrapped in burlap and rags in Fallujah and Al Saqlawiyah. Like many of his Ronin brothers, he was rarely without a book on downtime.

On a gray, cold late-January 2006 day in Fallujah, two weeks after I handed him and Boyer the intelligence report on Al Qaeda snipers, Kelso was sipping strong black coffee, his sniper rifle on the floor. He set his coffee down and leaned back.

"The American people have to know the truth on the street here; they deserve that from us. We know the ground truth of the war here; we know just how dirty and corrupt the Fallujah Police is, and we will not lie to our people. We will not lie to the parents of all of us who are going in harm's way here," he said, eyes bright, folding his arms.

Kelso carried an M40A3 sniper rifle, an M16A4, and an M9 9-millimeter sidearm at war in Iraq. Boyer's assistant team leader,

Kelso graduated from Marine Scout/Sniper School at Stone Bay, Camp Lejeune, in June 2005.

He was twenty-three years old in the winter of 2005–06. An Afghan vet, like many of his comrades in Ronin, Kelso had served in a Marine quick reaction force, with specific orders to guard President Hamid Karzai in Kabul. His total combat missions in Iraq and Afghanistan numbered well over 100.

His Arabic was solid in the field, definitely above conversational level, and he also spoke Spanish and German proficiently. Well skilled in a host of computer-programming languages, Kelso had also apprenticed to a locksmith. Along with Hodulich and Elder, Kelso possessed a great knowledge and understanding of rifles, machine guns, shotguns, and sidearms. (Ronin, on the whole, had a thorough, exact knowledge of small arms, which held true among the scout/snipers in my battalion, 1st Battalion, 3rd Marines, in the late 1980s also.)

Suffice it to say that if you can assemble it and load it, Kelso can fire it in the black. Sullivan said of Kelso on January 13, 2006, in Fallujah: "a very savvy, very intelligent young man and one of the brightest, most intelligent men in the battalion—a damn fine Marine."

On one operation, observing Route Ethan in Fallujah, I was watching an Iraqi Police shack. Lance Corporal Kyle Palmer, the watch before me, told me before I relieved him that anytime anything shady happened, any believed terrorist activity, the IPs would duck in their hole.

The IPs knew the attacks and IED bombings were coming beforehand. And it happened. Besides waving to their friends and chatting up random people passing by, it appeared that the IPs had nothing to worry about. So much so that they didn't even wear flaks and helmets.

At this point, I had an epiphany: The IPs never get hit by IEDs. We get hit by IEDs damn near daily. And the Iraqi Army got hit hard with a suicide car bomb last month, in December.

It almost seems like the Fallujah Police have a handshake agreement that they won't kill insurgents and terrorists placing roadside bombs, so long as the roadside bombs don't blow the Fallujah Police up.

I am not a cop or detective. I am a warrior and have to leave it up to higher-ranking people to decide how to act on the Iraqi Police in Fallujah's very shady behavior, which from my combat experience in Fallujah supports very strongly the conviction that the Fallujah Police are cooperating with terrorists and insurgents in Fallujah and western Iraq.

A few days before this mission of watching Ethan, we were observing the south side of Fran. Not far from where the Iraqi Police tried to kill you.

About ten meters left across Fran, right across from an Iraqi Police post, a roadside bomb [IED] went off. We had been observing that spot all day, but there was nothing but trash from our vantage point.

When the IED went off, the Iraqi Police reacted by making sure traffic went on as usual. That ensured that whoever set it off, if they were nearby, was able to escape by vehicle.

One Iraqi vehicle was peppered by shrapnel from the IED, but the Fallujah Police sent it on its way without so much as a cursory glance at whether there were any Iraqi civilians wounded or not.

All day long that day, the Fallujah Police had been hanging around that post, where the IED later went off, never more than fifty meters from where the IED was placed.

Whoever placed that IED did it in plain sight of the Fallujah Police or was an Iraqi policeman himself. Yet the Fallujah Police claim to have seen nothing.

A few days ago, in late January 2006, Ronin3 and a squad from Fox took a house to observe an objective thought to be interesting enough to warrant our attention. In other words, terrorist activity was thought to be going on in and around that house.

After we inserted and took over the house, a neighbor knocked on the door. The squad did not bring him inside, like we usually do.

The man called the Iraqi Police. Around noon, Fallujah Police showed up. The Fallujah Police put shooters on the

roof. The shooters were aimed at us. The Fallujah Police
yelled over the intercom with sirens, and flashed all their
lights on the vehicles paid for by American money, to make
sure that the entire neighborhood would know that we
were there.

I got on the radio with our scout/sniper SCC to call the Fallujah Police off. It took a while, but eventually they left.

But not before lining up to raid us, stacking on a wall, and
preparing to raid the house we were in. The Fallujah Police
drew a huge crowd and completely compromised us and our
mission. And left the area with an unsubtle message to all
Iraqi onlookers: "Don't worry, it's just the Americans."

How convenient for the terrorists in Fallujah that the Fallujah Police compromised us, exposed our position, and also
gave away our position to terrorists in Fallujah. That alone
made leaving the hide that night rather interesting. Like Special Forces says, a little too interesting.

Everything I've seen here has convinced me, for a fact, of
insurgents and terrorists penetrating the Fallujah Police.

When one of our former platoon members, Sergeant John
Matter, went to Echo Company as a squad leader, he got into a
firefight. Matter was hit with an IED and small-arms fire.
[Because of the needs of the battalion, Sergeant John Matter
became a squad leader in Echo Company, 2/6, in the middle
of his combat tour. Wounded on his first patrol with Echo, he
returned fire with his M.203, led a counterattack and was later
awarded a Bronze Star with V for Valor for his actions under
fire in Fallujah.]

His squad returned fire, killing several insurgents.

Fallujah Police on the scene, as reported by him, stripped
the dead insurgents' bodies of IDs and drove away with the
bodies. Muslim law on the dead says the bodies must be
blessed, cleaned, and buried with dignity within twenty-four
hours of passing. Iraqi law says that dead people must go to a
morgue for identification, if they are killed in combat here.
The morgues are in the hospitals.

But the Fallujah Police observe neither Muslim law nor Iraqi law.

They drove away with the bodies and dropped them into the Euphrates River. The names alone would have been useful information for Marine intelligence and Coalition intelligence.

It is highly likely, of course, that the insurgents who attacked Sergeant Matter and his squad were actually Fallujah Police themselves.

Every house I have been in has had Iraqis that love the Iraqi Police in Fallujah and hate the Iraqi Army. The local tribes love the Iraqi Police here. The Iraqi Police in Fallujah are all from the same tribes that supported Saddam 10,000 percent, that loved Saddam. The Iraqi Army here is mainly Shia, with a few Kurds, all from villages that suffered from the Sunni Arab tribes in Fallujah and western Iraq. There is no middle ground here.

Additionally, it is very troubling to me that the battalion, 2/6, has several high-value targets who cannot be snatched up to go in the pipeline to Abu Ghraib, supposedly due to lack of evidence. However, we have more than enough evidence to kill these same high value targets. These are terrorists, like Ahmed Sirhan, Diya Shakur Farhan, Shcikh Gazi Al Bowisa.

In fact, 2/6 has more than enough evidence, because I know for a fact that all the battalion has to do is tell one of us to take down one of the high-value targets, or all of them, and it is done.

The battalion won't order the kill on high-value targets, however, and these are terrorists—these are evil perpetrators.

Battalion S-2 keeps plugging away, seeking more evidence on high-value targets whom *we already know* are directly involved in planning and executing IED attacks and sniper attacks on our Marine brothers and on the Iraqi Army in Fallujah. S-2 tells us that if they get more evidence, they can put them in jail. "You don't understand the Big Blue Arrow," is what S-2 tells us. What I understand is terrorist snipers killed my brothers here, and nothing, not a damn thing, justifies refusal to issue kill orders on known terrorist and insurgent leaders. "Dead men don't give information" is what I get told when I ask why we are not being used to kill high-value targets, which is a classic scout/sniper mission: kill the enemy's commanders and all his high command. Know this: Dead men don't kill Marines, either. Dead terrorists open no offshore accounts. Dead terrorists plant no roadside bombs and plan no attacks. Dead men don't start terrorist cells. But alive men, that can't go to prison for so-called lack of evidence, can and do.

If 2/6 higher command, at the highest level, would let us set an example, or at least inform Fallujah that suspected terrorists will meet their doom by a single well-placed round, we might discourage a few people from placing roadside bombs. And a few are a hell of a lot more than none.

Instead, we sit on our hands, when any one of us would gladly take down any one of them and save Marine lives in Fallujah, including our own.

The Fallujah Police is the largest insurgent cell in Fallujah.

"The War on Terror is not about money or power. It's about a change. A change, a chance that my kids and their kids will be able to see America the same way that I did: a great place."

CORPORAL DAVID HODULICH,
RONIN2 SCOUT/SNIPER AND DEMOLITIONS SPECIALIST,
JANUARY 13, 2006

Corporal David Hodulich is one of the most committed, clever, and daring American warriors in the fight against Al Qaeda. Soft-spoken, witty, and knowledgeable on all small arms, Hodulich volunteered for the Marines at seventeen. Five-ten, broad-shouldered, and lean, Hodulich calls Springfield, Virginia, home and grew up near Washington, D.C.

In the spring of 2006 in Fallujah, he was nineteen. After witnessing Al Qaeda's attacks on the Pentagon on September 11, 2001, his life, like those of others of his generation, was profoundly changed. He is ardent hearted, without question, for victory over Al Qaeda in the Near East and all the world. We'd often find him reading journals and magazines of all stripes, gaining information on Al Qaeda and radical Islamic terrorism.

Never at a loss for conversation, he welcomed all dialogue on the guerrilla war in Iraq. Lance Corporal Andrew Smith of Baltimore and 2/6 Headquarters and Service company, a Marine infantryman, went out of his way to praise Hodulich's humble and cheerful manner, stressing that his camaraderie, fighting spirit, and easy-going nature all helped Smith survive the combat tour in Fallujah: "Dave Hodulich inspired me, over here, with his humility and courage. He was always there to listen, too. He helped us get through the hard times here. A good brother."

On clandestine actions, Hodulich was calm, steady, creative, and always thinking ten steps ahead of the enemy. He never moved without checking his 360, scoping in all directions down rubble-strewn streets in Fallujah and in date palm groves along the Euphrates, always making sure.

He often carried the M40A3 on missions and an M9 Beretta 9-millimeter sidearm on his hip. An expert rifle and pistol shot, he often shoots at ranges in northern Virginia and North Carolina. A demolitions specialist, he completed assault man's school, was assigned to 2/6, and later volunteered for Ronin. He graduated from Quantico Scout/Sniper School on July 29, 2005, and speaks conversational Spanish and Arabic. His Arabic in the field was often helpful to his team leader, Corporal Brian Areballo, on greenside (non-covert) missions when attached to Marine infantry in Fallujah and Al Saqlawiyah.

After handing Boyer and Kelso the intelligence reports on Al Qaeda terrorist snipers in Fallujah on January 13, 2006, I later talked with Hodulich about the terrorist sniper threat and the war in general. As always, he was thoughtful, insightful, and direct.

He asked if he could write an essay for the book. That essay follows.

A Marine Scout/Sniper in Fallujah

I am writing from Fallujah on January 13, 2006.

I'm a Marine scout/sniper in the guerrilla war here. I'm proud to be at war in Iraq. Sure, I know people who are against the war. Some are Republican, some are Democrats. I grew up near Washington, D.C., in Springfield, Virginia.

I watched the Pentagon burn on September 11, 2001. I was fourteen years old. I remember people at my high school losing friends and parents at the Pentagon. I saw the smoke pouring into the sky.

I remember September 11, 2001, very well. So the threat is real. No one can argue that we were attacked by Al Qaeda. We had a lot of debates on the war at my high school, but I always

believed that the war was justified. President Bush led us here
to take down a brutal dictator: Saddam Hussein. We've done
that. I had no doubt that the goal of the Iraq War was to
remove the threat of Saddam from us.

We did what we came to do. It was pretty kindhearted of us
to stay and try to help the people.

The Ba'athist tyranny is over. We don't have to worry about
Saddam funding terrorism, we don't have to worry about Saddam selling Scuds. You hear from Americans, "Iraq didn't have
any weapons of mass destruction." Well, tell the Kurds that.

Tell the people who got gassed at Halapja and so many
other places. Tell the Shia who were killed in their beds by
Saddam's *Mukhabarat* secret police, and lined up and murdered in the sand in Southern Iraq in broad daylight. We
need to stop feeling sorry for Sunni Arabs in western Iraq.

Sunni Arabs were the trigger pullers for Saddam.

There are some good people here. And yes, we don't try to
kill good people. But at what point are they more important
than us, or at what point are we more important than them?

I have tracked Al Qaeda cells here. I know the threat from
terrorist snipers here is real. I know that Al Qaeda is here. I
know that Al Qaeda has deep roots in Fallujah. I know the
brutal, diabolical nature of our enemy. I know what guerrilla
war means, I've lived it here. We cannot and must not lose Fallujah again to Al Qaeda.

I feel, to some degree, that the people here have more
rights than the people in the States. In the States, we could get
a warrant to search a mosque; here, we can't go into mosques
that we know are harboring terrorists and attacking us.

We have to be shot first, before we go into a mosque. Even
though we know there are terrorists in the mosques.

We allow the Iraqis to carry fully automatic AK-47 assault
rifles, weapons of war. But you can't own those in the States,
for good reason. Yet we are in a war here, and we allow the
enemy to arm themselves night and day. We must kill our enemies here, not placate them. And if you disagree with everything that I have said thus far, fine. I mean no disrespect at all,

saying that, I mean that straight up, strictly on the level. I welcome and appreciate the dialogue. Especially now, since I am in Iraq writing this and we are hunting Al Qaeda cells in Fallujah.

Americans have the right to disagree because generations of Americans have put it on the line to preserve that right. My generation is putting it on the line right now in Iraq and Afghanistan.

When I was a kid, I fell in love with America. I loved playing flashlight tag in the middle of the night. I loved lying out at the lake and staring at the stars with no cares. Playing ball with the guys I still hang out with—the fact is that I haven't been around that long.

I am nineteen years old. I've been blessed with good friends and comrades, graduated from Marine Scout/Sniper School at Quantico, and gone to war. My generation has been tasked with an awesome responsibility, here in Iraq and Afghanistan. At a young age, I realized that we are some of the luckiest people in the world.

I grew up in the shadow of the Founding Fathers. George Washington lived up the road, at Mount Vernon. Gunston Hall was down the street. Washington, D.C., is just twenty minutes by car from my hometown. Manassas was the site of two bloody Civil War battles. Mosby's Raiders rode up and down my side of the Blue Ridge. Colonel Washington and General Braddock marched on the road next to my school on their way to fight the French. Most people know so little about even the place they have lived their whole life. No wonder they don't understand why people like me go to war to protect a place larger than their own life.

Even Washington's generals in the American Revolution felt he fought wrongly at times during the Revolution. That seemed to work out, though.

Some people don't realize that the War on Terror is not about money or power. It's about a change. A change, a chance that my kids and their kids will be able to see America the same way that I did: a great place. My generation must ensure that happens; we must not fail.

I respect the sacrifices of all those who've served our country enough to realize that without my sacrifice, the sacrifices of all who've gone in harm's way before me will be in vain—and I respect them too much to allow us to lose this war.

I never want another generation of Americans to have their hearts sink, as my heart sank watching the attacks on September 11, 2001, and realize in that split second that nothing will ever be the same. On September 11, 2001, watching the smoke blacken the skies over the Pentagon, I knew that my generation would fight for greatness. In Fallujah in January 2006, I still know that.

I'm glad to fight for America. And as long as the American flag still flies, I'm OK to die for my people and forever be remembered by the red stripes on Old Glory.

So the next time you go to a ball game and sing the National Anthem, see a flag on a truck, or celebrate the Fourth of July, remember that the reason that flag still casts a shadow is not because some Marine scout/sniper got caught up in why we are fighting in Iraq and Afghanistan. He just served in combat in this war, knowing when he enlisted that he was going into combat, because he believed as I do that this is my generation's war and we must win it.

Some people say that there is nothing worth dying for; others say that there is nothing worth fighting for. For a small group of my generation, those of us who've seen action in Iraq and Afghanistan, your right to say that is worth fighting and dying for. My generation will not be denied victory. We will prevail.

Semper Fi.

"I totally agree, on the Iraqi
Police being penetrated by terrorists.
No question."

SERGEANT NELSON VERGARA,
RESERVIST WITH THE 25TH MARINES

Like Hodulich, Sergeant Nelson Vergara also witnessed Al Qaeda's assault on America on September 11, 2001. Vergara, a Marine reservist activated many times in the guerrilla war in Iraq, trained Iraqi police in Fallujah and Al Saqlawiyah from August 2005 to February 2006. He was thirty years old in the spring of 2006. He carried an M4 and a 9-millimeter sidearm.

Calm and frank, and no-nonsense when it came to talking about the Iraqi Police, Vergara grew up in Ridgewood, Queens, New York City. Five-ten, barrel-chested, and stocky, he took on a task that rivaled Don Quixote's for windmill-fighting: trying to instill professionalism and discipline into Iraqi Police in western Iraq, famed for their lax behavior, and sympathy for or outright allegiance to Al Qaeda and other *erhabi*.

A policeman in Washington Heights now, not far from Harlem in Manhattan, Vergara was in the "Three-Three," the 33rd Precinct in midtown Manhattan, on September 11. "Now my precinct is Washington Heights. A little after 9/11, I was working midtown," he said over coffee on February 12, 2006, in my small hooch on the top floor of Golf 2/6's mortar-scarred building. Arabic music and incense drifted down from our neighbors, Iraqi soldiers back from a patrol in Al Saqlawiyah.

Jamal, an Iraqi staff sergeant from Diwaniyah, Southern Iraq, brought us strong, dark, sweet Ceylon tea. Vergara thanked him in Arabic and sipped from his tea, going on, reflective and matter-of-fact as he talked about September 11 in New York City, the corruption in the Iraqi Police, and the need for far more effective counterterrorism in America and the world.

Three-Three Precinct, which covers 155th to 178th, it's north of Central Park. Spanish Harlem goes into Harlem, and then into Morningside Heights.

My brother works in Spanish Harlem, in the 23rd Precinct. NYPD calls precincts by their numbers, like the Three-Three. We don't call it the 33rd. From the twenties and up, we use single digits to name the precincts.

September 11th. The day that changed my world forever. Roger that.

I heard that the World Trade Center had been attacked. I headed downtown. I was in my regular car, not a police car.

As soon as I was driving, the second plane hit the tower.

Traffic was unbelievable—twice as bad as anything I've ever seen. The highway patrol cleared off the Grand Central Parkway, which goes into the Triborough Bridge, which goes into the city and the Bronx.

I was hauling ass. You could see the smoke from the bridge. Then the call came from Three-Three: "Don't go to the World Trade Center, report directly to the precinct."

I went to the precinct and put my name on a manifest. Immediately I was told, "Go to the George Washington Bridge. Defend it. Provide security. Expedite traffic. Let no one across the bridge." Then we got a false call.

A tractor-trailer pulled into the middle of the bridge and stopped. NYPD and Port Authority cleared the vehicle, which had come in from Jersey—it had gotten on the bridge from the NJ side. Searched it and cleared it.

Later that afternoon, I was blocking off a street by Columbia Presbyterian Hospital. The hospitals downtown were full. They were sending all the injured people uptown.

I went down to the site, to the bucket brigade, to help the search. In the beginning, I actually saw a couple survivors—they were emergency workers.

Dust and smoke everywhere. A lot of smoke. We were trying to remove rubble, as much rubble as we could.

Every firefighter in the city was there. We couldn't really do too much, they were trying to hose the rubble down, and there was so much fire under the rubble.

I did that for six months straight. Then I was temporarily assigned to the Chief of Department's Office. If the ESU teams or the fire rescue recovered a body, or body part—if anything was found—we would report it directly to that unit.

There was a garage underneath, and we'd gone into the garage. There was always the stench of burned flesh. Concentrated smell, of decay, of death. Then FEMA stepped in and made it mandatory to wear masks on-site at World Trade Center.

I remember the second day, or third day, and Robert De Niro appeared by the docks of the Lower West Side. At Battery Park.

He was crying. He shook our hands and hugged us. I met him three times. He also was at the Marine Corps Ball, November 10th, on the USS *Intrepid*, with Harvey Keitel. We usually get invited to go on the *Intrepid*, in our dress blues.

When De Niro came, I was working, still pulling rubble out of the World Trade Center. And he was doing a film shoot, down in Tribeca.

De Niro was very kind to us. Really lifted our spirits. I remember saying to him, "Nice to meet you, under the circumstances." He said to me, "How are you holding up?" I told him, "Pretty well."

He said, "I'm glad you are here." De Niro was teary-eyed, you could tell how upset he was. It'll always be something that is very present tense to me, as the years go by—9/11 changed my life. I can never forget that day.

I remember wanting to help as much as I could, and that by being a cop, I could do that.

We had a lot of support from the public initially, with a lot of units deploying to Afghanistan. When Iraq started, I wanted to do something. I'd finished my active-duty time, and I went reservist so I wouldn't lose my job in NYPD. And I found out a buddy of mine from Jersey was already mobilized, with Golf 2/25.

I found out from Gunny Leach, from Long Island, that I could mobilize: "We need '41s, mortar men, right now. How soon can you get over here?" I reported to Gunny Leach at Garden City, Long Island, and I was mobilized within a week.

Then, immediately, we reported to Camp Lejeune. We were there for two to three weeks. We went to Cherry Point and flew to Kuwait. Camp Shoup. Right up near the border, about a half hour from the border. It was pretty hard to get ammo. We got a convoy brief.

Crossed into Iraqi soil. Our objective was Al Nasiriyah. We made a base, which we called White Horse. About four klicks from where Jessica Lynch was ambushed.

We ran our ops from there. Stayed in Al Nasiriyah the whole time. Weapons Company went to Al Nasiriyah Museum—that was our new forward operating base.

We would go on patrols, do raids—same thing that's going on here, basically. We took a lot of incoming and small arms on those patrols. Everything—mortars, RPGs, small arms.

Our responsibility was pretty much the Iraqi Police, at that point. I remember an Iraqi policeman struck a little boy, by accident. I thought he was a little reckless. All of a sudden, the entire village came out of nowhere. Tried to pull the IP out of the vehicle.

They wanted to kill him. The little boy was bumped on his head and he was bleeding. The kid survived, he stayed in the hospital for a couple days. I thought, "Holy crap, these Iraqi Police need a lot of training, they need a lot of professionalism instilled in them, make them think, impress upon them the importance of common sense."

And that remains a huge challenge now, three years later, in training Iraqi Police. Trying to instill some ethics in them, a baseline of professionalism.

You try to make them think, What if you kill the good guy? You need a court system. Right. What's to say you won't make that mistake? What if you end up making a mistake?

We're teaching them our concept of policing, and one thing they have real difficulty understanding is "innocent until proven guilty."

The tribal laws make it even more complicated. Teaching an old dog new tricks is just as difficult here as anywhere else.

Their attitude is, "We want you to go; we want to continue our freedom without you." They are not ready.

They also don't understand that in law enforcement, if you want to improve, you are *always training*.

The number-one weapon that you have is your radio, not your weapon, not your pistol or shotgun. Your radio is your lifeline, your support, and your backup. They don't get that at all, either.

I asked my IPs, "What is your most important weapon?" and they all said, "My gun." Wrong.

I am always trying to teach them to use their radios. Never do things by yourself, always work as a team.

Last thing I was trying to teach them was how to respond to an ambush. You know well that only four Marines and three Iraqi soldiers were the only response to thirty terrorists in Saqlawiyah on October 26, 2005. You witnessed that.

The Iraqi Police response was "Get in a room and let the Iraqi soldiers and Marines deal with it." The whole idea of training is to get them to a point where they have confidence and can be far more proactive and take the initiative. There hasn't been any positive law enforcement models—no positive role models in this country.

I wanted to come here to give them confidence and give them the knowledge that I have, as a policeman and as a Marine. And teach them that your weapon should be your last resort. Human rights and law enforcement are all one. You have to respect that the suspect is a human being.

Roger that on the terrorist sniper threat. To avoid sniper fire, we're doing certain things that strengthen the walls and better secure the rooftop.

My focus is to do more vertical patrolling—get the IPs on rooftops, for instance. Make the terrorist think twice about going up on a roof to shoot at us, to know that there would definitely be the possibility of contact.

Just getting the IPs to understand situational awareness is a challenge. Know where the hell you are. For instance, never pat anyone down on the stairs, at the top of the stairs, because the suspect can back you up, get you off balance, and you're knocked backwards down the stairs.

I totally agree, on the Iraqi Police being penetrated by the terrorists. No question. October 26th in Saqlawiyah was a perfect example of that. So was December in Karmah.

I hope for the best, but I expect the worst. It almost feels like a losing battle. As soon as we finish training these guys, we get attacked.

A federal-level, Iraqi state-level counterterrorist command would be far more effective at fighting terrorism in Al Anbar—counterterrorist commandos, counterterrorism intelligence analysts, and counterterrorist operators, under their own command, reporting directly to the Iraqi government.

Structure it like Kurdish counterterrorist command, and communicate as the Kurds do: *Need to know means need to win.* That's the challenge, stateside and internationally, in taking down Al Qaeda: getting the bureaucratic walls down, getting the people in the field listened to at all levels.

A lot of it comes down to respect. You've got to respect that guy in the field, who knows what the hell he is talking about. He's lived it.

The Kurdish model on counterterrorism is incredibly effective. The problem in American culture is how much information is withheld, which the Kurds don't do—they don't withhold information, they don't block the passage of communication. They listen well, they communicate, and they execute. The Americans don't do that, or at least we didn't prior to 9/11.

"It is madness, what the Americans are doing by empowering the terrorist Sheikh Khalid. It is folly, it is madness."

AHMED, IRAQI INTERPRETER,
FEBRUARY 2, 2006

Ten days earlier, Ahmed, an Iraqi Arab interpreter, shed light on American decisions that have empowered Ba'athist sheikhs supporting Al Qaeda and other *erhabi* in Fallujah and western Iraq. Ahmed was fluent in Arabic, Iraqi dialects, English, Farsi, and German.

You could see the frustration in Ahmed's eyes before he spoke one word. He sat on the edge of a chair, smoking, shaking his head, quiet for a long time. It was difficult to get him to even agree to the interview: "The Americans don't listen!" he exclaimed, rubbing out a smoke. "What difference will it make? Do the Americans really care about victory here? Are they here to defeat Al Qaeda?

"My God, I do not know anymore why the Americans came to Iraq—they keep patting the Ba'athists on the back, helping them return to power."

I lit up his smoke and poured him a tea as a sandstorm gusted outside on February 2, 2006, in Fallujah and told him that if he gave Americans a chance to listen to him, perhaps they would. I reminded him that he'd been in Iraq three years, from March 2003 to February 2006, and he'd well earned his opinion in the field, under fire, and in many meetings between the Al Qaeda–connected sheikhs and imams in Fallujah and both the U.S. Army and the Marine Corps.

He seemed to warm to that, shrugging his shoulders and smiling slightly. Few people know more about Al Qaeda here, and how serpentine the threads run, connecting Al Qaeda, Black Flags Brigades, and other *erhabi* to the Fallujah City Council and Fallujah Police, than Ahmed. All told, the Iraqi Arab and Kurdish interpreters knew far more about Fallujah and western Iraq than the American military intelligence people. The 82nd exploited their knowledge from September 2003 to late March 2004, listening closely to their interpreters.

I sought many times, through Captain Sousa at 2/6, to sit in on Fallujah City Council meetings and also to interview different sheikhs and imams, as well as the Fallujah chief of police, one of Saddam's generals, Brigadier General Salah. It was Salah, Coalition Intelligence informed me, who told RCT-8 on December 26 in Fallujah, "All this country needs is a strong man back in power, like we had under Saddam." No doubt comforting words to the 300,000 Kurdish and Shia skeletons in the deserts of Iraq; and surely welcoming words to the 5,000 Kurds massacred in one day by Saddam's chemical weapons in Halapja in March 1988.

Sousa never delivered. RCT-8 never even replied to him, according to Sullivan (who went out of his way at meetings at RCT-8 to help me, to no avail), denying me the chance to speak with any of the Al Qaeda sheikhs on the Fallujah City Council. They had conspired in and paid for the Fallujah Police's two attempts in early January 2006 to kill me, according to a Kurdish military intelligence report I received on the twenty-fourth of that month.

I knew exactly how the scout/snipers felt, being stonewalled and ignored by 2/6 command; by the time I interviewed Ahmed, RCT-8 had done the same thing to me. Looking back, however, it was a blessing in disguise. I was forced to seek out more Iraqi Arab interpreters, who had been to all the meetings among RCT-8 Marine command, the Fallujah City Council, and Salah. Moreover, they had been in western Iraq longer, and deeper, than anyone else in-country.

Ahmed, like his fellow interpreters Muhammad and Malik
Peshi, delivered. He laid out Sheikh Khalid's connections to Al
Qaeda and other *erhabi* in a small concrete hut where two years
earlier, I'd listened to paratrooper scout Sergeant Joe LeBleu of
the 82nd advise Captain Scott Kirkpatrick of 10th Mountain Division about sniper missions near a mosque in Fallujah.

Sheikh Khalid was a wanted terrorist. Close to Ahmed
Sirhan, close to Zarqawi. Very high-value target, wanted for
financing, planning, and executing attacks on American and
Coalition Forces in Fallujah and all of western Iraq. Deep ties
to Zarqawi, known to meet personally with Zarqawi in Damascus, Ramadi, and Fallujah. Marines targeted Sheikh Khalid
from April 2004 to November 2004. He was a very high-value
terrorist target, a notorious terrorist. Like Sheikh Gazi Al Bowisa and Ahmed Sirhan. The Marines did not capture or kill
him. They tried; they made many raids to kill or capture him.
He was working closely with Sheikh Abdullah Al Junaibi.
    And they were well known to be terrorist sheikhs. All Fallu-
jah citizens know this. They financed IED attacks, mortar and
rocket attacks, bought AK-47s and RPGs, built and expanded
terrorist cells, handed out blocks of plastic explosives, and
planned terrorist attacks. They'd made their agreement with
Al Qaeda in April 2003, same as the other Fallujah sheikhs
and imams.
    They were meeting with Iraqi civilians, Fallujah citizens,
and at every Friday sermon, they would talk to people and
force them to make *jihad*: "You know, the Koran says we must
make *jihad*, because the Americans come to Iraq to steal the
oil. They are the Crusaders; we must make *jihad* against the
Americans." I tell this to the Marine commanders, and they
don't understand—they don't understand the significance of
this in Arab culture.
    A terrorist sheikh, who uses the mosque for operations
meetings, and the people know this and live in fear of him—
you have to kill him! If you do not kill him, it shows your weak-

ness. There is nothing worse in Arab culture than to show your weakness! And on such a scale, to show your weakness.

Bush does not want to kill the enemy here; he just wants to pay them off. Bush doesn't understand—it's not about money, it's about power. Ba'athists will do anything—you saw this before here—to regain the dictatorship.

Even the terrorist sheikhs on the Fallujah City Council were calling on the mosque loudspeakers, saying, "It is good for you to support the attacks on Americans." And they were using young people to carry out these attacks.

After Saddam fell, Zarqawi used these methods to get the young people to make *jihad*, to attack Americans and blow themselves up. Zarqawi, and Al Qaeda, telling them, "You will go to heaven and fuck the virgin girls." And some young people were convinced, and would do it for free, because the *jihadists* and Zarqawi persuaded them that they were going to go to heaven.

Sheikh Abdullah Junaibi was a famous guy in Saddam's government. He kept the volunteers list, to record who paid for AKs and other weapons and munitions, and the list of names. That list covers all Iraq. He made all the connections, to all the villages, for weapons and ammunition. Explosives, mines, bombs, mortars, grenades, and rifles.

Now Sheikh Abdullah Junaibi is a big-time terrorist in Fallujah and he has the Americans in his pocket. He uses the list to plan attacks on Marines and Coalition Forces.

Now, Sheikh Khalid, Sheikh Abdullah Junaibi, and the other terrorist sheikhs on Fallujah City Council—all appointed by the Americans—will go to mosques and drum up donations at the mosque to pay for *erhabi*. The mosques are a key financial base for the *erhabi*. Also, the mosques are central to the *erhabi*'s recruiting—financial base, armory, recruiting base, and operational center. The mosques are houses of war in Fallujah, and not houses of worship. This is the reality which the Americans know, at the highest levels, and which the Americans turn a blind eye to.

For instance, the *erhabi* put a big box in the mosque and let the people know, this money is going for the *erhabi*. They will say, "This money is going to the *muhjahadeen*, to fight the holy war, etc." The *erhabi* raise money easily in the mosques in western Iraq.

Now, when Second Fallujah was over, the Marines put in a new mayor and new Fallujah City Council. The Marines appointed Sheikh Khalid to the new Fallujah City Council. I first heard this, I wept.

The Marines appointed Sheikh Khalid Hamood Mahal Al-Jumaili to the Fallujah City Council in December 2004. Just after Second Fallujah—Al Fajr, second battle of Fallujah. Sheikh Khalid is a known terrorist, with deep connections to Zarqawi and Al Qaeda. He was one of the most-wanted terrorists in Fallujah and western Iraq prior to Al Fajr. This is madness. The Americans are their own worst enemy. Sheikh Khalid remains on the Fallujah City Council, as we speak. He continues to support Al Qaeda. The Americans appointed him. That is like inviting Osama Bin Laden to dinner at the White House and appointing him to the Joint Chiefs of Staff.

Bush is lost in his thinking; he is mad. And not only Bush, but the Americans, in general, over here in command. It is madness. Three years ago, I crossed the berm from Kuwait into Iraq, with Americans at war.

I have served as an interpreter for many American units in Iraq, both U.S. Army and Marines. 3rd Infantry Division. 82nd Airborne Division. 1st Marine Division. 2nd Marine Division. 1st Marine Division, again.

The Americans leave, I stay, and I translate for new Americans. The Americans refuse to win here; nothing has changed since 2003. It is worse now than it has ever been since the beginning of the war.

The new Americans and the old Americans have one thing in common; it is sad for Iraq and it is tragic for freedom in Iraq: They want to please Saddam's generals, they want to please Sunni Arab sheikhs and imams, they want to please the

Mukhabarat, they do not understand the horror that we Iraqis faced under Saddam.

They do not understand that they have empowered Ba'athists to support a return to Ba'athist dictatorship.

The Americans do not understand the horror of Saddam. They make decisions as if Saddam never existed, as if the Ba'athists are all now somehow different than before, as if the genocide Saddam perpetrated against the Shia and Kurds never happened.

Do the Americans read history? It is frightening to me, sad, frustrating, and terrifying to know the decisions made by the Americans, to get the Ba'athists back in power.

The Americans do not understand that their decisions, like their decision to appoint the terrorist Sheikh Khalid to the Fallujah City Council, strengthens Al Qaeda in Iraq, strengthens Black Flags Brigades.

The American decisions in Iraq give Osama Bin Laden what he wants: a major Near East recruiting, operations, and training base in the heart of the Near East, Iraq.

And these Al Qaeda terrorists, supported by the sheikhs that the Marine commanders have empowered, wreak havoc and mayhem every day on Iraqi streets. Bush is insane, in what he has perpetrated here.

They will terrorize any land they set foot in, including on American soil. It is madness, what Bush is doing by empowering terrorist sheikhs like Sheikh Khalid. It is folly; it is madness.

"The mosques in Fallujah

and western Iraq are terrorist COCs? You're asking me for the record, yes or no answer? Yes. That is a very accurate statement. The mosques in Fallujah and western Iraq are terrorist command-and-control centers."

MAJOR MICHAEL MULLER AND MAJOR TIMOTHY MURPHY,
MARINE ADVISOR TO THE IRAQI ARMY IN FALLUJAH,
25TH MARINE REGIMENT, JANUARY 9, 2006

Major Michael Muller of Tucson, Arizona, a bright, inquisitive, and fearless tank commander who had volunteered to be a Marine advisor to the Iraqi Army in Fallujah, sat at an operations desk with maps and photos piled all about it, a satellite photo map of the city behind him with red dots marking successful raids by the Iraqi Army.

Iraqi Army soldiers guarded the rooftop and the walls of the compound. The compound's main building had good sight lines—you could see over the entire city and down each side of the building clear to the ground, without obstructions.

It was the winter of terrorist snipers in Fallujah. Corporal Jay Elder of Ronin3, a senior scout/sniper, had warned me in mid-November 2005: "Do not hesitate to eyeball sight lines, any place you sleep or spend any time in. The rat bastard terrorist beast is out there, and the beast is hungry." With Ronin denied countersniper missions throughout December 2005, I detached from the scout/snipers and attached to countersniper missions with the Iraqi Army.

Muller was grinning this day, as was his nature. Mud covered his boots. He scratched at his short blond hair and halloed his comrade, Major Tim Murphy, who had enlisted in Marine infantry in 1986 and went on to get an officer's commission. Like Muller, Murphy served as a Marine advisor to the Iraqi Army from August 2005 to February 2006. It was January 9, 2006, in Fallujah, and Muller was scanning a target list of Al Qaeda terrorist snipers and other *erhabi* in the city.

Murphy, an artist and teacher from Brooklyn, joined him and checked out a target photo, saying, "I will take this guy down, brother." Muller nodded in agreement, still grinning. Matter of fact, I rarely saw Muller not grinning. He handled the ups and downs of that winter in Fallujah, on the street and in the mud, with a smile, a wave, a 9-millimeter sidearm, an M4, and grenades.

Three days earlier, at 3:15 in the afternoon, Murphy had been all smiles too, with the terrorist sniper cell leader Bilal Ibrahim Dari Al Kubasi in tow. Murphy, built like a light heavyweight and quick on his feet, came out of a small house in central Fallujah with the terrorist Al Kubasi in one hand and his M4 in the other.

Fallujah kids clapped and smiled at us as we hustled up the street, Iraqi Army soldiers flanking us, some of them jogging, their AK-47s held from the hip. Muller slapped me on the back and said, "Terrorist sniper cell leader, Bilal. Solid raid."

Bilal Ibrahim Dari Al Kubasi, six-foot-one, wearing cuffed black trousers and a collared shirt, looked as if he'd been sleeping in a lot of different places—wrinkled clothes, scraggly salt-and-pepper beard, and dark circles under his eyes. He'd led a terrorist sniper cell in Fallujah and had planned and executed mortar attacks on Marines and Iraqi Army soldiers.

As we hurried for an Iraqi Army rusted pickup truck, Iraqis eyeballing us in the narrow streets, Murphy said, "Bilal is wanted for kidnapping, additionally. We've been hunting him, and we took him down today, thanks to Iraqi Army human intelligence. Entire operation to take him down was all Iraqi Army human intelligence driven."

Kids in the neighborhood swarmed out again as we got close to the Iraqi Army pickup and flex-cuffed him.

Murphy got on the truck and said to me, gazing around at the children in the streets, "These kids know he's an evil perpetrator.

They know the deal. Great to see they are happy that we took him down." I stayed on the foot patrol. Two hours later, with the Iraqi Army on patrol, we were hit with a roadside bomb and small-arms fire, in the action that wounded Lieutenant Keane.

Three days later, in Major Murphy's operations room, feeling damn happy to be alive, I could see gray clouds flooding the skies over the Euphrates west of us. A prayer call echoed from a mosque as an Iraqi Army patrol went out the wire, and I knew insurgents and terrorists in the minaret of the mosque were marking us.

Sheikh Abdul Sattar (occasionally spelled Sittar), imam of Jama Al Raqueeb, near the Fallujah train station, was marking Iraqi Army patrols with *jihadi* rants from his mosque loudspeakers every day I patrolled with the Iraqi Army from December 27, 2005, to January 13, 2006. One of the terrorist sheikhs named by Ahmed as in deep with Al Qaeda, and a member of the Fallujah City Council, Sheikh Abdul Sattar ran the *jihadi* fireworks at Jama Al Raqueeb.

The Iraqi Army compound I'd stayed in bordered on the high, massive stone and concrete walls of Jama Al Raqueeb. I'd earlier noted to both majors, and also to 1st Sergeant Chris Colby, that Sheikh Abdul Sattar was marking our patrols with his loudspeakers, blaring *jihadi* rants as soon as we'd step out the wire on patrol and as we'd return.

They'd agreed and added, like Muhammad in Al Saqlawiyah, that Al Qaeda and other *erhabi* keep lookouts in the mosques at all times. That way, each time an American or Iraqi patrol enters or leaves its compound, the *erhabi* can mark it with a *jihadi* rant, setting Coalition forces up for IED attacks, RPG attacks, and combined-arms ambushes.

Major Muller, like Major Murphy, saw no downside to the aggressiveness, initiative, and savvy of the Iraqi Army in Fallujah. And as Muller had said to me on January 6, "Not bad men to have around; they've saved your life twice now." Like many Marines, both Muller and Murphy referred to Iraqi *erhabi* as the *"muj."*

Muller: "The mosques in Fallujah and western Iraq are terrorist COCs? You're asking me for the record, yes or no answer? Yes. That is a very accurate statement. The mosques in

Fallujah and western Iraq are terrorist command-and-control centers. The bottom line is that we allow the enemy to hide behind his religion and use their mosques to stage attacks and to store weapons.

Jama Ma'adhiya is one such mosque. That's the mosque near the site of an ambush on December 16, 2003, the mosque that gives terrorists and insurgents significant support. Where 10th Mountain Division held, with a classic counterattack. The Old School Warrior Kings, Bohlen's men [referring to an action in *Among Warriors in Iraq*]. There was a big battle at Jama Ma'adhiya nearly a year after that action, in the second battle of Fallujah, Al Fajr. Probably the most brutal battle in Al Fajr was in Jama Ma'adhiya.

One unique advantage we have as advisors is we get the unfiltered information directly from the Iraqis. Sheikh Abdul Sattar is a real bad guy and very much like a mob boss. Correct, he is in the mosque right near the Iraqi Army compound you're in, Jama Al Raqueeb.

The way the *muj* gained power in Fallujah, after Saddam fell, is that they went to every imam and sheikh in April 2003 and said, "You will not support the Coalition. You will not give a pro-Coalition sermon and statements over the loud speaker—and if you do, we'll kill you." Correct, Al Qaeda and all other *muj*.

At the same time, they offered tremendous rewards, cash and other gifts, if they support the insurgency. In the more powerful mosques, that extended to, "If you don't support the insurgency, we'll kill you."

The more I came to understand this, the less I liked Islam. Their religion is all inward focus to begin with. Self-sacrifice is a foreign concept to them. Most of them only understand self-service.

The imams delivered the sermons. About two months ago, the imam of the big blue mosque delivered a pro-Coalition sermon. And they murdered him. Sheikh Hamza. The whole city knew he'd been murdered. On the heels of that, a reminder from Zarqawi: If anyone else does this, we'll kill them.

I've run into Fallujah Iraqis who speak English: "I thank you very much for what you're doing, but I can't help you or they'll kill me." Our neighbor was passively helping us, clearing garbage from in front of us and informing us of suspicious activity, and the terrorists slit his throat.

I agree with Major Muhammad, the Iraqi Army intelligence officer you spoke with on December 27, 2005: yes, 70 percent of the Fallujah Police support the *muj*. That is accurate.

The only way that one of our contracted Iraqis helps clean our compound is that he tells the terrorists that we made him do it. It's what he has to do to stay alive. No way he can tell them, or anybody else, that he gets paid.

Sheikh Abdul Sattar. Nasty. Right, his mosque is Jama Al Raqueeb. We are the only battalion that's rolled up any sheikhs, that I know of. We've rolled up two.

Major Murphy was in front of this mosque. He heard mortars coming out of the mosque. We reacted and surrounded with IAs. We were attempting to get permission from RCT-8.

Colonel Ra'ad, a very intelligent, aggressive, and incredibly competent Iraqi Army battalion commander, did not hesitate to go into the mosque. Colonel Ra'ad entered first and found a massive weapons cache: mortar base plate, RPG warheads, mortar fuses, mortar firing tables, and this was all without metal detectors.

Finally, once we got approval, Echo Company engineers came in, and we pulled huge weapons cache out of the mosque: grenades, C-4, more RPG warheads, RPG launchers, RPK, small-arms ammunition, etc. Massive weapons cache.

I was testing for powder residue. One, the mortar firer, tested 100 percent positive for residue. The imam's quarters are in the mosque, of course.

Lieutenant Colonel MacVarish, our battalion commander, pushed higher headquarters hard to buy time to completely exploit the site. However, there was a lot of pressure to get out of there quickly.

The saving grace was that the more we searched, the more we found, and you couldn't argue with success! Lieutenant

Colonel MacVarish was in favor of rolling up the sheikh and ultimately got approval to do just that. The sheikh claimed that everything had been buried before May 2003; the Iraqi Army soldiers had found the mortar rounds, and everything else, above ground, of course.

Colonel Ra'ad lost all respect for the mosques in Fallujah on that day. He is a Muslim, and he sees mosques being used as houses of war as a complete desecration of Islam. And, of course, nothing in the Geneva Convention protects mosques being used as houses of war.

We had Echo Company, 2/6 line infantry Marines, get ambushed from a mosque about a month ago—kid threw a hand grenade in sector 16.

It took about forty-five minutes to get approval for entry. The IPs went in first, then the IA, then a few Marines. We found buried fuses.

To actually exploit a site with metal detectors is very slow, takes about six to eight hours to complete a thorough sweep. Two more mosques penetrated by the *muj* nearby. One is the mosque on Route Henry, Jama Furqan. Huge minaret. Jama Furqan is the mosque you passed each time you were nearly killed, on January 3rd and January 6th.

First time we went in there, we were doing a cordon and search in a nearby area. One of Iraqi Army soldiers said they saw two American males and one American female, dressed in *dishtashas.*

I'd earlier that week received reports that two American men and one American woman were reporting on the insurgency by living with the insurgency. The terrorists have embedded journalists: Americans, reporting on insurgents and terrorists who are killing Americans.

A week or two after, we noticed some individuals surveilling us from the mosque. So our executive officer, Lieutenant Colonel Ahmed, entered Jama Furqan with Iraqi Army soldiers, went up into the minaret, and talked to the Iraqis surveilling us. They claimed, "Oh no, we're only stringing lights." There's always IEDs near that mosque, within 100 to 200

meters in all directions. You and Lieutenant Keane were hit
with an IED near there just a couple days ago, on January 6th.

Now we're back to Sheikh Abdul Sattar's mosque. Jama Al
Raqueeb.

We've got reports from some time that Sheikh Sattar is a
known terrorist. Interrogations of *muj* often point back to
Sheikh Abdul Sattar. He gives anti-Coalition sermons all the
time. That's his trick bag.

Back in October and November, it was grenade season, it
shifted to sniper season, now it's more IED season. We had
many grenade attacks within a block of Sheikh Abdul Sattar's
mosque by thirteen-to-fourteen-year-old boys. And they were
throwing grenade-sized rocks, trying to get us to shoot one of
them and cause an international incident.

We had a super Iraqi Army soldier, who realized they were
being spied on and cut a satellite patrol and baited the
grenade throwers. Two grenade throwers raised up, and the
IAs butt-stroked them. They captured three of them. We even
captured another grenade thrower.

Sheikh Abdul Sattar is on the Fallujah City Council. Often,
Sheikh Sattar calls Colonel Ra'ad right after we roll up a
known terrorist.

Sheikh Abdul Sattar vouches for the man and says he is a
good man. This happens far too often to be a coincidence.
Colonel Ra'ad really hates Sheikh Abdul Sattar. He actually
hates all the sheikhs in Fallujah who have sold out to the *muj*.

Murph [Major Tim Murphy] and I saw a kid, right outside
the door of Jama Ma'adhiya, in the cemetery, digging with a
shovel in a pile of dirt. The kid dashed in and a man came
out, dressed like an imam, and said that nothing is happening. We found a piece of UXO [unexploded ordnance, such
as a mortar, mine, bomb, artillery shell, or rocket]. We came
back two nights later.

Murphy: And right where that kid was digging, we found
three 155s [155-millimeter artillery rounds, used by Al Qaeda
and other *erhabi* to make IED. The September 29, 2005, IED

in Al Saqlawiyah, for instance, was made of two 155s wired together—daisy-chained, in grunts' parlance].

Muller: What we've seen done recently is that locals are raising the height of the walls, so that you can't see into the Jolan cemetery. All of them are near Jama Ma'adhiya. There's more insurgent and terrorist activity to that mosque, no doubt. They also flash lights down April and Henry, to signal the front trace of Echo Company patrols, at night. At day, the houses nearby use pigeons to signal our patrols to terrorists and insurgents.

Murphy: Two days after the raid that nailed the 155s, another Iraqi Army patrol was patrolling adjacent to the Jama Ma'adhiya. A grenade came out of the mosque. The grenade killed one of the Iraqi Army soldiers.

Right after this, a call for prayer from all the mosques, *except* the mosque the grenade came from. There was no call to prayer for the rest of the day from Jama Ma'adhiya.

And no imam came out from the mosque—so Colonel Ra'ad entered the mosque and said, "Why are you not curious about what just happened outside your walls, and why are you not making the call for prayer?"

The imam said, "I have diarrhea."

Mortar fire came out of a mosque, Jama Badawi. The guy we detained who'd fired the mortars was an elder at the mosque.

Muller: Jama Badawi. Very dirty. Sheikh Sa'ad Ismail Shankhah. That was the name of the sheikh that we rolled up. He was the mortar attack sheikh—he was behind that mortar attack. Massive cache of mortars in that mosque. His cache. He has confessed to being a terrorist imam.

He actually turned up many terrorist-connected elders, such as Imam Muhammad Ahmed Muhtar in Fallujah; the imam Sheikh Mohammad Ahmed Muhtar in Fallujah also.

Jama Badawi is bad news. We had an Iraqi Army patrol out there on 14 December, out after curfew. As they were patrolling along, they noticed a man looking around the corner, watching them. They doubled back. The man was still watching them. Turned out, he was an imam and his house was connected to the mosque.

Iraqi Army entered his house and found huge amounts of proterrorist, anti-Coalition, anti-American CDs, videos, etc. Iraqi Army wanted to roll him up. [RCT-8 ordered his release because the elections were the next day, and RCT-8 didn't want to offend the Al Qaeda–connected sheikhs on the Fallujah City Council.]

We grabbed his passport and turned over his cell phone to RCT-8. He's still at large, right now. His videos showed how to use a multiple rocket launcher. Also, he had videos that had filmed IED attacks, RPG attacks, and small-arms attacks on American and Iraqi troops in Ramadi.

Murphy: One thing that may change dramatically is in order to exploit a mosque site, you must have metal detectors.

The insurgents and terrorists bury their weapons in mosques—in some cases, as deep as four feet. Unless you have a metal detector, you're not going to find their weapons. Up till now, we've had to rely on 2/6 for that capability.

We have now ordered our own metal detectors so that IA can conduct their own raids, so they don't have to rely on limited American assets.

I've been on active duty for well over a year. I'd like to spend the next ten years eradicating these individuals who are Al Qaeda. I now have two sons, and I'd like to see to it that they're not going to have to come over here; that we get the job done. I don't think the War on Terror is going to be over for at least twenty years, at least.

We do a lot of staff-related work as Marine advisors, but when we go on patrol, we're observers. When events occur, we often find ourselves acting as super squad leaders, however, since we have the most experience. Part of our job is, when necessary, to step in and lead. We all talk about it. There hasn't been one second when I've seen any of us take cover. Forward momentum all the time.

The importance of having a grunt out there is never more real. For instance, on November 13th, when we were out on patrol, we heard a mortar launch. We heard the round cutting through the air. "I just heard a mortar launch," I said.

By the time I got done saying that, it impacted, maybe five seconds later. I heard, from the sound of it, very close and to our northwest. From the fact that the launch and impact was only five seconds apart, no charge on the round, and the tube must've been cranked over at a low angle. Which means it could've been launched from someone's yard with a high wall, like an open area surrounded by a high wall.

The only place located close to us like that was the mosque, about 200 meters away.

I was thinking that people were going to hide the mortar and escape. I patrol every day here. We had some guests, an Iraqi Army sergeant major, and the squad leader had a lot of pressure. The patrol leader knew where the mortar had come from. Colonel Ra'ad, who was 800 meters away in his head-quarters, had a theory it had not come from the mosque.

I got the guys to turn around and go to the mosque. I was certain the mortars had been launched from the mosque.

We left security at the mosque, to be absolutely sure that the mortars had been shot from the mosque. We stopped at the mosque and posted security. A team of IAs went into the mosque. I was standing right outside the door of the mosque.

By the way, the exact second that the mortars were launched was the very beginning of the call to prayer. A recent discovery: Calls to prayer hide the sound of the mortars being launched.

People were filing out, all males, and the IAs said, "No, if you're in, you're staying in." The IAs came out and said, "Come in. We're sure that we've found something."

So I went in and looked for the imprint from the mortar base plate. While this was happening, Major Muller with elements from our Iraqi Army battalion showed up. IAs whooped and hollered from the wall adjacent to the imam's house. The

IAs had found evidence of the mortars being fired from the mosque. They were psyched, and we were too—high fives all around. Over by the wall, several RPG rounds, mortar base plate, a compass, a mortar site, mortar firing tables, mortar rounds, and small-arms ammunition. All of it was in pristine condition—clearly and obviously recent material, lubed up, greased, and wrapped in plastic.

Then Marine engineers began fully exploiting the site. Machine guns, RPGs, C-4, other munitions, and grenades, all buried in the mosque.

We tested the congregation for explosive residue and detained a couple of them.

We took all of the weapons and munitions, stacked all that, and lined up the imam and the congregation behind it, like a high school football team photo. Took the photo.

Pretty late at night; all that was left was Colonel Ra'ad, his security team, and Lieutenant Colonel MacVarish. One of Colonel Ra'ad's soldiers went over to the imam's house and arrested him. We took the imam away.

The big challenge for the Iraqi Army is logistics. Operationally, they are fully capable of independently carrying out counterinsurgency operations. Outstanding human intelligence, no question about it.

"Imagine if you manned the NYPD in 1940 with the Cosa Nostra. That's Fallujah in our time. You've manned the police with the Mafia."

CAPTAIN MARTY KEOGH,
BLACK LABEL GUN TRUCK PLATOON COMMANDER,
WEAPONS COMPANY 2/6, FEBRUARY 10, 2006

Promoted from first lieutenant to captain in July 2006, Captain Martin Keogh inspired everyone that ever rode with him in combat in Fallujah. He led from the front of his platoon, Black Label gun truck platoon of Weapons Company 2/6, whose company commander was the irrepressible "Tommy Z," Captain Thomas Ziegler, since promoted to major. Ronin1 team leader Sergeant Efraim Parra said of Keogh, "When we know that Keogh is picking us up, on an extraction from a covert mission, we are damn happy. He is a straight shooter and one of the best commanders we know. Ronin respects him because he treats us like men, and he is one helluva squared-away officer."

Keogh was always careful to have a .50-cal on his point gun truck—Keogh rolled on point himself—and an MK19 40-millimeter grenade launcher on his tail-end Charlie. Six gun trucks were under Keogh's command in Black Label.

His men loved him. Higney, his radioman, called him "The Sir" and said, "The Sir listens to us, brother. I can't honestly say that about all officers. But I'm proud to say it about him. He knows how corrupt the Fallujah Police are. He's an honest man." Agreed.

The words that come to mind immediately, remembering Keogh in Fallujah, are respect, integrity, and listening. Keogh knows how to listen, and he knows how to lead men in battle.

About five-ten, lean, and swarthy, Keogh hails from Newark, Delaware. He graduated with a degree in literature from the U.S. Naval Academy in 2002. He runs marathons, drinks cold beer, and commands Marine infantry. He often sang "Danke Schoen" on patrol in Al Saqlawiyah and Fallujah, getting a holler out of his wheelman, Private Raban "Anthony" Kimungu, every time. "The Sir knows we hate that song, brother—I mean, it's a lounge singer's tune, you dig, 'Danke Schoen,' Lord—but since it's The Sir singing it, we can deal with it." Keogh would sing it as he spotted roadside bombs and stayed on the hunt for Al Qaeda night and day in Fallujah in the winter of terrorist snipers.

You knew he was hard-core, deadly serious about taking down Al Qaeda and other *erhabi*, and you knew at the same time, all the time, that he was always looking out for his men. His men respected him and would follow him anywhere, and no better words can be said about a commander. He received the prestigious Tarawa Award for the most outstanding lieutenant in the Marine Corps in 2006; his parents accepted it on his behalf, while we were still in combat in Fallujah.

Like Major Muller and Major Murphy, he too was impressed with the Iraqi Army in Fallujah. Keogh was one of the very few officers, likewise, who agreed to go on the record about the Fallujah Police. Apart from Major Sullivan, Major Murphy, Major Sullivan, and Keogh, no other Marine officer in Fallujah would talk about Al Qaeda's penetration of the Fallujah Police. Keogh, like Kelso and all of Ronin, shared Hemingway's gift for moral and physical courage, moreover.

As Kelso said on a hasty raid on January 22, 2006, near the Blackwater Bridge, hustling down a sidewalk, "The Iraqi Police behind those machine guns are guarding Al Qaeda near here, and they are guarding terrorists and insurgents all throughout Fallujah," pointing to three Iraqi Police pickups with mounted PKC 7.62-millimeter machine guns, the police behind those machine guns wishing us to our graves with their stares.

On February 10, 2006, I got a chance to interview Keogh in Fallujah.

I think that purely out of frustration, I came up with the idea to integrate my Marines with the Iraqi Army. The Iraqi Army are really committed here.

My main thought: We need to get the Iraqi Army on the tip of the spear. Lieutenant Jones, our Weapons Company executive officer, really helped, of course. Captain Ziegler didn't hesitate to move it forward.

A challenge, certainly, though. Learning the Arab mind is probably the equivalent of learning thermodynamics. For people who are focused on things literary—I am a literature man—it's tough, it's ridiculous. Everything is upside down over here, compared to any Western culture. When you listen to the Iraqi soldiers, however, you get real insight into the situation here and to taking down our enemy.

I just thought, you know, to use an Iraqi would be a gold mine. That was my thought: We need to get the Iraqi soldiers on the tip of the spear. Use them and support them, learn from them.

I was looking for a terrorist in the marketplace who owns a tailor shop. So I used a couple Iraqi soldiers to find him.

The first time I actually tried this, we were hit with a suicide car bomb. We were on the western flank of that.

We saw a guy pitch a rifle. We cornered him. No way in hell I could ask what happened. No interpreter with us, no way to ask.

But an Iraqi Army sergeant major and three Iraqi Army soldiers were with us, thank God, and the integration was beautiful.

Magical part of it was that the Iraqi Army sergeant major knew how to talk to them, knew his audience, varied his tone and approach with all ages. Magical to watch him do that; it was unreal. The tailor shop was in the heart of the souk.

All I did was provide security. They hunted down the tailor shop guy. It was amazing. We took him down together.

Since then, I have not done it again with them. I'd like to, but there is a new Marine advisor element in town. Major Murphy, Major Muller, and their guys are rotating out, redeploying.

The Iraqi Army know the street, they've got the juice. They have the in with the people. So much of it is nonverbal, too, just knowing the culture and the street. The Iraqi Army soldiers are fearless, and they want to take down terrorists and insurgents. Fighting spirit is high, and it is real.

The most elementary thing of dealing with this, you know, you wouldn't bring somebody from Worcester, Massachusetts, to show you around Newark, Delaware.

The Iraqi Army soldiers are the key to unlocking the cultural divide.

And they *enjoy* being with us. That's the huge good news. I'd say, it's like the icebreaker. You know, when you're walking outside and you're seeing Iraqis and Americans together, on counterinsurgency.

Yes, part of counterinsurgency is shocking people, surprising the hell out of your enemy, and deception is very important. Fundamental to victory, deception, no question. Crucial.

Deception is critical. The triangle here is uniting Marines, Iraqi Army, and Iraqi Police. Once they're on board, it's game over. That's a heckuva challenge, getting the Fallujah Police on board. Excruciating challenge. The problem in Fallujah with the Iraqi Police is that they are Fallujans.

Imagine if you manned the NYPD in 1940 with the Cosa Nostra. That's Fallujah in our time. You've manned the police with the Mafia.

You need outside elements in the Police, in order to grow here. But now they are all like-minded. It's the same fuck-up that is being allowed to happen with Hamas policing Palestine. That can't work. Why would you start out with problems? Why not start with a clean slate? But we didn't start with a clean slate here, not at all. When you man the police with the Mafia, don't be surprised when they act like Mafia.

Look, when you start out with insurgents/terrorists in the police force, you're causing problems for yourself.

What I know from night and day patrols and raids in Fallujah is you have to eyeball the street, eyes-on, no substitute for human intelligence. I really believe that looking right at the street and knowing what's going down—that's crucial. I know that for a fact. Knowing what's going down night and day here, seeing exactly where the IEDs are being laid.

If you don't eyeball the streets and the rooftops here, and if you don't know what's going down in the mosques, you can't win. That's vital to victory to here. And Major Dan Sullivan has really helped me, really been a rock in the storm. Major Sullivan has always steered me in the right way. The Iraqi Army integration is effective, it is working for us and for the Iraqis. Our counterinsurgency operations, with the Iraqi Army on point, are incredibly effective.

We are taking terrorists and insurgents down. The Iraqi Army is tough, smart, and very ingenious. Ten years from now, I hope we can look back and say we made it happen, and that the Iraqis are not suffering any longer.

I just want my kid to get on a train and know that he's not going to blow up, regardless of what country he's in.

"The IPs are marking our patrols for the terrorists and insurgents here . . . by lighting up their vehicles when we go out the wire."

CORPORAL JAY ELDER AND CORPORAL STEPHEN LUTZE,
RONIN4 SCOUT/SNIPERS, JANUARY 15, 2006

Elder: The IPs are marking our patrols for the terrorists and insurgents here, of course, by lighting up their vehicles when we go out the wire. Last night, we patrolled on Fran, and we were with U.S. Navy SEALs at this point. [US Navy SEALs and Ronin were on combined operations in late December 2005 and January 2006). Turned the corner going north, and IPs came from behind us and turned the dome light on and turned their red and blue lights on. They were mocking us, and their body language was really offensive. It was kind of obvious that they were mocking us.

The second truck behind that truck had his brights on, silhouetting us down the street with his high beams.

My overall vibe of the Iraqi Police is that they are all dirty. They are all penetrated by Al Qaeda and other *erhabi*—some directly supporting terrorists, others terrorists themselves, some giving information and looking the other way when terrorists set up IEDs on us, for example.

We've been hearing that directly from Iraqi counter-terrorist forces. They were extremely professional. They were dedicated fighters. Johnny Walker, Rex, and Abdul all

Ronin Platoon. First row, left to right: Sgt. Efraim Parra, Cpl. Brian Areballo, S/Sgt. Christopher Williams, Cpl. Darren Smykowski, and Cpl. Derrick Boyer. Back row, left to right: Cpl. Bobby Parker, Cpl. Justin Novi, Cpl. Dudley Kelso, Cpl. Noah Fleming, Sgt. John Matter, L/Cpl. Jim Owen, Cpl. Stephen Lutze, Cpl. Danny Milstid, L/Cpl. Jon Zwirblia, HM3 Joshua James Gutierrez, L/Cpl. Jason Hillestad, Cpl. Dave Hodulich, L/Cpl. Billy Getscher, and Cpl. Jay Elder.

Cpl. Justin Novi, Ronin4 assistant team leader, and Cpl. Bobby Parker, Ronin1 assistant team leader, on a C-130 from Kuwait to western Iraq, September 21, 2005. Novi is holding a Barrett .50-cal sniper rifle.

Ahmed Sirhan, leader of the insurgent Black Flags Brigade and one of the most wanted insurgent/terrorist leaders in Iraq. On September 29, 2005, Cpl. Derrick Boyer, Ronin3 team leader, was ordered not to kill or capture Ahmed Sirhan at the moment this photo was taken.

Cpl. Dudley Kelso, Ronin3 scout/sniper, in the reeds along the Euphrates River at Al Saqlawiyah, October 15, 2005.

Cpl. Justin Novi using a spotting scope on a reconnaissance and surveillance mission in western Iraq, October 2005.

Kelso sights in his M40A3 7.62x51mm NATO rifle on a sniper mission in western Iraq, October 2005.

Cpl. Jay Elder on reconnaissance and surveillance in Fallujah, November 2005.

Cpl. Darren Smykowski, Ronin4 team leader, on a mission in Fallujah, November 17, 2005.

Ronin4 back inside the wire, Fallujah, November 22, 2005. Left to right: Cpl. Stephen Lutze, Cpl. Darren Smykowski, Cpl. Justin Novi, and Cpl. Jay Elder.

Iraqi Sunni Arab family welcoming Ronin3 on a November evening. Cpl. Derrick Boyer and Cpl. Danny Milstid are on the floor; Cpl. Jay Elder, wearing a black watchcap, sits on the sofa.

Cpl. Derrick Boyer on reconnaissance and surveillance in western Iraq, November 28, 2005.

Immediate aftermath of a suicide bomb attack on "Super 7 ton" trucks and humvees, Fallujah, December 11, 2005.

Private Raban "Anthony" Kimungu wearing the helmet that a terrorist sniper had shot through in November 2005. Photo taken in January 2006.

Lieutenant Muhammad of the Iraqi Army leads an insurgent cell leader to a "gun truck" (an armored pickup truck), Fallujah, December 13, 2005.

Cpl. Stephen Lutze, Ronin4, after a reconnaissance and surveillance mission in Fallujah, December 2005.

First Sgt. Chris Colby, of the Boston Police Department and the 1st Battalion, 25th Marine Regiment, in a Fallujah cemetery where Al Qaeda stored weapons in graves, December 21, 2005.

Searching for weapons in a Fallujah cemetery.

Capt. Marty Keogh, Black Label gun truck platoon commander, never missed an opportunity to gain human intelligence. On the right is Corporal Higney. Fallujah, February 9, 2006.

Keogh (left) with Staff Sergeant Rose (right) in Fallujah, February 2006.

10:16 A.M., March 10, 2006, at Checkpoint One in Fallujah: the wake of the suicide attack that killed L/Cpl. "Bunny" Long.

Checkpoint One, two minutes later.

Cpl. Mike Loper, Jim Beam platoon antitank man and machine gunner, manning an Mk19 40mm grenade launcher and a light machine gun after his last mission in Fallujah, April 3, 2006.

Music was the only thing that kept the scout/snipers sane. Cpl. Justin Novi and Cpl. Danny Milstid in Fallujah, March 12, 2006.

Cpl. Jay Elder aiming in with a SAM-R rifle.

Cpl. Dudley Kelso on radio watch for Ronin3, waiting for intel on a mission in western Iraq, March 2006.

On firebase in Fallujah, April 12, 2006, three days before leaving Iraq. Left to right: Cpl. Brian Areballo, Cpl. Jay Elder, "Doc" Gutierrez, and Cpl. Dudley Kelso.

talked with us: their language skills were very competent. They told us, "We'd rather shoot the Iraqi Police than look at them."

The Iraqi counterterrorist forces touched on, in their own way, that the Iraqi Police are terrorists, and the corruption in the government is a big part of problem.

What the Iraqi Police are doing: Let's say an insurgent or terrorist gets hit. The Iraqi Police are first on the scene, check all the IDs and make sure they're not Iraqi Police, and then dump the bodies in the river rather than take them to the morgue. If the dead insurgents/terrorists are Iraqi Police, then the Iraqi Police destroys the IDs and dumps the bodies in the river, same-same.

We've been informed that if we see this, that we are allowed to engage the Iraqi Police. They have been warned. Lutze, does that confirm with you?

Lutze: Yes. Solid copy. Everything you've seen, I've seen at least once in Fallujah—agree completely with you, brother.

Elder: My theory on this right now is that insurgent cells are primarily focused on shutting down our observation posts. Our Marine guards standing duty at observation posts are sitting ducks, easy targets for them.

They already know that we're almost out the door, already, a lot of Fallujah is being given up to the Iraqi Army. We're seeing a lot more high explosives in Fallujah since Iraqi Police manned checkpoints with Marines, like at ECP-1. The only conclusion is that Iraqi Police at those checkpoints are letting explosives get smuggled in Fallujah; it's no accident.

Yesterday I called in some construction workers digging on a curb. Digging on a curb but not pulling anything out. They weren't there to prepare it for pouring concrete, that's for sure. I was sure they were digging to prepare the hole for a roadside bomb, for an IED. Called it in on the horn, on the radio. "They're digging on the side of the road. Check it out." Iraqi Police phoned forty-five minutes later, talked to the owner of the construction business, but didn't check out the actual IED site.

No one ever checked out the actual IED site. No Iraqi policemen came out and eyeballed the digging. In a city where roadside bombs go off like clockwork. We're trusting the Iraqi Police far more. For what reason? Majority of the Iraqi Army, on the other hand, are not dirty.

"If there is a man-eating lion
near your village, do not send the
entire village to kill the lion. Send one
lion hunter to kill the lion. Your best
hunter." Masai proverb, East Africa

CORPORAL DARREN SMYKOWSKI, RONIN4 TEAM LEADER;
CORPORAL JUSTIN NOVI, RONIN4 ASSISTANT TEAM LEADER;
CORPORAL BRIAN AREBALLO, RONIN2 TEAM LEADER;
AND CORPORAL JAY ELDER, RONIN4 SCOUT/SNIPER AND GRENADIER

In the winter of terrorist snipers in Fallujah, with the Iraqi Army using great human intelligence assets to take down terrorist sniper cell leaders, 2/6, RCT-8, and 1st Reconnaissance Battalion refused to use American warriors who are specifically trained for countersniper missions in guerrilla war and conventional war: Marine scout/snipers.

Yet Corporal Darren Smykowski had led Ronin4 in Fallujah on countersniper missions from November 15 to December 1, 2005, without being compromised. We set up on rooftops and in rooms; low-crawled over broken glass, gravel, and concrete shards; stayed covert; and Ronin4 made clean infiltrations and extractions on every mission I saw them on—top-drawer clandestine ops. Corporal Brian Areballo's team, Ronin2, was also in Fallujah in November, carrying out daring covert countersniper missions.

There is a Masai proverb on man-eating lions: "If there is a man-eating lion near your village, do not send the entire village to kill the lion. Send one lion hunter to kill the lion. Your best hunter." Lions are not stupid. They can scent from way off, sense many hunters approaching, and bolt and return. The terrorist snipers in Fallujah, I had no doubt, were not stupid either. Diabolical, yes, but not damn fools.

RCT-8, 2/6, and 1st Reconnaissance Battalion were not keen on African proverbs, however. They removed the best lion hunters we had, Marine scout/snipers, who knew the village, Fallujah, very well, night and day, and had carried out excellent reconnaissance and surveillance missions there in November 2005. Then they sent lion hunters who had never lived in the village to track the terrorist snipers: a company of Recon Marines, plus U.S. Navy SEALs and U.S. Army Special Forces snipers.

Unlike Ronin, none of these assets had prior experience on the streets, in the alleys, and on the rooftops of Fallujah.

Not only did the best lion hunters we had remain in guard posts, behind concrete, while the man-eating lions were on the prowl in Fallujah in the winter of 2005–06, but the lion hunters sent to kill the terrorist lions were, so to speak, from an entirely different region of Africa.

When your scout/snipers already know the terrain like the back of their hand, and they are the most highly trained assets in the U.S. military for countersniper missions—along with U.S. Army snipers—you listen well to them, heed their counsel, and send them out to track and kill the terrorist snipers. The Marines did the opposite: stonewalled them and ignored them.

After RCT-8 ordered me at 3:00 A.M. on December 1, 2005, to stand down from Marine scout/sniper missions, I had the good fortune to share a coffee and conversation with Smykowski before returning to Camp Bahria. He brought up, again, the wisdom of the African proverb.

In late November, we'd heard word that 1st Reconnaissance Battalion was going to "own Marine scout/snipers for all December." Now it was happening, and all bad news: Ronin was being ordered on guard duty at observation posts, making the men sitting ducks for the terrorist snipers. "We'll sit behind concrete and barbed wire, watch for muzzle flash, and then, blink of an eye, kill the terrorist snipers right after they shoot at us or shoot at our Marine brothers?" Smykowski said. "That's retarded. That's waiting for your enemy to kill you. This is a complete waste of our assets.

They're sending the whole village to kill one lion, or a few lions.
Wrong answer. Send your best lion hunters who know the village.
Who know it well."

Six weeks later, he, Areballo, Elder, and Novi detailed just how
badly RCT-8, 2/6, and 1st Reconnaissance Battalion failed to listen
to Ronin and failed to employ them on countersniper missions,
which have historically been a key scout/sniper operation in guerrilla warfare.

> **Smykowski:** We are far more qualified than Recon [refer-
> ring to all Reconnaissance Marines, and specifically in this
> case to 1st Reconnaissance Battalion] for countersniper mis-
> sions. Countersniper is one of our core missions, by the way.
> Recon did not listen to us, all of December.
>
> In truth, no one listened to us. All Recon did was have the
> audacity to call me on the radio and ask, "What are these build-
> ings like? How tall are they? What's their structure? Can they
> hold fifteen people?"—calling in ten-digit grids from a map.
>
> Because they didn't know the terrain. They don't know Fal-
> lujah anywhere close to as well as my team, and all Ronin
> teams, know Fallujah. Incredible waste of us, the entire month
> of December. We are specifically trained to kill enemy snipers.
> Terrorist snipers were killing our brothers. And we were
> ordered to sit in guard posts and wait to be shot at.
>
> **Areballo:** Finally we got out of the guard posts. We began
> the combined ops with the SEALs. Check this out: The SEALs
> had never operated in any city environment before. That's
> what they told us. So not only were they fresh to combat in
> Fallujah, they were fresh for urban combat, period.
>
> But they knew that we knew the turf. They respected us,
> unlike our own command. And they came to us for a lot of
> questions; they were very fresh in the game. Look, if you took
> snipers who'd never set foot in Baghdad before and gave
> them Baghdad missions—bam, you're in Baghdad, and it all
> looks like Dodge City to me, and so on—the SEALs were in
> that spot. Nobody at RCT-8 thought of the simple tactical real-
> ity, "How well do SEALs and Recon know the terrain?"

The battalion thought by bringing in SEALs, that they could accomplish more. They brought all these assets. But what the battalion didn't understand, and what RCT-8 didn't understand, was that we were far more trained, far more experienced, and we knew these streets and alleys far, far better than any SEAL. It's the man-eating lion and the village, exactly, and we are the best lion hunters on this turf.

And what we talked about in late November with Ski: You predicted that all the special ops assets, the SEALs and Recon, wouldn't nail the terrorist snipers, because RCT-8 has a piss-poor human intelligence network here from the get-go, and you need solid human intel to take down enemy snipers on urban turf. And this is urban turf, Fallujah. Right. Our analysis in late November was correct. And you were right.

Smykowski: Then—oh, this was brilliant—2/6 was telling us we'd clear rooms with our 40s. Clear rooms with sniper rifles. Sniper rifles for close-quarter battle! Right, they were going to take away our M-4s, suppressors, and sidearms, even our SAM-Rs. We're in an urban environment without a weapon suitable for close-quarter battle? No one trains for CQB with sniper rifles anywhere, it defies all combat logic. That's madness.

Yet our own battalion was telling us, "You can clear rooms with an M40." It's crazy. You can't even use a light machine gun now, with our rules of engagement. It makes much more sense to just use our SAM-Rs, because they are fully automatic and you can control that rifle easily. You have to personally identify everything, and that's why a light machine gun is pretty useless now.

Areballo: You can't control where the rounds are going all the time, on the light machine gun, and it lets out a spray of rounds. You can't take well-aimed shots from it. Not an effective weapon, with our rules of engagement.

Smykowski: A real problem in the battalion is failure to communicate. My team nearly got killed by friendly fire, blue on blue. My team worked with Naval Special Warfare and SEALs. We did that until just recently. Fox Company Marines nearly lit us up, blue on blue. Failure to communicate, and the failure came from Fox.

We were in a hide, with Navy SEALs, on reconnaissance and surveillance for a high-value terrorist target. Every male in a nearby house had been flex-cuffed and arrested. We called it the Axis of Evil house.

2nd Platoon Fox nearly lit us up. They saw people on the roof and freaked out. They started lighting up the house, firing at us.

The SEALs threw an air panel out. [Air panels identify friendly fellow Coalition forces to all other Coalition forces, which is common knowledge to U.S. Army and Marine units.] They kept firing at us.

We talked to 2nd Platoon Fox later and they said they heard our cease-fire but they didn't know it was us. What, did they think terrorists and insurgents are now speaking fluent English? Man, the SEALs threw an *air panel!*

On top of that, 2nd Platoon Fox stacked on that house, got ready to raid it, and I had to yell out, "Hey, don't hit this house! This is Ronin4 out here!" It was fucking retarded.

They told us later, "We were all amped up and we were all talking and joking, and we freaked out even though we knew where Ronin4 was at."

Here's the failure to communicate: I know they had our pos rep [position report, exact location of a Marine or his unit]. I know that they knew *exactly* where we were.

I had just talked to their platoon sergeant on the radio. I'd reminded them that I told them, "Hey, we've got eyes on you. We're on the northwest corner of Dave's Field. We're in the corner house, in the only all-brick house in the area." Everyone in Fox Company knows Dave's Field.

They knew that was where we were at, but they still opened up on us. It's not cool being lit up by friendlies, because you can't return fire. All you can do is lay there and hope you don't get wasted. Man, the SEALs were pissed. I mean, the SEALs threw down an air panel, which says it all.

Areballo: December was a goatfuck. All of December,
denied what we can do better than the SEALs, Recon, or anyone else: countersniper missions to take down terrorist
snipers. It was a month of static positions, aside from two
actual missions with the SEALs. The colonel used to boast
about us stateside: "My snipers will be taken care of in Fallujah." He'd call us in front of the whole battalion: "These are
the new snipers, and they're solid." Then we got here, and we
are just shit on.

Because "you're not producing results." Don't deny us kill
shots on terrorists, then. Don't deny us perfect reconnaissance
and surveillance positions. Don't piss down our backs and tell
us it's raining.

If you don't give me freedom of mission, I can't give you
results. What did we do throughout December? We sat behind
concrete and barbed wire. There are targets all over Fallujah
that our own command denied us.

Novi: When Sergeant Matter went to Echo, he was
ambushed on his first patrol near OP Henry, near Route
Henry. Somebody was on the wall of the mosque Jama Ma'adhiya, videotaping.

After the firefight, Iraqi Police were taking all the IDs off
the dead insurgents, throwing them in the backs of the cars.
Found those seven bodies the next day floating in the
Euphrates. Same bodies. The Iraqi Police didn't take them to
the hospital, because then you'd have to ID the bodies, and
you get the names. We'd get the names, too. No body, no ID,
however.

But if the names are names of Iraqi Police themselves, you
see the situation. The Iraqi Police covered up the insurgent
attack because the Iraqi Police in Fallujah *are* the insurgents
and terrorists.

The Iraqi Police made sure that their Iraqi Police buddies
who were killed on that day were not identified. Roger that,
we got the intel from you, on Iraqi Arab doctors and nurses at
the hospitals in Fallujah who are locked on with Al Qaeda and
other terrorists and insurgents. When the doctors and nurses

at the hospitals and clinics are cooperating with terrorists and insurgents, and actually terrorists and insurgents themselves, then you can see the depth of our troubles here.

The Iraqi Police snatch teams, like the Iraqi Police that snatched up those dead Iraqi Police with masks on, killed by Sergeant Matter and his squad—it's easy for the insurgents to use the Iraqi Police like this, because the Iraqi Police can't be fired on. Military lawyers, the JAG, said we can't. Sergeant Matter wanted to engage them; he knew they were insurgents.

The Iraqi Police are never going to clean up this town. They will never allow Fallujah to progress. The Iraqi Army definitely needs to be in charge.

Fallujah needs martial law. The police are the insurgent cell in this town, exactly. Major Muller and Major Murphy are accurate—confirm their observations 100 percent. That is exact to what we've seen go down here.

All the Iraqi Army needs to end it here are live rounds. It's common knowledge that the Iraqi Police in Fallujah were all *muj* before. They are still *muj*; nothing has changed. You watch the Iraqi Police rotations, coming on and off their posts. How they move and where they move. Never wearing flaks and helmets, because the Iraqi Police in Fallujah don't fear Al Qaeda here, *because they are Al Qaeda.*

They'll respond to IEDs before anyone—the Iraqi Police in Fallujah know exactly where the IEDs are going off ahead of time.

You'll see them go up and down Fran on vehicle patrols and then you'll see them disappear for ten to fifteen minutes. Then an IED will go off on us or on Iraqi Army. Then they'll come back—they are already en route. They know exactly the positions of those IEDs, because they cooperate with the *muj* in laying the IEDs.

Elder: The battalion S-2 and RCT-8 do not understand how to get human intelligence, how to gain human intelligence sources, and how to develop a human intelligence network. That's all fundamental in guerrilla war, but they don't have a clue how to do that. It is striking that the Iraqi Army nailed that terrorist sniper cell leader Bilal; that is awesome. All off human intel.

The SEALs tried to establish an actual network, with one individual who lived across from the CMOC [Civil-Military Operations Center], and knowing that the guy was cab driver. Who gets around the city better than cab drivers? But it was never pursued, to the best of my knowledge.

Fox knew about it and passed it on; I was there when the SEALs did a lot of their debriefs. I was interested in seeing how the SEALs intelligence would be disseminated. And it wasn't disseminated. The SEALs were stonewalled. It went nowhere.

The blue on blue with the SEALs: Me and Ski were near the northwest corner of Dave's Field, and Sergeant Soto's guys engaged. Roger that. Ski had just called them on the radio, let them know *exactly* where we were. Fox was supposed to brief them on that, additionally, before they went out the wire: sniper hide of Ronin4 and U.S. Navy SEALs.

Soto's Marines had been lit up by an IED seventy-five meters from our position, and they had been moving to the northwest. They were coming toward our position, and it was like they were getting sucked in by the enemy. We could see they were ripe for an ambush, at that moment.

We called it in: "We have eyes on; we are observing for enemy activity," to find out who is shooting at them.

That information was passed to the COC [Fox Company command and control center]. And the COC knew the day before exactly where we were. We'd called in our position the day before.

One of Soto's Marines was pointing to an individual running away, looked to be a triggerman, running north. I engaged at that time with a suppressed weapon on that individual. Soto's squad lit up the northwest corner, from where I'd shot—it was blue on blue at that point.

Soto's squad was lighting us up. We did not return fire. I am not going to kill another Marine, no way in hell.

The SEALs had air panels on the side of the roof, and we shot green star clusters, and what it all boils down to is that higher knew where we were at, but *nothing* was disseminated to the squad on patrols.

Staff Sergeant Stowers, Soto's platoon sergeant, told us that Soto's squad had never been told of our position. But we had communicated on the radio to his squad. It's a fundamental problem in 2/6, a basic failure to communicate, at all levels.

We did a debrief, and a Navy SEAL, I'll call him Chief James, told us that the COC never disseminated that information about our position and our mission to that squad before it went out on patrol.

Another little quirk of that mission was that the house we set up in was a known terrorist safe house. But no one told us that before the mission.

Correct, after the mission we were informed. I know for a fact that the SEALs were asking about that area—their instincts and their human intelligence, before the mission, drove them toward that house.

All the intel gurus decided that it was now the time to tell us. No one talks in this battalion. 2/6 is a retroactive battalion.

Novi: It's the Big Blue Arrow. We don't know what's the Big Blue Arrow.

Elder: The Big Blue Arrow, roger that. When we ask the intel gurus why they deny us key intelligence on our enemy here, they smirk and say, "It's the Big Blue Arrow. We can't explain it; it's just the way the missions need to be."

That's coming from people who don't have 1 percent of the time we have on the ground here, out the wire. It's madness. And everybody is a sniper employment officer. EGB, Inc.: Egos Gone Berserk, Incorporated.

Novi: Roger that. Everybody wants to tell us how much they know about our job. All ideas are open on how to employ scout/snipers, *unless it is from our platoon.* The battalion does not listen to the operators, to us scout/snipers.

Elder: Remember in *Kingdom of Heaven,* on not listening to scouts. Very instructive, that movie, on the essential truth of listening to scouts in war. Excellent, telling, straight to the core of all reconnaissance in war.

Remember Custer. Don't do it; don't go over there. Listen
to your scouts; listen closely. We are not in business to jack you
over; we are here to help you survive and win.

Custer didn't listen to his scouts, and he got waxed. 2/6
chain of command all the way up, except for Major Sullivan,
does not give us the respect and does not listen to us.

Novi: My buddy Plaza has been with me since boot camp.
He's in Fox Company now. His lieutenant put Plaza in for a
Navy Achievement Medal with Combat V for Valor. Plaza is a
lance corporal. He received that combat medal for actions
here as a squad leader.

Lieutenant Colonel Aiken then found out that a lance corporal is leading a squad. Because he has to check off on the
paperwork for the medal. Now, there's a corporal in Plaza's
squad who guarded the president at Camp David. Which
doesn't mean jack, in the grunts. Having guarded the president has nothing to do with small-unit leadership in the field,
and at war.

But the colonel said, "Either the Camp David corporal takes
over the squad, or Plaza gets moved to Echo." Plaza was
removed as squad leader. Plaza got shot on patrol, he led his
squad damn fine in combat, he's an outstanding squad leader,
and he had done nothing wrong. Plaza was thinking about
reenlisting. Not anymore.

Elder: The main reason the Marine Corps doesn't reenlist
good Marines is because of failures of leadership by Marine
commanders. [Rather than reenlist in the Marines, Jay Elder
volunteered for the U.S. Navy SEALs in the early summer of
2006.]

A U.S. Army sergeant came up to one of our SAW gunners,
a private first class, and said, "I can't believe you're carrying a
SAW." He thought this was incredible, for a PFC to be carrying
a light machine gun, because that's a lot of responsibility. Tra-
ditionally, the Marine Corps has given responsibility to Marines
who've earned that responsibility, especially in combat.

Plaza is hands-down one of the best squad leaders in Fox—
well, he was before our battalion commander stupidly had

him relieved of that squad. That's not even a battalion commander's responsibility in the first place.

The Marine Corps is supposed to carry on the tradition that the best Marine in the squad is the squad leader. Plaza is the best Marine in that squad. Lieutenant Colonel Aiken, fundamentally, is not concerned with combat effectiveness. And we are in combat here.

"The essential dilemma is this: The right money is going in the wrong places. The American money that strengthens the Fallujah Police strengthens Al Qaeda in Fallujah. And paves the way for the Ba'athists to return to power in Fallujah, Baghdad, and all Iraq. . . . Fallujah is still their goal. Al Qaeda owned Fallujah from April 2004 to November 2004. Al Qaeda wants Fallujah back."

SERGEANT SALAH, PRIVATE SEERWAN, AND
PRIVATE JAMIL, IRAQI ARMY SOLDIERS, FALLUJAH,
JANUARY 3, 2006

Private Jamil came from Diwaniyah, and Segeant Salah from Samarra, both historic cities in southern Iraq, and Private Seerwan was from Dahuk, Iraqi Kurdistan. Three together, they saved my life in the Mexican standoff on January 3, 2006, in Fallujah. Earlier that day, they'd graciously allowed me to interview them in their hooch on the Iraqi Army compound directly north of the Fallujah train station. We'd just come off a morning patrol, through winding streets and down alleys rich with the scent of burning joss and sheep dung and oil can fires, Iraqis warming their hands, glaring at us as we passed, the patrol going very quickly.

Scoping for IEDs and terrorist snipers, we hustled, two hours flashing by in a panorama of Iraqis walking to morning markets and women in groups of four and five carrying carrots, eggplants, tomatos, onions, and olive oil in plastic bags, their long dresses dragging in the mud. We dodged from storefront corners to concrete abutments, alley corners to stoops, checking our 360s at every chance we got.

Rain had hammered us all that winter, gray skies rolling in the mornings, Iraqi Army soldiers gathering by oil can fires on our compound, lighting cigarettes and making sure there were no lines of sight on them, no way a terrorist sniper could line up a shot on us. The morning patrol on January 3 was no different— gray and cold and wet, scoping rooftops for snipers and watching every alley corner very carefully.

The men slung their AK-47s and light machine guns in their rooms when we got back and boiled water, joking about the rain and the cold and whether the Lebanese tabla drumming surpassed that of India. Seerwan ended that argument with the observation "What we need in Fallujah is less terrorists and more women from New Delhi. Now, that and some brandy would end the fighting here, and to hell with the tabla drumming!"

We drank tea and smoked cigarettes with the translator, listening to Moroccan music, before I began keying them in at ten in the morning.

Jamil was from Diwaniyah and twenty years old that winter, a short, very stocky young man with thick brown hair. Jamil was Shia, like Salah, and his family had suffered greatly under Saddam's regime: Six uncles, three brothers, one sister, and eight cousins had been killed in their beds by Saddam's *Mukhabarat.*

"That is what the war comes down to for us," he'd said the day before on patrol, handing out candy to Fallujah kids as a heavy-gutted, shaved-head man in long gray robes and a black jacket stared daggers at us on Route Henry, a block away from where we were hit with the IED a few days later, on January 6. Smoke drifted over the streets from fires in abandoned lots. Sheep and cows grazed on trash and straw thrown on the corners of alleys, Fallujah kids tapping the sheep with long sticks.

"My children will not suffer the horror that my family suffered, that I witnessed. We will not let the Sunni Arabs ever have that kind of power again."

Salah, twenty-three years old and lean, with a thick black mustache, soft-spoken and jovial, reflected on Jamil's remarks of the previous evening, nodding, a musing look coming over him.

"I cannot argue with Jamil; he speaks truth—the war is just that personal for us, just that real. We must never let the Ba'athists gain that kind of power again, and the Ba'athists are Sunni Arabs. The Sunni Arabs began the civil war against us in 1968.

"The dictatorship killed our relatives, our loved ones, our friends. You'd find the kid sitting next to you in high school with his throat cut, in the sand. You buried him and asked no questions. You knew this was the *Mukhabarat*." Salah carried an AK-47 with a paratroopers stock. He was married with a one-year-old son, of whom he was very proud: "My baby boy is a free spirit, free from Saddam! Free from the Ba'athists! Oh, he will not taste the bitter fruit that I knew, all my years until 2003! I tell you, that is my great motivation here, that gives me fighting spirit: to do all I can to ensure that my son grows up and prospers in a land free from Ba'athist dictatorship."

Seerwan, like his comrades, grew up in the shadows of death and oppression. For him, too, the guerrilla war in Iraq is personal: His father, mother, and two uncles and their wives were hung by the Ba'athist *Mukhabarat* and Iraqi Army in July 1988 near Ameydi, Iraqi Kurdistan, an ancient mountain town about 40 kilometers south of Turkey and roughly 100 kilometers east of Iran.

Saddam's Army raped his aunts before hanging them, he'd told me on the evening of December 27, the first day I'd patrolled with his platoon. "Do you know that pain, brother?" he'd asked me, his forehead wrinkled, copper-colored skin pocked and scarred on his face.

"To see your own mother and father, your uncles and aunts, hanging naked at the end of a rope, the women bleeding from between their legs. I was five years old. I cried all that day and night. I have never cried since.

"The *Mukhabarat* that did that were Al Bowisa tribe, the tribe led by Sheikh Gazi Al Bowisa. And the heart of Al Bowisa tribe is right here in Fallujah. Did Saddam ever dream this day, brother, when he would be in jail and Kurds would patrol in Fallujah?" he said, a slight grin on his face now, lighting up a smoke in the cold winter rain.

I was fortunate to patrol with the Iraqi Army from December 27, 2005, to January 13, 2006, in Fallujah. The Coalition suffered from a lack of interpreters in western Iraq and may still. I had very few opportunities to interview soldiers—there were four foot patrols a day and hasty raids that went down on a moment's notice, and the one interpreter for that Iraqi Army company was on leave most of that time. But luckily, on the morning of January 3, the interpreter was around.

Jamil: Ba'ath and *Mukhabarat* are still the foundation of *erhabi* in Fallujah, combined with Wahabis now, and Salafis. When you are talking about Wahabis and Salafis in Fallujah, you are talking about the same people.

Remember, Osama Bin Laden is Salafi. The Wahabis are here and in Afghanistan, in force. They have strong support from the imams in Fallujah and western Iraq.

Seerwan: People in Saddam's army, in all command positions, were very nearly all Sunni. Very good thing to have disbanded Iraqi Army, as the Ba'athist colonels and generals would have used it as a foundation to regain Ba'athist power and reestablish a Ba'athist regime, no different from Saddam's. Different in perhaps only one aspect: perhaps more brutal than even Saddam.

Salah: The Sunni Arabs in Fallujah want what Sunni Arabs throughout Iraq want: a return to Saddam. They will chant at us on patrol, "Long live Saddam," and "Down, down to the Shia!" The Sunni Arabs despise having Shia officers in command now, and Kurdish officers, also, in command in the new Iraqi Army. I understand that many Americans criticize Bremer for disbanding Saddam's army. Had Bremer not done so, there would've been Shias rioting in the streets, and you would've lost the Kurds, additionally.

Seerwan: Disbanding the Iraqi Army was one of the best things Bremer did—the mistake was in supporting so many Sunni Arab sheikhs and former Ba'athist Iraqi Army generals, like Ghanim Al Basso in Mosul. Huge mistake, that, and we've paid for it in blood. Iraqi blood and American blood.

Jamil: You know, under Saddam, if you were Shia in Tikrit, Fallujah, or Ramadi, the police would arrest you and put you in jail. Your crime was that you were Shia. Those days are gone, Allah be praised. We will not allow that to happen to our children. Now, Sistani is a good leader for us.

Salah: Right now, our army is small. But the more we train and get larger, and very importantly, improve our logistics, then we can take over the war fighting here by summer 2007.

Seerwan: The terrorists are traveling back and forth from Jordan, Syria, and Saudi Arabia. They all have safe houses in Fallujah. Fallujah is still their goal. Al Qaeda owned Fallujah from April 2004 to November 2004. Al Qaeda wants Fallujah back.

Jamil: The police here, and many of the people in Fallujah, still support *erhabi* and say to us every day on patrol, "The Iraqi Army are bad and the Marines are bad; the Americans are evil." Kurdistan is the great victory for us, a real template. We don't have terrorists in Kurdistan. The Kurds don't need Americans to help them defeat Al Qaeda in Kurdistan. The Kurds are doing it very well on their own.

Salah: In the entire country, step by step, we are making progress. The elections succeeded. The *erhabi* did not stop the elections. We carried out free elections for the first time in our history. I feel very grateful to have voted on such a historic day—all three elections, actually. What a marvelous, beautiful day. Saddam is gone, Uday and Qusay are dead, and we voted for our own constitution and parliament. Magnificent.

Jamil: Our primary needs: We need uniforms, boots, and less corruption in the Ministry of Defense and Ministry of Interior. We are not receiving our full salaries. Some of us are wrapping duct tape around our boots, because we are not getting our regular issue of clothing and boots.

Salah: I have one year in the Iraqi Army now, but Marines have donated most of what I wear to me. The Marines have been very kind to us, and we are grateful. We are not getting enough food, also. One meal a day is not enough. We need good boots and uniforms. And also, many of us have been in combat for over one year now, without promotions—not even to lance corporal.

Jamil: Also, we need humvees—our vehicles are not even military vehicles. We ride in pickup trucks. A real problem is a cultural and historic one, concerning corruption: There is a legacy of theft, from Saddam's era, which plagues Iraqis at all levels of our society.

Seerwan: Yes, comrade, but I will tell you the real problem here, what is truly at issue here: The Marine commanders are turning a blind eye to the corruption in the Fallujah police. This is a huge, monumental mistake. The United States is heavily arming Iraqi Police in Fallujah. The United States is arming its own enemy—do the American people understand this?

Jamil: It is madness. Only the American Marine officers like Major Murphy and Major Muller understand this, and they do not hesitate to criticize the Fallujah Police for their support of *erhabi*. Personally, I think Major Murphy and Major Muller are very brave to stand for the truth. They are men of honor.

Seerwan: We talk of this often, of the honor of these two great Marines. Major Muller and Major Murphy! Arizona and New York! They are the lions of America! They do not fear the *erhabi*—they strike at Al Qaeda here, and they never protect the Fallujah Police. Yes, they are men of honor! They do not fear to speak the truth of how the Fallujah Police are terrorists here. Major Murphy and Major Muller—if all the American officers were as brave and honorable as these two men, our troubles in Fallujah would most certainly be in the past tense.

Salah: It is sad that these two majors are not commanding generals. We wish to see them as commanding generals. For I see corruption in the Marine command here, from lieutenant colonel and above.

Seerwan: The higher-ranking Marine commanders know that the Fallujah Police are supporting terrorists and refuse to do anything about it. I do not understand this, but I assure you, our Iraqi Army commanders will not hesitate to crush the Iraqi Police in Fallujah. We are ready.

Salah: Seerwan speaks truth. This is the truth on the street in Fallujah, the truth no one can hide. The Fallujah Police tell us on patrol, "We will make Fallujah a graveyard for the Iraqi Army," but like all Sunni Arabs, they do not understand that Saddam is not coming back. What happened to Uday and Qusay will happen to the Fallujah Police. If the Americans do not solve the problem, we will.

Jamil: The Marine commanders, and the Americans in general, look at the Iraqi Police as the solution to security in western Iraq. This is madness. The Iraqi Police in Fallujah carry Glocks and we don't, for instance. Brand new Glocks.

Salah: Exactly! The Iraqi Police are driving brand new Nissan pickup trucks and cars; the wax is still shining on these cars, they are so new. But we patrol in duct-taped boots and buy our own candles for light because the electricity is always gone to hell in a handbasket.

Seerwan: The essential dilemma is this: The right money is going in the wrong places. The American money that strengthens the Fallujah Police strengthens Al Qaeda in Fallujah. And paves the way for the Ba'athists to return to power in Fallujah, and Baghdad, and all Iraq.

Salah: In this way, many times, the Americans are their own worst enemy here. It is Bush's support of Ba'athists in post-Saddam Iraq that has cost the lives of many American warriors here, and Iraqi people also. In Fallujah, Baghdad, and Mosul, the police are friends of *erhabi*.

Jamil: The police in Fallujah talk on their cell phones to *erhabi*, including Al Qaeda, every day and night—always reporting on our patrols, our movements, our size, our weapons, all the time.

Salah: A real and urgent problem with the Fallujah Police is that they are from Fallujah and surrounding areas—hopelessly corrupt. These tribes loved Saddam. Their motivation for supporting *erhabi* in Fallujah is all for a return to Ba'athist dictatorship, which would benefit the tribes in Fallujah immensely, just as it did under Saddam.

All our lieutenants, like Lieutenant Mohammed of Basra, and all our commanders understand this well, as we do. I will tell you this: In this entire country, there is a reckoning coming. The Buddhists came from India, which is not far from Mesopotamia in the ancient times. The Buddhists say bad karma comes back to haunt you. You reap what you sow, in this world. Karma never lies. I say the Buddha speaks truth.

Seerwan: I am a Muslim, and I find truth in that Buddhist saying: The bad karma of the Sunni Arabs, like the Al Bowisa *Mukhabarat* who killed my family—that will fall like a tidal wave on western Iraq if the Sunnis continue arming, financing, and manning the ranks of the insurgency.

Bush is tying our hands now, and protecting the sheikhs and imams from the Iraqi Army. Bush wants the Ba'athists back in power.

But we can tell the Americans to leave, at some point. In fact, the sooner we tell the Americans to leave, the better.

Like my comrade Salah has said, the bad karma of the Ba'athists comes back on them like a shadow from a storm.

There will be a reckoning.

We will never forget the horror Saddam perpetrated on our people. And we will never, never let that Ba'athist horror touch our villages again.

"Bush traded justice for

stability and got neither. The stability here is the chaos of Al Qaeda, and if Bush's intention was to reinforce Al Qaeda in western Iraq, then his intention was true. . . . Because that is exactly what Bush has done here. The Bush plan does not support stability, it supports terrorism."

LIEUTENANT MOHAMMED,
IRAQI ARMY PLATOON COMMANDER,
JANUARY 11, 2006

Lieutenant Mohammed led Iraqi troops in Baghdad, Baquouba, Fallujah, Karmah, and Al Saqlawiyah from September 2003 to April 2006. In the winter of terrorist snipers in Fallujah, his soldiers were quick to praise his leadership. The twenty-four-year-old taught his men how to patrol vigorously and smartly, how to raid and win, and how to always look out for one another. I rarely saw him need to speak on patrol, as he executed hand and arm signals professionally; his men respected him so much, he only had to talk briefly with his sergeants, on occasion, and they would do what he asked.

Like many Iraqi soldiers and officers from Southern Iraq, the lieutenant's family, too, had suffered from Saddam's rule. Lieutenant Mohammed is Shia. "Nearly all my family was killed by the *Mukhabarat* after Bush called for us to rise up against Saddam in 1991," he'd told me on December 27, 2005, in Fallujah, recalling President George H. W. Bush's call to arms in the wake of Kuwait's liberation, when the forty-first president urged Iraqis to take down Saddam, but then at the drop of a hat, refused to back them up.

Shias like those in Lieutenant Mohammed's family, and Kurds like friends of Seerwan, inspired by the American call to arms in the immediate wake of Kuwait's liberation, rose up against Saddam. "The American president was calling us to take arms against Saddam, to end his dictatorship. How could we have known he was lying?" Lieutenant Mohammed said to me as we came off a patrol on December 30, 2005, in Fallujah. The Shia and Kurd revolt, lacking U.S. support, was crushed in weeks while American policymakers shrugged their shoulders and turned a blind eye.

Lieutenant Mohammed had a girlfriend in Basra and friends throughout Basra, Diwaniyah, and Al Nasiriyah. He carried a Walther PP9 9-millimeter sidearm on his right hip, a clip jacked in and four clips strapped on the side, and an AK-47 with a black plastic stock and Czech markings. He always had a clip jacked in his AK and eleven clips in faded green canvas magazine pouches slung over his vest.

About six feet tall, slim, copper-skinned, with his eyes set back deep in his face like a falcon, Lieutenant Mohammed was eager to go on the record about the Fallujah Police. We sat down in his operations center on January 11, 2006, and sipped strong, dark, sweet Ceylon tea. He pulled out his smokes, lit one, and began.

The IPs drive at night, run their lights, and communicate with terrorists—the IPs *are* the terrorists! It is Iraqi Army, not Iraqi Police, who secure Fallujah. We secure Fallujah; we patrol the streets. We capture *erhabi.*

Yes, the IPs are the terrorists. We captured an IP yesterday, driving a car without documents. No registration, no driver's license, and no plates.

Exactly the kind of car that the erhabi use to transport weapons, munitions, medicine, and terrorists. Also, exactly the kind of car the erhabi use for suicide bomb attacks and to transport and place IEDs.

The Americans told us, "No, you cannot detain this man, because he is a Fallujah policeman." Allah! Oh, the Americans are very naive when it comes to the Fallujah Police. The Amer-

icans have failed to kill or capture the following terrorists,
since Al Fajr:

Omar Muhammad Bendar: He is a Fallujah policeman,
twenty-five years old, native of Fallujah, and leads a terrorist
cell in Fallujah. Very bad man, yes, we have made the Americans aware of him. The Americans refuse to kill or capture
him. If we take him down, the Americans control him—the
Americans will detain him briefly, then release him. Do you
capture a man-eating lion to cage it, then release it back
into a village?

Ah, but the Marines here, the Marine command, merely
wants to cage the terrorists in the Fallujah Police, then
release them back on the street. In truth, the Marines rarely
capture the Fallujah Police; it would make their investment
look bad. Omar Muhammad Bendar remains on the Fallujah Police.

Mohammad Abdul Aziz Ali Egabe Al Essawi: You gave us more
help to take him down than the Marines. We are still on the
hunt for Mohammed Al Essawi—the field intelligence you
gave us is a big help. [Lieutenant Mohammed is referring
to field intelligence on a radical Islamic imam in the
Shark's Fin that I got out of a Sunni Arab Iraqi man while
on patrol with Marines on December 18, 2005. Over tea
and cigarettes on December 27, I mentioned this to Lieutenant Mohammed, because I knew that the Marine S-2,
Captain Harlow, was not communicating with the
scout/snipers, not giving them key intelligence on terrorist
snipers, and I suspected that Harlow also was not giving key
intelligence on terrorists like Mohammed Al Essawi to the
Iraqi Army in Fallujah. Lieutenant Mohammed confirmed
my instincts on Harlow, thanked me, and turned over the
intelligence on Al Essawi to the Marine advisors, and also to
Colonel Ra'ad, his battalion commander.]

The Marines did not tell us about the imam in the
Shark's Fin who is the only imam in this area from Al
Essawi tribe. That was excellent fieldwork by you, to recog-

nize that on the spot and act on it. This Al Essawi imam,
yes, he is a radical Islamic imam. Now that we know that the
only Al Essawi imam in this area is at that mosque, and he is
a radical Islamic imam, we can act on that intelligence—to
take down Mohammed Al Essawi.

His mosque would be a perfect meeting place for
Mohammed Al Essawi and other terrorist leaders in western
Iraq.

Ahmed Khamis Sirhan: Leader, Black Flags Brigade.

Mohammed Khamis Sirhan: Financier of Black Flags Brigades;
one of the three Sirhan brothers at operational core of
Black Flags Brigades *erhabi.* Our last intelligence on him was
that he is in Dubai; he spends more time in Dubai than his
brothers, who all spend some time there. It is like the oasis
in a desert for camels: All the terrorists drink from the
same oasis, Dubai.

Sheikh Rafia Al Rawi: Al Qaeda–connected sheikh notorious
for his deep support of *erhabi* in Fallujah and western Iraq.
Key in the planning and execution of fall 2003 assassination
attempts on Colonel Jeffrey Smith and Lieutenant Colonel
Brian Drinkwine, 82nd Airborne, in Fallujah.

Ahmad Khathair Abbas: One of the notorious Abbas brothers,
erhabi financiers and cell leaders. Pays for many IED attacks.
We remain on the hunt for all of the above.

All of Saddam's officers and *Mukhabarat* lived in Fallujah
and Ramadi and the villages in between. This is very, very
strong pro-Ba'athist area, and they want a return to Ba'athist
dictatorship.

They want the power back, and all the privileges that went
with it. Correct—they miss the gold Kalashnikov and the black
Mercedes.

Under Saddam, if anyone refused the Ba'athist orders in
Fallujah and western Iraq, Saddam would order that person or
village murdered by the *Mukhabarat* and Iraqi Army. Now the
erhabi want Ba'athist power again.

Iraqi Army commanders were all Ba athists. Many of them
were Sunni Arab, like Saddam. Notice that the *erhabi* are pre-
dominantly Sunni Arab, in all of Iraq.

The Marine commanders met all of the demands made by
the Iraqi brigades in April 2004, demands made to Marine
commanders.

I saw this as a huge mistake. The Ba'athists again controlled
Fallujah, as under Saddam. Then you had Al Fajr in November 2004.

You know, in the old regime officers were all from the western area of Iraq—from the ground we are standing on now.
Even a lieutenant from western Iraq could order a major or
colonel from Southern Iraq to be their servants—the Sunni
Arabs in the Iraqi Army command, like the present police
chief of Fallujah, had all the power. And thought they were
superior to all Iraqis.

I have been in the Iraqi Army for two years now, since January 2004, in Baghdad, Al Kut, Fallujah, and Al Saqlawiyah.

The IPs have great supply and support from the U.S., so
they feel confident at all times that they can get away with supporting *erhabi* in Fallujah. The IPs know that Marine command prefers the Iraqi Police to the Iraqi Army—all of the
Marine decisions, the American decisions, favor the Iraqi
Police in Fallujah. Marine commanders let the Fallujah Police
control checkpoints—how do you think the terrorist snipers
have been getting in and out of Fallujah, to kill Marines?

Those are Fallujah Police who are giving the terrorist
snipers easy access to Fallujah. I'll bet the Marines didn't tell
you that the Fallujah Police take down information on Iraqi
Army soldiers, at checkpoints, whenever we go on leave. Then
the Fallujah Police turns that information over to Zarqawi/Al
Qaeda in Iraq. Al Qaeda, because it has that information on
us, can then target my men and their families.

Iraqi Police in western Iraq can only become IPs with agreement from Al Qaeda and other *erhabi*. If they don't make that
verbal agreement, they don't put on the police uniform. Once
they make the agreement, they must cooperate with Al Qaeda

and other *erhabi*. If they don't cooperate and turn over information on Americans and on the Iraqi Army, then Al Qaeda will kill them.

Look at what happened on January 3rd. My IAs wanted to search a vehicle, but traffic police released the vehicle. The Fallujah Police wanted to kidnap you and kill you. Yes, my men are right when they say, "The Americans are arming our enemy here, backing the Iraqi Police in every way." Very accurate, yes.

And the Fallujah Police know that they have the Marine commanders in their pocket. They know that they control the Americans.

The Americans are turning a blind eye to Al Qaeda in Fallujah. The Fallujah Police are the *erhabi*; they just change uniforms at night. In daytime, they wear the blue police uniform. At night, they wear *dishdasha*, wrap the *kaffiyah* around their faces, plant IEDs to kill the Marines and my men, and attack us with RPGs and small arms.

The police in Fallujah know that they have new supplies and weapons and trucks from the Americans; they know this. The Fallujah Police are so arrogant and cocky, they tell us when we are on patrol, "We will make Fallujah a graveyard for the Iraqi Army. Al Qaeda owns Fallujah, thanks to the Americans."

Two days ago, on January 3rd, here is what we heard when we monitored the Iraqi Police radio: "Eleven patrols are ready to move for this corner now, and kill the Iraqi Army." Eleven patrols—that's eleven pick-up trucks all mounted with PKC machine guns, heavy machine guns. And they already had six IP gun trucks on the scene, all with heavy machine guns! You saw what happened—even with the Marine advisors supporting us, we could only put three IA Nissans and one Marine gun truck on the scene. You and I, and all my men, we are lucky to be alive, brother.

Right, that went over the radio, and their IP captain told them to hold in place. This IP captain is a known terrorist, by the way; he has led mortar attacks on American Marines in Karmah. [On March 6, 2006, I witnessed Keogh and his

Marine infantrymen flex-cuff and arrest this IP captain, Fallujah Police Captain Munther Muhammed Hais, on the terrorist
target list for mortar attacks that killed Marines and Iraqi
Army in Karmah. Two hours later, Regimental Combat Team
Five, in command of 2/6, ordered him released "because we
can't upset the Fallujah Police." Keogh was so upset he
wouldn't talk about it, but one of his machine gunners, Lance
Corporal Joshua Watson from Johnstown, Pennsylvania, told
me, "Morale is shit now; we have no fighting spirit. This is
bullshit to take down a known terrorist and then release him,
complete RCT-5 fuck-up: this rat bastard had a brand new
phone bank, to set off IEDs, in his house. He will plan and
execute more attacks on Marines and IAs, for real."]

Look closely at what happened that night, on January 3rd:
They put six PKCs and thirty police *within two minutes* on that
corner. They could've manned it with eleven more PKCs and
ninety more IPs in a heartbeat. And you don't see any duct
tape on their boots and shoes, do you? Meanwhile, we had
one company of Iraqi Army on call, with thirty soldiers and
three PKCs, total. That's all.

The IPs get special training in Jordan, new and excellent
weapons, and the very best vehicles and support. All of this,
and the IPs are thoroughly penetrated by Al Qaeda. Zarqawi
owns the IPs, and if you own the police in Fallujah, then
essentially you own Fallujah.

Fallujah is again a great home for terrorists because of the
American plan for "2006, Year of the Iraqi Police." Bush is
playing right into the hands of Al Qaeda in Iraq. The Americans are arming their enemy here.

My men and I know something, however. We are Iraqi
Army. We are from all walks of life, and from all of Iraq that
was murdered under Saddam's rule. The Iraqi Army is Iraqi.
We are of the Iraqi people; we are Iraqis. We are not an occu-
pying force. We understand that the terrorist threat in Fallujah is real.

We are the only force in Fallujah, also, that is committed to
killing Al Qaeda. The Americans have not proved here, at all,

that they are committed to killing Al Qaeda. We have taken down more Al Qaeda and far more *erhabi* than the Marines, and we will continue to do so, because we are not confused about our enemy here.

We know that the Americans know that the Fallujah Police supports Zarqawi and Al Qaeda. I am very, very frustrated and confused about the Americans in Fallujah: Why does Marine command make this plan to invest in the Fallujah Police, a den of thieves who want Saddam back and enjoy supporting Al Qaeda?

I've heard American Marine commanders tell me, "We established the Iraqi Police in Fallujah because we support stability in Fallujah."

Your American writer Hemingway once said, "Don't confuse motion for action." I think of that when the Marine commanders talk to me about the Fallujah Police and stability. I think Hemingway would say, "Don't confuse stability with justice." Because we had thirty-five years of Ba'athist stability, and there was no justice in it, nor any peace but the peace of the dead. The only peace in Iraq under Saddam was the peace of the dead and a piece of the action.

That translates to me that the Americans think buying off the sheikhs and imams and setting up a police force just for the sake of saying, "We established the Iraqi Police in Fallujah," is all an exercise in the Americans patting themselves on the back.

You know, "We built a police force, now we can leave." But the Marine commanders' words run contrary to what is actually happening on the streets of Fallujah.

Bush traded justice for stability in Iraq and got neither. The stability here is the chaos of Al Qaeda, and if Bush's intention was to reinforce Al Qaeda in western Iraq, then his intention was true. Accurate. Exact. Because that is exactly what Bush has done here. The Bush plan in Iraq does not support stability, it supports terrorism.

Power is not in Iraqi hands here. A continuing problem is the American cycle of detain and release. Plays right into the hands of Al Qaeda. We capture a known terrorist target. A high-value target. But the Marines will not send him on to Abu Ghraib. The American strategy on fighting terrorism here is "detain and release." The terrorists know this, and it further increases their confidence that they rule Fallujah.

The right money is going to the wrong places? Yes, that is correct. Bravo to Seerwan, he hits the bulls-eye. And not only in Iraq.

Also, the wrong people are in the right places. We need the right money going to the right places, and we need the right people in the right places. Get the Ba'athists *out* of power! That remains a real problem in Iraq. And the U.S. military, in all of Iraq, is appointing Saddam's generals into the Iraqi Police.

Wherever you look and see American hands involved with Iraqi Police, you will find Al Qaeda and other *erhabi* have penetrated that police force. The terrorists know the checkpoints in Fallujah very well, and they will attack the checkpoints with suicide bombs, because the Americans have opened the door for the terrorists here to do just that by embracing the Fallujah Police. Their main target is Entry Checkpoint One (ECP-1).

PART THREE

"Fighting for reconstruction aid in Iraq is like fighting for a woman's virtue in a bordello."

"The weakness of the U.S. is we refuse to send undercover teams into the mosques. Al Qaeda knows this, the erhabi know this, and they exploit our weakness here, 24/7. Mosques are forward operating bases for terrorists."

—SERGEANT EFRAIM PARRA, RONIN1 TEAM LEADER, APRIL 9, 2006

I n tents in the sand on Camp Bahria, Ronin and Marine infantry
waited to roll IED roulette on trucks through Fallujah on April
11, 2006.

"Choppers or seven tons?" Areballo asked me in the morning.
"Seven tons," I told him, and he squinted, sunglasses hanging down
off his neck.

"IED roulette once more," he muttered, reflecting on the later
movement on seven-ton trucks from Fallujah to the Taqqadum Air
Field (TQ), looking west. West was a plane to catch, the end of our
combat tour.

None of the scout/snipers or infantry talked of the elections in
Iraq in October and December 2005 and their historical significance. Al Qaeda roamed Fallujah at will in April 2006, aided by
Ahmed Sirhan's Black Flags Brigades and the Fallujah Police,
financing and plotting suicide bomb attacks on us, such as the one
on March 10, 2006, that wounded Corporal David Soto, Marine
infantryman, whose interview appears in this section.

And the scout/snipers, more than anyone, knew just how badly
Marine command had failed to take down Ahmed Sirhan, Diya
Shakur Farhan, Sheikh Gazi Al Bowisa, Fallujah Police Captain
Munther Muhammad Hais, and other terrorist and insurgent lead-
ers in Fallujah and western Iraq.

Ronin was just damn glad to be alive, as we all were in April
2006. January, February, and March saw us rocked with suicide
bombs, IEDs, terrorist snipers, and RPG attacks. The 1st Battalion,
25th Marines, arrived in late March and early April, replacing 2/6.
The Marine reservists, many of them from Boston and other ports
and villes of New England, were courteous, professional, and generous with their wit and gifts they'd brought from stateside. Their
scout/snipers listened very closely to Ronin, heeded their counsel,
and proved the truth of Milstid's observation in Fallujah on
November 14, 2005: "Respect is a two-way street."

For Soto, it was a combat tour he will never forget, one marked
by friendships made, the love of his wife, the respect of his comrades, and a suicide bomb that killed Lance Corporal Long at

Entry Checkpoint One (ECP-1, manned by Fallujah Police and 2/6 Marines), just as the Iraqi Army had warned in January 2006, with their prophetic remarks on how deeply Al Qaeda has penetrated the Fallujah Police.

"The IPs always know where the insurgent/terrorist attacks on us are; they know beforehand. They're always on the scene immediately."

CORPORAL DAVID SOTO JR.,
FIELD RADIO OPERATOR,
APRIL 1, 2006

orporal David Soto, a twenty-four-year-old Marine, father of two boys, from O'Donnell, Texas, survived the worst suicide bomb to hit Fallujah on 2/6's combat tour, on March 10, 2006. Wounded with shrapnel in his left thigh, calf, and behind the knee, he suffered a grade-three concussion and 45 percent hearing loss. Half-deaf, bleeding, and nearly knocked out from his wounds, he got up, shouldered his M203, and got back in the fight, killing one *erhabi*.

Not only was Soto one of the bravest men I have ever had the good fortune to meet, but he is certainly one of the toughest—and his insight on Al Qaeda's penetration of the Fallujah Police was earned in blood.

He left West Texas in the summer of 2002 and volunteered for the Marines as a field radio operator, graduating from boot camp at San Diego Marine Corps Recruiting Depot in late September 2002.

His wife, Priscilla, has stood by him all his time in the Corps, and he wanted to make sure that his thoughts for her were right up front: "Priscilla, I love you and would not have survived combat here without your love."

They have two little boys, Dorian and Abriam. He flipped open his wallet as we flew over Germany on our flight to Kuwait on September 17, 2005, and smiled proudly, talking of his family from across the aisle on the World Airways flight.

Six and a half months later, he slipped his M.203 over his shoulders, sat down on a bench, and smoked, quiet now. The scars on his forearms were beginning to heal. Cotton puffed out of his right ear. He told me that he still had ringing in his ears, but his balance and coordination were back, three weeks after he'd survived the suicide bombing.

Brother, it's always good to know that we served our country. I'll tell you for a fact why I volunteered for the Marines. I joined the Marine Corps to make my life better, to make my family's life better. My wife supported me.

That's why I joined the Marine Corps, to make our lives better. It's hard. I have to sacrifice the quality time that I want to spend with my family. And miss my sons' lives—I've got two sons. I've missed the first years of their lives.

Now I know how Marines in past wars felt, missing their families. Being so far away from their loved ones, and at war. It's hard. To me, it's hard being away from them, but now my wife understands.

She understands the sacrifices that I've made, being away from them. She supports me and understands that this is my job—this is what I do. She supports the decisions I make, and if it wasn't for her supporting me, I wouldn't be here today.

I wouldn't be a corporal and I wouldn't be alive, because I wouldn't really care what was going on around me. Her support has really made me the Marine I am. And I thank her every day, for her support, for her love.

The day of the suicide truck bomb attack was the eighth anniversary for my wife and me—I first met my wife and fell in love with her on March 10, 1998. We got hit on March 10, 2006, at ECP-1.

Long shouted at the dump truck, *"Aroja! Aroja!"* which means "Go away!" in Arabic.

At that point, the truck had stopped. Long was not far from me, about thirty feet away. He stood on top of an eight-foot barrier, made of Hesco barriers filled with sand and rock. He was waving at the truck and shouting.

At that time, the bomb went off. It sounded like missile going off, a zooming sound and a huge blast. All I saw was red. My ears were ringing. It pushed me against a Texas barrier, made of concrete. I fell to the ground. I was in shock. I finally realized that we were getting attacked.

So I low-crawled. And I finally got up. I grabbed my weapon in the high-back gun truck, my .203. I came to my senses.

I saw Marines low-crawling to take cover. I ran inside our little COC house. When I walked in, I found Marines yelling, screaming. I thought, "Security, security," and I shouted to Marines, "Grab your weapons! Get on the walls and provide security!" And at that time I could hear Sergeant Roberts yelling, "We're getting mortared, take cover!"

I was at the wall now, the north wall. I looked toward the on ramp, and saw two cars burning. And pieces of the dump truck burning, on fire.

I started yelling, "It's a VBIED! It's a VBIED!" [vehicle borne improvised electronic device—in layman's terms, suicide car bomb] during that whole time. My senses started coming back to me. I started looking for a triggerman or anyone else who's not supposed to be there. Remote detonated or command detonated—if I found a triggerman, I knew it was command detonated.

I looked over at the potato factory and I saw a man running away, wearing a white *dishtasha*. I started yelling, "Agulf! Agulf!" which means "Stop!" in Arabic.

He failed to stop. I was screaming at him to stop. He wouldn't stop.

I took my weapon off safe. I sighted in on him. I shot my whole magazine off, on single-shot. Then I did a quick magazine change. I kept shooting at him. I shot another five rounds off my second magazine.

I saw him fall. Then I saw an Iraqi Police truck coming down the military bypass. I shouted, "Cease fire! Cease fire!"

At that time, I jumped over the Texas barrier and patrolled on my own. I could see shrapnel and pieces of burnt flesh all around me. I turned around and looked toward Mobile, to the highway, MSR.

On the overpass, there was a white car stopped. It looked like he might have been videotaping it, and I shot two warning shots toward it.

Then six Iraqi Army soldiers in an IA Nissan and Corporal Norton and Corporal Picazo rode up to the overpass together. I was just walking and shouting. Still looking for *erhabi*.

And that's when Sergeant Snell picked me up and took me to the hospital. I took shrapnel to my left thigh, left calf, and behind my knee. They pulled all the shrapnel out at the hospital. 45 percent hearing loss in my right ear. The docs say the hearing should come back. Also, I had a grade-three concussion. And they thought I had a T3 spinal injury, but there's nothing wrong with my spine, thank God.

Yes, I have seen a lot of shady activity by the Fallujah Police. They always say, at the checkpoint, "Oh, he's OK, he's OK, he's my friend," when someone wants to enter at ECP-1 without a badge.

We tell them, "No badge, no Fallujah." Some of the IP officers will countermand us, and we can't read Arabic—they give us their IDs and tell us a story, but we can't read Arabic, and when the terp's not there, it's very hard. Without an interpreter, there's not much you can do. The terp is not always there, and then it's very, very hard. So many of the people trying to get through are related to the police.

And the Fallujans get really pissed off when you tell them, "Look, your ID is fake. I can't let you through."

I do think that we are arming our enemy here, by supporting the Fallujah Police so much. That checks clear with what I've seen on the ground here. Roger that.

The Iraqi Police dragged that man I shot, dragged him away. They left no trace of the body, but their tire tracks went

right up to where the guy fell. Why were they so quick to get
him the hell out of Dodge? Why didn't they let us get his ID?
And you know, that's not the first time that's happened here.
It happened with Sergeant Matter and his squad. Countless
other times.

I didn't shoot a full magazine and five more rounds at a
ghost. I killed that guy, I did what I was trained to do. I saw
him drop. I dropped him. The Iraqi Police truck's tire tracks
rolled right up to where I dropped him.

The IPs have a history in Fallujah of very quickly removing
bodies off the street, anytime we shoot and kill someone here,
and disappearing the bodies. Then we find the bodies in the
river. The IPs always know where the insurgent/terrorist
attacks on us are; they know beforehand. They're always on
the scene immediately. Like the snipers say, "That's why we
don't have very many confirmed kills, because the IPs pull the
bodies off the street and throw the bodies in the river. Without the bodies, we don't have the confirmed kill."

Seventy percent of the IPs are directly supporting terrorists.
Agreed, Major Muller and Major Murphy are accurate. They
know the deal.

There were about twenty-four to twenty-eight Marines at
ECP-1 when we were attacked, during that changeover. The
easiest time to attack any guard post is during a changeover.
The Fallujah Police know when the changeovers occur, of
course, because they are right there at the checkpoints, all the
time. None of them were outside when we were hit on March
10, 2006.

That was a coordinated attack on our ECP-1, including AK-
47s. Now, looking back at the weeks prior to the attack, there
was some very, very strange activity by the Fallujah Police at
the potato factory. Every other day, at the busiest time of the
day, when the Fallujah Police know that we are out on the line
searching vehicles, Iraqi Police trucks and police cars rolled in
and out of the potato factory.

It was bizarre. I mentioned it, and that was it. There's no
rational explanation for that activity. But if you wanted to

smuggle weapons and munitions into Fallujah, from *erhabi* caches in the potato factory, that would be an easy way to do just that. Back in October, we searched the potato factory and found nothing, but we haven't searched it since, to the best of my knowledge.

And it's a big place—even Gunny Robertson said, "We need a whole company to search the potato factory, not twenty-two Marines." There are a lot of rooms, a lot of small doors. A lot of places to hide guns, plastic explosives, TNT, ammunition, mortars, and so on.

I'd like to dedicate this to my wife, Priscilla, and my two sons, Dorian and Abriam: Wherever I may die, my heart will always be with them.

"Fighting for reconstruction
aid in Iraq is like fighting for a
woman's virtue in a bordello."

CORPORAL BRYAN DAVIS,
MARINE INFANTRYMAN AND FIRE TEAM LEADER,
MARCH 24, 2006

A good friend and comrade of Corporal Stephen Lutze, Corporal Jay Elder, and many other Marine scout/snipers, Corporal Bryan Davis completed his third combat tour in Iraq with 2/6. About six-one, a twenty-two-year-old from Madison, Indiana, Davis is the kind of guy who will always look you in the eye, look out for you in combat, and never steer you wrong. Possessed of a sly wit, always squared away for missions, he and his squad leader, Sergeant White, were always picking the scout/snipers' brains for field intelligence on Al Qaeda and other *erhabi* in Fallujah. And Davis, like many Marines in Fox Company, listened closely to Ronin's suggestions and advice.

Lutze made coffee in the late afternoon of March 24 in Fallujah, and we talked as single shots of enemy small-arms fire burst outside the massive concrete and stone walls of the snipers' hooch on the top deck of the Fox Company firebase in the heart of Fallujah. More than two years earlier, in the fall of 2003 and winter of 2004, Sergeant Joe LeBleu and paratrooper snipers of the 82nd Airborne lay prone on the roof one floor above us under trash and netting, while Delta Force snipers in hides 300 meters to the southeast covered the streets south of Fran.

"I was here for the invasion," Davis said, thanking Lutze for the coffee. "Then we went to Okinawa for eight months. Then on to Afghanistan. Now here for a second time, three years after my first combat in Iraq. We pushed up in 2003. We secured Babylon."

Davis sipped coffee as he continued, talking about Corporal Albert P. Gettings, a twenty-seven-year-old Fox Company Marine from New Castle, Pennsylvania, who was killed in action in Fallujah as he tried to pull a wounded Marine out of the line of *erhabi* fire.

Gettings was definitely the guy that everybody liked. An outstanding Marine and a great American. He always had a kind word for folks; he was a damn good man. A lot of folks say that about someone when they die, but it was absolutely true about Gettings.

I don't know anyone who didn't like Gettings. He was a good friend and comrade to many Marines. He was in 1st Platoon, Fox Company. Gettings was hit, and he fought on. He was brave. He was trying to pull a Marine out of the line of fire. He died trying to save a Marine's life. Brother, that is courage. God bless Gettings, and may he rest in peace—Semper Fi to him, he's on higher ground now.

I honestly didn't expect to go home. I wasn't planning on surviving. I feel very fortunate to be alive. I guess that speaks to how seriously I took it. I wanted to give it everything I had here, to make sure I got the job done right. I think that maybe that was because it wasn't our first time in a combat zone. But it was a first time with a mission to capture or kill terrorists. I mean, that's what they told us at the beginning of this mission, at the beginning of this combat tour.

Fighting for reconstruction aid in Iraq is like fighting for a woman's virtue in a bordello. The whole idea of not really knowing if it's right for us to be here, and on the same side of that coin, if we're really being effective.

I really don't see us having that much of an impact, in the long run. The biggest thing that I struggle with is the fact that we're trying to spread democracy in this nation, and knowing a little bit about Islam, that it's a very fatalistic culture and society here.

Democracy in America was formed as a model government with Christian religion and Western philosophy backing it up, at its foundation. The reason democracy will never work here is that the Arab world is run off religion and not secular democracy. Look at our country in its infancy—we had people wise enough to realize that separation of church and state is vital.

In the Bible, there's a saying, "If a man doesn't work that day, he ought not eat." That's a pretty sound picture of capitalism, the good side of capitalism: incentive, initiative, and self-reliance. Those are classical Western values, Israeli values, and Kurdish values. But they are not classical Near Eastern and Central Asian values. From what I've seen in Iraq, not classical Arab values, either.

For instance, when I was in Afghanistan, I really noticed it. You'd be driving down the road, and you'd have to swerve off the side of the road. Because there would be a dude kneeling down right in the middle of the busiest road in Kabul, praying. We would talk to the driver and ask, "What is this guy thinking? That defies every bit of common sense known to man."

He would say that they pretty much have no fear, because if it's their time to die, then Allah will make it their time to die. What I got from it is that Muslims believe that they pretty much have no control over their lives. If they're growing up poor, then it's the will of Allah, and they will remain poor. If they're growing up rich, then it's the will of Allah, likewise, and they will remain wealthy.

Having said that, going back to democracy and trying to make it work in Iraq, it's like mixing water and oil. Because in America, for instance, we grow up hearing about hard work. Get your education, stand on your moral fortitude, and all these things put together, with the right drive and motivation, we can basically live the American dream.

Looking at Iraq, those things are absent. They possess none of those qualities in their culture, outside of Kurdistan. For us to have this imaginary idea that if we just put more money here and try harder with Iraq, that it will work in the end— hope is not a plan. Look at communism: The huge failure is that they removed the human factor. That is the failure in communist theory, and how communism played out, for real.

And the human factor is not there to develop democracy in Arab culture here. For that reason, I really don't see this working.

The Arabs are planning on the next IED they'll plant, not the next teacher they'll pay and the next health clinic they'll build.

With the Arabs, we're talking about making them free. We've started giving them freedoms that they never had under Saddam. But the problem is, they're like little kids. They can't handle those freedoms.

Basically, all we are here is a bunch of babysitters. And the babysitter never disciplines a child—a babysitter cannot discipline the child.

Even if we could do our real job, I'm not sure that it would be a success. Listen to our gunny, he really nailed it. Gunny Harrington, our gunnery sergeant, really got to the core of it: "Twenty percent of this country fucked over 80 percent of this country. The Sunni Arabs killed the children of the Shia and the Kurds. And that 80 percent that got fucked over, they are never, never going to let that happen again." Brother, that is accurate. In the black.

Absolutely, it makes sense to redefine victory here. Makes damn good sense to me, and this is my third tour in Iraq. Victory means we deny Al Qaeda a base in western Iraq, Baghdad, and the Sunni Triangle. Fuck dying for reconstruction aid, it's bullshit.

We take down Al Qaeda and go home, end of story. If that means martial law and 50,000 Kurdish *peshmerga* in western Iraq, Baghdad, and the Sunni Triangle, right on. Let the Iraqis win the war—it's their war at this point.

I see it in the form of little things, telling details, like how they name our operations—for instance, Operation Mister

Rogers Neighborhood. Taking away our viewpoint by language, forcibly telling us in this way that we're not in a war, according to Pentagonese. This is all meant to say, "We're your friendly neighborhood killing machine." We're your kindler, gentler Marine Corps and don't mention the word *war*.

The day that we were doing one part of this Operation Mister Rogers Neighborhood, we were handing out soccer balls. For at least a couple days prior, we'd known about some suicide vehicles. We knew what they looked like, and we knew that there was a big possibility that they'd be coming back to see us. But the day that they blew up at ECP-1, the suicide truck bomb, we were handing out soccer balls.

We were the unit that reacted to that. On the REACT there, we questioned, "Why are we handing out soccer balls, when we should've have been looking for those dump trucks?" We had the intel, but at some level of command, 2/6 command decided it was not a priority for us to search for those dump trucks, but it was definitely a priority to hand out soccer balls.

The other thing I don't understand is how there are certain ways you force yourself to think. There's a certain way you force yourself to think in the war, and it breeds a lot of contempt and hate toward Sunni Arabs. To have a clear conscience, and to do what you may be forced to do in the next two minutes of combat, you have to hate them. Because you don't kill people that you like.

They are doing us a great disservice by ordering us to "wear laughs and smiles." That was our specific order on March 10, 2006, the day of the suicide bombing that killed Lance Corporal Long and wounded Soto—"Laughs and smiles, everyone, laughs and smiles. We've got to make this the Fantasy Island feeling in Fallujah"—just before the suicide truck bomb went off at ECP-1.

Five minutes later, we were racing down Fran, watching ECP-1 burn down and knowing that Long was dead.

This whole "hearts and minds" trick bag in the middle of a guerrilla war really plays a game with your mind. I just said to myself, when we got there, this is anything but Fantasy Island, and anyone who thinks that is a damn nut.

They can't have their cake and eat it too. They want us to bring victory, but they want us, at the same time, to be the nice, kind, and gentle Marines. We are shock troops; that's who we are. We are the Hounds of Hell. We are Marines.

Our mission in life is to fire, leap over brick walls, reload, and kill the enemy. If you run out of live rounds, unsheathe your fighting knife and be happy: You'll never need to reload your K-Bar. You can't change 231 years of Marine history, of training us to be hard-core warriors, at the drop of a hat. We didn't get that nickname from the Germans—Devil Dogs, the Hounds from Hell—by handing out teddy bears and soccer balls.

The cost is far more than just monetary cost. Because it costs each one of us a little bit of our sanity every time we do something like that.

It stresses the hell out of me when we have to go out and do the humanitarian side of this mission, because it is pointless. And it gives the terrorists and insurgents here more opportunity to kill us. It breeds confusion in my mind.

With all that being said, I've often wondered if you presented that case to the Senate, or a Senate committee. If they read that, would they really understand? If you presented this as a case to them, it seems to me that hands-down they should agree.

There should pretty much be no other solution other than to revamp our actions here or leave. Either there are some hidden agendas or we're only here for the oil, but I don't buy that at all about the oil. We turned the oil back over to the Iraqis. It all seems to come down to a money issue.

The thing that people back home in America don't understand, for the most part, is they don't understand our duty as Marine infantrymen, and the military in general. Secondly, they somehow think that we love combat, like we enjoy war.

In reality, from what I've found from all my brothers that I've been with, is that we would rank high among antiwar activists. Nobody knows the human cost of combat better than us, no one. Most people who are actually in a war are among the most antiwar people there are, and rightfully so. I'm not saying that war is a needless thing, because at times you must fight—there are things worth fighting for. Jeffersonian democracy in Iraq isn't one of them; they have got to want it, and they simply don't want it. The Kurds want independence, and let them have it. The Kurds fought that sonofabitch Saddam with everything they had, fought for their freedom. Right on. The Kurds are going to be free and independent, anyway.

But I don't think that war as it used to be will ever happen again—for instance, World War II–type conflict. It will never be that way again, where clear lines are drawn, where you always know your frontlines.

"The weakness of the U.S. is we refuse to send undercover teams into the mosques. Al Qaeda knows this, the *erhabi* know this, and they exploit our weakness here, 24/7. Mosques are forward operating bases for terrorists."

RONIN1, APRIL 2006

onin1, led by Sergeant Efraim Parra from Brighton, Colorado, held over watch on streets and fields south of Fran on January 27, 2006. We'd hustled up in the darkness, a cold wind blowing from the Euphrates at zero dark thirty, and Corporal Bryan Davis's fire team from Fox Company had passed us as we entered a gated compound.

An Iraqi father let us in, and we talked to him in his kitchen, telling him we needed to be upstairs. He gathered his wife, daughter, and son in the kitchen and led us upstairs. Lance Corporal Jason Hillestad and Lance Corporal Billy Getscher secured the courtyard and ground floor. We had Corporal Stephen Lutze with us for extra backup; he carried a light machine gun that day and moved freely throughout the house.

On the top deck, a steel door led to the roof. Sergeant Parra crawled out onto the roof, an M4 cradled in his arms, his 9-millimeter sidearm on his right hip. "Keep low," he whispered, as Corporal Bobby Parker stood in the shadows near the doorway, an M40A-3 shouldered.

Certain the roof was clean, and having checked all sight lines, Parra low-crawled back and asked me if I would help them on over watch. I agreed. Once back inside, in a shed smelling of goats and dust and joss, we dug through old musty blankets, picking out a few to cover windows and rest sniper rifles and spotting scopes on as Parker scoped the streets. A baby wailed down an alley, and a siren blared in the night.

Parra was twenty-five years old, about five-eleven and solid as a brick wall, and an American of Mexican descent—"Spanish and Aztec are my people, brother, and I call Colorado home." With more than seven years in the Marines and over three years in Ronin by January 2006, Parra was the most experienced scout/sniper in the platoon. He whispered to Parker about the reconnaissance and our hide, and Parker nodded.

Everyone in the platoon shared Elder's opinion of Parra: "Outstanding combat judgment, very savvy. Parra will never lie to you, and he has an uncanny understanding of reconnaissance and surveillance. All our team leaders are sharp, but I've gotta give the nod to Parra, and that's no knock on the other team leaders, by no means. Three years plus behind the scope, three years as a for-real scout/sniper, the real McCoy, that's *beau coup* experience. And he's always thinking, the wheels are always turning, mind like a steel trap." Parker pointed something out to him, looking through a night vision scope, and Parra nodded and patted him on the back.

Parker calls Maryville, Tennessee, his hometown, "probably the best place on earth. I can see the mountains all around my home." Maryville is near both the Little Tennessee River and Big Tennessee River, in the Smoky Mountains. Twenty-one years old, he volunteered for the Marines on June 9, 2002, as an assault man, like Hodulich. Both of them qualified as 8541s, and Parker did his schooling at the Stone Bay Scout/Sniper School, near Camp Lejeune, North Carolina, in the winter of 2004. It is a ten-week scout/sniper school, same as Quantico. Parker had praised Stone Bay highly before we went on the mission, saying, "You go to school with the people who are motivated. Sergeant Sullivan was a great instructor, very knowledgeable and capable. They still use his techniques in Afghanistan. He was my primary instructor."

We didn't see Getscher and Hillestad again until the late afternoon, when the skies darkened and streetlights flickered down streets thick with garbage and stinking dark puddles, Iraqi men huddled against the sides of mosques and on street corners, warming their hands over oil can fires. We scoped the minarets of the mosques for terrorist snipers.

In the kitchen, waiting for the call from Fox 2/6 for us to swoop back to the Fox 2/6 firebase across Route Fran, Getscher stood quietly, cradling a light machine gun. Like Hillestad and Boyer, he was a Marine scout/sniper from Maryland.

Getscher grew up in St. Mary's County, where Catholics first settled in Maryland in the 1600s. Nineteen years old in January 2006, he volunteered for Marine infantry in October 2003. Before volunteering for scout/snipers, he'd been a grunt in 1st Platoon Golf 2/6, with Twiggs as his platoon sergeant. This was his first combat tour, and Parra had said of him, "very reliable, exactly the guy you want on tail-end Charlie. No freaking out with a machine gun on my team. That's not gonna happen with Billy Getscher. No shitbirds in Ronin, that's a law. Billy knows how to handle a light machine gun. He knows how to handle the SAW [squad automatic weapon]. He's clutch, listens well and communicates well, solid young Marine." About five-eleven, slim, humble, and clever, Getscher grew up not far from Hillestad, as the crow flies, in southern Maryland.

Lance Corporal Jason Hillestad carried an M16A4. His home is Waldorf, Charles County, southern Maryland. Twenty-two years old in January 2006, he graduated from Westlake High School in Waldorf in 2002. Charles County is horse country, though Hillestad said that the horse farms were falling prey to developers' shovels. "It's more built up now than when you were in the Corps. For instance, there are less horse ranches, less breeders, and less farmers. A few tobacco farms still exist, too." Deceptively strong, built like a free safety, Hillestad was also about five-eleven. Like Hodulich and Lutze, Hillestad devoured books. He volunteered for Marine infantry on September 22, 2004. In March 2005, he joined Ronin1.

With Lutze on tail-end Charlie and Hillestad on point, we moved out in the gathering night toward the twin spires of a mosque, the nearest landmark for Fran. We sprinted across Fran, a

Fox Company patrol coming back in with us, and hustled across mud and gravel, Lutze grinning in the evening as we got back to the scout/snipers' hooch on the top deck. A good mission: clean covert entry, undetected, twelve hours of reconnaissance and surveillance, uncompromised, and clean covert extraction.

In April 2006, waiting in the tents, sandstorms lashing at the canvas and dust clouding inside the tents, on days that felt far more like winter than spring, the men of Ronin1 had their say.

SERGEANT EFRAIM PARRA,
   RONIN1 TEAM LEADER AND SCOUT/SNIPER, APRIL 9, 2006
   I joined 2/6 scout/snipers back in November 2003. I was a sergeant. This November will make three years in this platoon. I don't get out until 2007, and if I stay with them until then, I'll have four years.

My hometown, Brighton, is in northeast Colorado. It's out in the prairies. It's all farmland. Folks are building new homes everywhere. If you go south, toward Durango and Grand Junction, there are Indian reservations.

December was the worst here. December 2005. The frustration was intense. You just had to hold it together. All we did was just sit in observation posts [OPs]. All we were was an extra set of eyes at the OPs, and waiting for the enemy to shoot another Marine.

Then we were supposed to counter that, once the enemy had shot at us again or killed one of us. We were sitting ducks, waiting to be shot at. 1st Recon was getting their missions from Camp Fallujah. And when we belonged to 1st Recon, they didn't use us either. 1st Recon kept us static, that whole time.

Pretty much every Marine in the platoon voiced their opinion at that time to the team leaders, platoon sergeant, and so on: Why don't we find different jobs? Why don't we move out 200 meters from the OPs? But every time we'd tell our platoon commander for us to do something different, it was just like nobody cared.

All the guys in the platoon started to get real frustrated, doing the same things over and over. What would've worked much better was using our actual 2/6 assets to bait the insurgents. We could've used CAAT [Combined Anti-Armor Team], gun truck teams like Black Label and Jim Beam, and us together, as a hunter/killer team. We trained for that last summer. Set a pattern, intentionally, and bait the terrorist sniper.

It works, because we saw it here with Black Label [Black Label gun truck platoon, led by 1st Lieutenant Marty Keogh]. They were going to insert us one night. We were supposed to get inserted at 1800 [six P.M.]. We were told the curfew was at 1800. But the people of Fallujah did not know that the curfew was at 1800. They still thought the curfew was at 2300 [eleven P.M.].

When we were driving around, to see a good spot to insert, we finally got to hit the house we were going to insert at. We needed bolt cutters to get into the house. So we called up Black Label to get us some bolt cutters. When they came back around, two *erhabi* fired an RPG at Black Label high-back, missing it by just a little.

The RPG skidded off the hood of the high-back. The reason why they got hit was they'd created a pattern by moving in the same area, over and over.

We'd set the bait and they'd taken it. Had we done that starting in mid-November, it likely would've been different here. We might have saved some lives here. But you have to listen to your scouts in the first place for that to happen.

We are lacking in human intelligence. I'm talking at all levels. If we had more people, clandestine assets, who would actually go into the mosques, we'd really start taking down Al Qaeda.

For instance, Iraqis who would go into the mosques and actually get hard intel that way, it would help us tremendously to stop attacks on U.S. soldiers and troops, and would definitely help stop attacks on Iraqi Army soldiers and civilians.

The weakness of the U.S. is we refuse to send undercover teams into the mosques. Al Qaeda knows this, the *erhabi* know this, and they exploit our weakness here, 24/7. Mosques are forward operating bases for terrorists.

For a fact, Special Forces A teams would be a great asset here. Especially if you used them as before, when SF and Delta were here, when you were here before. There are numerous other ways they could be of great, great benefit to us—with scout/snipers, for instance.

Right, if we split up an A team, attached two of them to each of our Marine scout/sniper teams, not only would we be better off on reconnaissance and surveillance and sniping missions, we'd be incredibly more effective at getting information from Iraqis.

What would've made it better for us was if company commanders had a better understanding of how to employ scout/snipers. As far as what we bring to the table, for the battalion to fight more effectively. The officers' sniper employment school is there for Marine officers to learn how to employ scout/snipers.

The mistake that we made was not sitting down the company commanders and the platoon commanders, and giving them a sniper employment class. So that way, they have a better understanding of what we can do.

Even if our platoon commander and platoon sergeant didn't do it, it should've been up to our team leaders to sit down with the company commanders and platoon commanders. Then give them a brief on what we can and cannot do.

Roger that on the African proverb. The Masai nailed it. You don't send the whole village to kill a man-eating lion, you send your best lion hunter. We sent the whole village, and we didn't even send our best lion hunters, either—Marine scout/snipers.

You know, if I was an enemy sniper, and I saw all those people moving around, I would not come back. I was attached to Echo Company, at the Fallujah Train Station, at that time.

I told Echo Company, if it was me, I would kill a few enemy to bring morale down, kill a few and then move out. And come back, eventually. Our morale went down when the terrorist sniper killed our guys. Morale is so valuable in war; it has so much impact on everything. Fighting spirit gives you that edge over your enemy—invaluable.

And he then saw what our reactions were to his killing us, and that was in the beginning. Then RCT-8 sent out everybody and their mothers after the terrorist sniper.

Then, the second time, he took out more targets, he killed more of us, because we gave him more targets.

These are all good guys. I wish they weren't getting out. 2/6 gave them a bad taste of the Marine Corps. They got sent to scout/sniper school at Quantico and Stone Bay to master the art and craft of sniping, and they were crushed here in 2/6. Just crushed.

Other battalions, I'm sure they have scout/snipers who reenlist, who got a chance to do what they get paid for. Being a Marine scout/sniper, that's who we are. That's what we do.

Gettings and Snider were my comrades. [Corporal Josh Snider of Echo Company 2/6 was killed by a terrorist sniper, while standing post, in late November 2005.] I was trying to kill that enemy sniper for them. I was Gettings' platoon sergeant in Afghanistan. It would've meant a lot to me to kill that enemy sniper. And Snider, we took him out on a mission with us. He was solid. He was going to go to college in Colorado and snowboard. Snider was from Maryland, like Billy Getscher and Jason Hillestad.

CORPORAL BOBBY GENE PARKER,
RONIN1 ASSISTANT TEAM LEADER AND SCOUT/SNIPER, APRIL 3, 2006
We were still successful, on reconnaissance and surveillance throughout our deployment here, and in our intelligence gathering. Battalion had a problem with us not killing people. If you deny us kill shots, however, who the hell is at fault there? Not us. You can't deny us kill shots and then talk smack about us.

But when something happened and we did kill people, battalion would say, "Why did you kill them?" You wanted to say, "Because this is war, idiot." But you didn't say that. Damn truth, though.

When we actually took someone down, battalion did not shake our hands and tell us, "Well done."

Just getting along with everybody was a challenge—and our higher-ups did not understand about employing snipers. Then they'd treat us like we were cowboys for talking about employment, as if we don't understand sniper employment. Roger that, everybody thought they were the gods of sniper employment but refused to listen to us, actual Marine scout/snipers, in regards to sniper employment. Roger that, Egos on Parade, Inc.

Usually it was the lieutenants and gunnys who'd chide us and tell us how we should be employed. This battalion got a boot drop of lieutenants before we got over here. So you've got lieutenants on their first combat tour ever, with less time in the Marine Corps than me or Sergeant Parra, talking to us like they are the wizards of reconnaissance.

Gunny Via, he did us no favors. Weapons Company, Wild Turkey gun truck platoon commander, but nothing like Keogh—Keogh knows how to listen to scouts. Keogh is *bad*. Gunny Via's got no idea about how to employ us. This is his first combat deployment, and all he did was throw his rank around.

For example, we were sitting in the back of the humvee, open back, near ECP-1 [Entry Checkpoint One, hit by a suicide bomb on March 10, 2006]. Our humvee was out in front of all the other vehicles. Me, Parra, Brian, and Fleming were in the back. Brian was standing on the outside. I was standing on the right side. I was outside the truck. Billy was in the truck that Gunny Via was in.

The turret gunner was standing up and he dropped his SAW. He picked it back up and let off an eight-round burst on the left side of the truck. If he had been just four feet right, he would've shot Brian Areballo, Sergeant Parra, and Noah Fleming. Dead.

Gunny Via's reaction: "Shit happens." Not even a "By your leave," and "My turret gunner won't touch that SAW again." Now, it's a law in war that when you set patterns, your enemy notices and uses those patterns to kill you, to ambush you, put a sniper on you, hit you with RPGs, and so on.

If you're predictable, you're dead. But Gunny Via sets patterns left and right. Turns around in the same spots. Drives over the same holes. Predictable as the sun coming up in the morning.

Runs the same routes every day. That's just asking *erhabi* to lay IEDs on you, they see how you roll the same routes every day.

That's how come Wild Turkey has been hit so many times, because the terrorists and insurgents have a field day with anyone who sets patterns. Wild Turkey is easy to target because of Gunny Via.

Then we left from ECP-1. Farewell to the mad SAW gunner. We went and set up in a building to the east of the hospital, on Fran. We were setting up in there, and Fox Company's quick reaction force drove by in two humvees, with the high armored sides.

They were not using night vision goggles [NVGs], so they spotlighted all the buildings. The spotlights shine 10 million kilowatts strong.

They saw our tripod on our sniper rifle and stopped in front of Areballo's house, and he lost communications, because Fox Company had electronic warfare devices on their vehicles. So now we had no communications with anyone. Our field radio was useless. It gets better.

They backed up in front of our house. As they backed up, they hit the tripod of our sniper rifles again with their spotlight.

We could not raise them on the horn, because their electronic warfare had killed our communications. We could see by the look in their eyes that they were going to attack us.

We were all laid out in the prone and we started shouting, "We're Marines! We're Marines!" and they got out of their trucks, ready to raid that house with no NVGs on, and came on, weapons at the ready.

We kept shouting, "We're Marines! We're Marines!" but they kept coming on. Sergeant Parra screamed at them, "Are

you fuckin' stupid? There's Marines in here!" That's when
they finally realized that there were indeed Marines in that
abandoned building.

Fox 2/6 Marines said to us, "Oh, OK, you're Marines." That
ruined our hide. Fox 2/6 compromised us. Everybody and
their uncle in Fallujah knew where we were at. I look back on
that now and can only say it is by the grace of God that I'm
talking to you, because Fox 2/6 was raiding us, all weapons at
combat ready, ready to light us up. Blue on blue.

All because Gunny Via never told Fox Company in the first
place that we were in that hide. He never told Fox where our
hides were, even though that was his duty. We were in Fox
Company's area of operations.

Failure to communicate. So I got on the radio once Fox
left, and we regained communications.

"Ronin1 will go to Ronin2's hide, because Ronin1 had lost
communications and couldn't get his field radio back up."

Gunny said, "Negative. You will stay in your house because
Fox Company knows your position."

I said, "Fox knows where we are now, but did you tell them
before our mission where our hide would be?"

There was a dead silence for a few moments, then simply,
"Negative."

I said, "thank you." And that was it.

Battalion didn't listen to us, from jump street, and battalion
didn't give us targets to hit. They didn't use us to support
raids, in over watch positions—classic guerrilla war stuff. I
always wanted to be a Marine scout/sniper. That's why I volunteered in the first place. I was going to stay in for twenty years,
but 2/6 smashed that.

But we were good. Like Brian said, "We are Ronin and we
are one." We were tight and we hung tough. We worked good
together. It's a good time to be alive. I hear there's whiskey
and beer at Shannon Airport in Ireland. Let's make it to that
bar—hell, yes.

LANCE CORPORAL JASON HILLESTAD,
RONIN 1 SCOUT/SNIPER

Not using the intelligence that we had, that was the worst of it all. A lot of advantages and opportunities were missed because as a battalion, we just sat in the defense. Blatant disregard for field intelligence from battalion.

For instance, we heard while we were at Echo 2/6, at the Train Station a couple times, that there was solid intelligence on insurgents gathering at different locations in the city. But the defensive posture of the battalion was so powerful, we were never ordered to attack.

Another time, helos [helicopters] picked up heat signatures of a large gathering in the middle of the night. The next day, that was when all the observation posts got hit. This was in early December. Terrorist snipers hit us the next day, all over the city.

The feeling that I got when we were at Echo was that the company commander was afraid to engage, for fear of casualties. To be fair, the defensive posture of the battalion did not encourage the company commanders to be aggressive.

Also, with the high-value terrorist targets [HVTs], like Ahmed Sirhan, we didn't have the intelligence that you had. You told us more about Ahmed Sirhan than our own S-2. No one told us that he was the leader of Black Flags Brigades, for instance. S-2 didn't tell us, also, that a couple of days before, we were going to carry out reconnaissance and surveillance on a different terrorist, another high-value target, that a squad of grunts from Fox had been to the same location—the terrorist's auto repair shop.

They sent us in, which is a wasted mission, because you've already got the enemy's radar up.

You don't send in covert assets *after* you've used your line grunts, you send us in *before* so we can do the reconnaissance and surveillance. Then you raid. We can likely nail the guy ourselves, for that matter. At the very least, you provide your infantry with real-time human intelligence by sending us in before the raid, not after. [U.S. Army commanders in Mosul and Fallujah in 2003–04 routinely did exactly what Hillestad is saying, sending their scouts and also Special Forces assets on real-time human intelligence missions prior to raids on high-value terrorist targets.]

The battalion commander did not understand how to employ scout/snipers. Countless examples of that. Worst one was on Observation Post Henry, in Fallujah.

We did one mission across from OP Henry in December. We were on the northeast side of OP Henry, watching OP Henry. Reconnaissance and surveillance for terrorist snipers. It was completely static, but at least we were looking out for Marine infantrymen in that OP.

Then the battalion commander sent all the scout/sniper teams to Al Saqlawiyah for a week and did absolutely nothing. While we were at Al Saqlawiyah, a terrorist sniper killed Corporal Josh Snider at OP Henry.

So the battalion commander moved us out of Al Saqlawiyah and put us at OP Henry. We stayed static at OP Henry, sitting ducks for the next terrorist sniper. I've got to get out of 2/6!

Another failure was that the battalion refused to let us use bait. In guerrilla warfare, it is absolutely essential to use bait.

For example, the weapons caches: leaving the weapons caches. Be covert about what you've found, also, instead of blowing it up and letting every village nearby know that you've found it. Sit on that cache with covert assets—your scout/snipers, for one—and wait. If you use that weapons cache as bait, you can kill the enemy: It's classic guerrilla warfare.

Echo Company blew up a cache one time and then told us, "Now you can sit on it and wait for the insurgents and terrorists to return." That's retarded. Your enemy is not coming back to that cache after you've blown it up; he's not that stupid.

The Fallujah Police are absolutely just as crooked and dirty as Kelso has stated. The Iraqi Police did some shady shit when

Sergeant Matter got bushwhacked on his first patrol as a squad leader, with Echo. The Iraqi Police came out of nowhere, rolled up in their pickup trucks, threw those dead *erhabi* on the back—the Iraqi Police in Fallujah knew *exactly* where that ambush was going down.

One time, also, the Iraqi Police spotlighted us. We were with SEALs going across Fran, from Fox COC. Headed on foot with the SEALs for about 200 meters east. The Iraqi Police saw us, hung a U, and then spotlighted us as we entered the building. The Iraqi Police wanted to make sure that everybody and their brother in Fallujah knew that we were in that building.

We had guys already in that building. That was in December 2005, on the joint countersniper ops with the SEALs. The SEALs were professional, motivated, and good guys. We flowed together on the small unit ops.

Less than a month ago, I shot one insurgent. He was creeping around our building late at night, out in the Shark's Fin. We had two teams, Ronin1 and Ronin3. We had used that hide a couple days before.

There was a hallway outside of our room. I could hear the glass kicked on the floor. I knew that someone had entered. Fleming woke me up.

"We're sure someone is setting up a booby trap," Fleming said.

We cleared the rooms and we could hear the guy coming back inside. I hit him with the Surefire [high-power flashlight attached to a rifle]. He freaked out and tried to run through the door, toward us. He was running right at us.

We already had our weapons up. We lit him up.

Roger that, we came through the fire together. Lot of nights laying in broken glass and mud and rain. Made it through the winter of the sniper, mercy. We have great guys in the scout/snipers. Sergeant Parra is a solid team leader. I'm happy to be headed stateside. The feeling of accomplishment is just not there, however. Otherwise, I'd want to stay.

LANCE CORPORAL WILLIAM GETSCHER,
    RONIN1 SCOUT/SNIPER, APRIL 4, 2006

I joined the scout/snipers because a lot of people I talked
to said it was considerably more challenging than a line
infantry company, and that you better yourself. I wanted to
better myself, so I decided that it was the place to go.

Me and Hillestad, Novi, Hodulich, and Lutze all came in
together. Right, we were the PIGs. The HOGs made sure we
earned our places on the teams. I got put on Sergeant Parra's
team right away.

This was my second combat deployment. My first was in
Baghdad. Our first mission was actually out in Al Saqlawiyah, at
Golf 2/6 area of operations. We were checking out enemy mor-
tar sites, because of all the mortars being fired on Golf 2/6.

We were out in the country, in the bushes and reeds, hunting the enemy mortar teams. We were set up in farms. We had
two guys, Sergeant Hope and Corporal Keller, from Golf with
us. It was a six-day op.

No such luck, though, finding the enemy mortar teams.
Then we went back to the train station. We were directly
attached to Echo Company. We didn't have very good luck
finding the enemy.

In December, we were attached to 1st Reconnaissance Battalion and the SEALs. 1st Recon didn't want anything to do
with us. 1st Recon sent us out to the OPs, to the observation
posts. It sucked. Complete static over watch. We sat behind
concrete and barbed wire.

But the SEALs understood how to use Marine
scout/snipers. The SEALs used us. That was their call. We
attached to the SEALs and went on a couple missions with the
SEALs. They were real professionals. They treated us with
respect. They were cool, very solid operators. We schooled
them on what we do at Quantico and Stone Bay. The SEALs
were pretty good guys. Hodulich had SEALs in his
scout/sniper class at Quantico, by the way. He respected the
hell out of them, and he told us that was the same with them:
they showed him a lot of respect, too.

The most frustrating thing? Oh, no question about it, the way 1st Recon handled us on the countersniper operations. The winter of the sniper. Terrorist snipers all over Fallujah, and we were ordered to stand guard. 1st Recon backhanded us to the OPs, and we didn't do jack. All we did was stand guard. We had our scopes and rifles, and we stood guard.

The IPs are some shady motherfuckers. Mad shady. I'm pretty sure that most of them are dirty. We were at OP Henry when Sergeant Matter's squad got ambushed. Our scout/snipers saw the IPs rush up and grab the dead insurgents, throw them up on IP gun trucks, and speed away. I'm sure that there's a few good IPs out there. There just aren't that many.

We had a pretty tight team, Ronin1. We were all pretty much the same height, so we could interchange our gear. We have been called, from time to time in the battalion, the best team. Not bragging or nothing, but we were solid. This place sucks, but we made the best of it. Hell, yes, it feels damn good to be getting home! This is the best part of the deployment.

Thanks to everyone in my family in Maryland, and my friends, for their prayers and support. No one has ever talked down to me about being a Marine, criticized me for being in the military and the choice I made to be in Marine infantry and scout/snipers.

People have respected me, back home, and that means a lot to me. My dad has always backed me 100 percent. My mom has everyone in the church praying for me. The last time I saw her, after I came back from Baghdad, she hugged me and broke down and cried. She really didn't think I was safe until I was back in Maryland and she could see me with her own eyes.

"We know our enemies here, but we are essentially defending our enemies from our friends."

CORPORAL MIKE LOPER,
MARINE INFANTRYMAN, ANTI-TANK GUNNER,
JIM BEAM GUN TRUCK PLATOON,
WEAPONS COMPANY,
APRIL 8, 2006.

orporal Mike Loper from Virginia's eastern shore, a mariner before he was a Marine infantryman, glanced toward huts and houses a kilometer away in the desert north of Fallujah on January 22, 2006, stirring instant coffee, sugar, and powdered creamer into a canteen cup filled with boiling water over a small gas flame. The gas burner was his pride and joy. "Any waterman worth his skipjack knows you always carry a burner, brother, life without coffee ain't worth living," he said, merry in the winter sun near the Fallujah train station.

Inside the train station, Sergeant Parra examined a map, going over a mission for his scout/sniper team, Ronin1. Jim Beam's gun trucks, along with Black Label's gun trucks, had supported Parra's team on many missions. Indeed, Weapons Company aided all of Ronin, in Fallujah and Al Saqlawiyah, earning the respect of the scout/snipers with their professionalism and calm under fire.

Both gun truck platoons had just come off missions to refuel, clean weapons, gear up, and move out again, hunting roadside bombs, terrorists, and insurgents in the winter of the sniper.

Loper was seventeen when he volunteered for the Marines on September 27, 1999, at Parris Island. An anti-tank gunner (TOW gunner, 0352 military occupational specialty), he grew up on the Chesapeake Bay in Cape Charles, Virginia. His people are watermen on both sides of the family. He plans on working on boats off the shores of New Jersey and Long Island after getting out of the Marines in late 2006. About six feet even, he was cheerful, low key, burly, and red-faced from the desert sun. He'd mastered all small arms and carried an M4 assault rifle and a K-Bar fighting knife.

My hometown is Cape Charles, Virginia, and my people are people of the sea. We know the Chesapeake and the Atlantic. We are watermen. That's where my grandfather had his business, since the early 1940s, where the Coast Guard Station is at Cape Charles. He was a commercial fisherman.

That's what I'm going to do when I get out—I'm going to clam with my dad. He's working out of Point Pleasant, New Jersey, right now. That's northern Jersey.

My first tour here was the invasion. The night we crossed the line of departure, crossed the berm from Kuwait into Iraq. It was the darkest night, no illumination. Actually kind of cold, that March. March 11, 2003, we had started to push up from Kuwait. I'd already been in country since September 2002, with 1st Marine Expeditionary Force.

The second one, we were in Baghdad. That was just a guard mission. Very boring, very monotonous. Stood post, guarded the palace. Took a lot of incoming. Mortars and rockets. Did a few combined patrols with the Army in the Red Zone. Basically, we served as a guard force/quick reaction force for the Green Zone. That was pretty much it on that tour.

The Fallujah Police are the largest insurgent cell in Fallujah? Roger that. Kelso is dead-on. That is correct. Hell, yes, I second that. Exactly.

The Fallujah Police let the terrorists and insurgents into the city. It's an ever-revolving cycle around here—about every four months, Al Qaeda ratches it up another notch.

In the city of Fallujah, over time, the populace is building back up, and the bigger the population in Fallujah, the more terrorists you have. It's been passed down from RCT-8 to us, through Major Sullivan—and Major Sullivan is a damn good man—that we have to keep a lid on the terrorists in Fallujah, at 10 percent of the population.

If Major Sullivan was in command in Iraq, we'd have a no-bullshit guy in charge, and we need more commanders like him. He's the best we have. Now, the 10 percent acceptance rate on terrorists here—that's the going number now. Doesn't please Major Sullivan, I have no doubt; don't get me wrong, doesn't please him or us. But dig this: 10 percent of Fallujah means 20,000 people. So the higher-highers have decided that 20,000 terrorists in Fallujah can be appeased. Reading history, that's a mistake; you appease terrorists, and you find yourself in a world of hurt.

What you saw on March 6th was typical, not uncommon at all. When Regimental Combat Team Five [RCT-5, replaced RCT-8 in late January 2006] ordered the terrorist Fallujah Police Captain Munther Muhammed Hais released.

Fallujah Police Captain Munther Muhammed Hais is a for-real high-value terrorist target, roaming Fallujah and western Iraq at will, killing Marines. And Marine command, RCT-5, let him walk. But that's not uncommon here. It's a goatfuck, no question.

The Big Blue Arrow, like Novi and Kelso have said, points to someone else's agenda in this war, and it's not our agenda. It's about who has the money right now; it's about who has the pull.

The people who have the money and the pull now are the Sunni Arabs. But Sunni Arabs are the same people who recruit, finance, arm, man, and back the insurgency; they *are* the insurgency. We should have fought and won this war in 1991. We are here now because the forty-first president did not keep the saber unsheathed; when you draw that sword, brother, know what the hell you are doing. "Easy to be hard, hard to be smart." Truth. We earned that proverb in blood in the Marines, over 231 years now, since 1775. And if you draw that sword, disappear the scabbard.

Guerrilla war history says you fight a sniper with a sniper. 2/6 and 1st Recon didn't read guerrilla war, apparently—you fight a sniper with a sniper. The Masai said that, on taking down a man-eating lion! Righteous. Roger that, you send your best lion hunter out on the savannah, that lion is not stupid. But our scout/snipers well and truly got fucked. 2/6 fucked over our scout/snipers.

We can kill one wolf or we can kill the pack. I prefer to kill the pack.

If you're moving covert and quiet, light and fast, as Ronin can operate if you simply let them, you have a much better chance at killing the pack.

But we're in a strange situation here: It's March 31, 2006. On Wednesday, March 29th, we got real-time intelligence that a Saudi guy was driving a suicide car bomb and we knew exactly where he was stowing his vehicle. Suicide car bombers have attacked our ECPs here, as you know. We also had his tag number. Name, physical intel, whole nine yards.

Instead of ordering us to capture or kill the guy, we were ordered to ECP-1. Roger that, we had all the intelligence we needed to take down a known suicide bomber. And 2/6, our own battalion, denied us the mission.

Which just made us targets for the suicide car bomb, once we got to ECP-1. When the Fallujah Police at the checkpoints are letting terrorists and insurgents through, you're up against it. We know our enemy here, but we are essentially defending our enemies from our friends. Every time we've taken fire, we've been in the vicinity of a mosque. Thank God that we have survived.

"Common sense and history
dictate that you must listen to your junior troops if you want to win a guerrilla war."

RONIN HEADQUARTERS ELEMENT,
APRIL 10 AND 11, 2006

Lance Corporal Jon Zwirblia grew up in Worcester, Massachusetts. Twenty years old when I interviewed him, he began writing poetry under the tutelage of his advanced-placement English teacher, Mrs. Pedone, at North High School. Zwirblia, an American of Polish blood, was the chief communicator for Ronin and key to the headquarters element of the scout/snipers. Along with Lance Corporal Jim Owen and HM3 Joshua James Gutierrez, he supported Ronin on many missions in Fallujah and Al Saqlawiyah.

Zwirblia had two years on active duty in the Marines by April 2006, and three years as a poet. At seventeen in Worcester, he said, "I first started writing poetry. Yes, I showed my poetry to my AP English teacher, Mrs. Pedone. She talked to me about improving my skills as a poet, and poets whom we were studying at the time. She also gave me insight into grammatical points and punctuation. From her, I learned so much about Walt Whitman, and definitely Robert Frost. We studied Emily Dickinson, also. She is very thought-provoking, very powerful. Emily Dickinson is something else, wicked poetry. We studied Shakespeare, also. Ah, Shakespeare, the master.

"I was really into Robert Frost and Walt Whitman. Those are my two favorite poets. Frost's metaphors, and his symbolism. And the feeling that he portrays, a deep feeling. He really gets deep into the soul. Everyone faces the fork in the road, you know, 'The Road Less Traveled.' Frost is deep and soulful, and I really enjoy reading his work. There's such exuberance in Whitman's work, the song of the common man, song of the heart. Whitman is fantastic."

Zwirblia was often hunched over a notebook near the Fox command-and-control center, writing and rewriting poems, when not on duty. *Leaves of Grass* and poetry anthologies were stacked near him, his 9-millimeter sidearm on one hip and his rifle leaning against a wall. He was a young poet at war and one of the best radiomen in the Marines. About five-ten, stocky like a wrestler, he missed New England, talking often of the stone walls in green fields bordered by deep forest, and the docks Melville walked before he shipped out on whalers for the South Pacific.

Lance Corporal Jim Owen hails from New Bern, North Carolina, south along the Atlantic seaboard from the poet Zwirblia. Owen was twenty years old in the winter of the sniper. New Bern, named after Bern, Switzerland, is about an hour west of Morehead City and an hour north of Camp Lejeune. "There's a lot of farmland, thick pines, and a lot of underbrush, just like Camp Lejeune," Owen said in Fallujah on April 10, 2006. He carried the SAW in Iraq, on tail-end Charlie on many missions, carrying the light machine gun on rear guard. He was broad-shouldered and about five-eleven—strangely, almost all of the scout/snipers were right around that height—and he could carry a load.

Owen graduated from New Bern High School in his hometown in June 2002, volunteered for Marine infantry, and reported to Fox Company 2/6 on June 27, 2003. They'd just come back from Iraq, and he became a point man in 1st Platoon Fox 2/6, carrying an M16A2 assault rifle, the predecessor to the M16A4. Right before Fox Company left for Afghanistan in August 2004, Owen volunteered for Marine scout/snipers.

In headquarters element, he worked the computer and the photograph files. Doc liked to kid him, calling him "our scout/sniper computer geek number one." Owen would grin and reply,

"Just make sure you don't run out of morphine there, you, medical geek number ten—that and Motrin. Remember, Navy corpsmen are here for Marines' entertainment."

HM3 Joshua James Gutierrez, known as "Doc" or "Doc Gute" to Ronin, graduated from the Woodlands High School in June 1998 and was twenty-six years old in the spring of 2006. He grew up in Woodlands, Texas, north of Houston—"East Texas, brother, very flat and very humid, more pine trees than God made grains of sand, a very pretty place. My wife loves it, too. In the summers, its hell's half acre, mighty hot." Gutierrez graduated from Great Lakes Navy boot camp on October 31, 2002. "Since high school," he said, "I'd wanted to join the service. My dad wanted me to go to college. Well, I went to Southwest Texas State. The ratio is eight girls to every one guy. After three years, I decided to join the Navy. I had a break from classes and went to the recruiter and said, 'Sign me up.' I knew that I wanted to be a corpsman."

The Doc carried a 9-millimeter sidearm in the field. About six-one, with black hair and coal-black eyes, he attached to missions with all Ronin teams throughout the combat tour. In the cold, gray, wet winter in Fallujah, he'd wear a long, khaki-and-light-green waterproofed jacket, balaclava over his face and throat, and hand out smokes at the end of Ronin's missions.

A reflective, thoughtful man, he never lost touch with his wife the entire combat tour. Doc Gute is a good man and a top-notch corpsman, in the tradition of Navy corpsmen in Marine infantry units, like those I was fortunate to serve with in the late 1980s: Michael Hartman, "Buddha Doc," a former Peace Corps volunteer from Fort Lauderdale, Florida, and Doc Testori, who called Vegas home whenever we came in from the field.

Three together, the Poet, Big Jim, and Doc weathered the winter of the sniper and many IEDs. On April 10 and 11, 2006, I had the good fortune to listen to them in Fallujah.

LANCE CORPORAL JON ZWIRBLIA,
  RONIN CHIEF COMMUNICATOR AND FIELD RADIO OPERATOR
    I've written three poems in-country. I haven't rewritten and revised all that I would like to, but I am rewriting now. New poems.

The work that I've been doing over here is dark, due to the situations around the battalion. Some of the feelings I've had, of real boredom and monotonous time, and personal emotion. It's been a rough grind, this combat deployment, especially for this platoon.

So my poetry now, here, is dark, because of the situation. Dark is honest right now. You've got to be honest with yourself, you know. At the same time, I'm happy to do my job.

December. Just the worst month ever. Roger that. I sat on an observation post on top of a roof, on top of Fox Company, that we fit three people very uncomfortably on for twenty-two days straight. It was easier just staying on the roof around the clock. Winter of the sniper.

Three men on rotation throughout the days and nights. Doc Gute, Staff Sergeant Williams, and me. We just stayed up there, sleeping on a mat when we were not on countersniper over watch. I'm not complaining about the hardship; that's just what you endure. But our trained snipers in our platoon were not employed effectively in the countersniper operations. We felt that at the time. We would've been much better employed setting up hides in the city and taking houses. We have four-man scout/sniper teams, but they were not used effectively.

It was hard, roger that, when we'd hear that the terrorist sniper had struck again. Losing Marines is always hard. Especially for the families of our brothers. We felt like, "Let's get out there and counterattack; let's do our jobs." When the battalion needed us, we were always ready.

But nobody listened to us. Maybe they'll listen to us now. It's a damn shame that we were chained and shackled in that December.

Ah, the three-man patrol along the Euphrates. A heckuva long way we patrolled in that neck of the woods with only three men. November. That three-man patrol was very difficult. We patrolled from Golf's firm base in Al Saqlawiyah all the way to our objective point on the Euphrates River.

It was challenging mentally in the daylight due to all the people being around, farming, doing their daily activities. We had to stay covert. It made it difficult to maneuver and achieve our objective.

Emotionally it was tough, because it was just three men. I carried an M16A4 and my M9 [9-millimeter Beretta sidearm]. Doc had an M16A4 and an M9. Staff Sergeant Williams had a SAM-R and an M9.

We hugged the river line and stayed covert in the reeds and orchards. Most of the orchards were dead, due to the winter. And we were weaving in and out of the tree line, hopping canals. It was November, near the Marine Corps birthday.

We did this twice. First time we did it, Doc got a mild concussion jumping over a canal. He hit a tree, after slipping in the mud. The second time we did it, it was near Marine Corps birthday. Both times we reached the objective at nightfall.

The second time, we held security all night. Carried out reconnaissance and surveillance. Scoping for any enemy activity, mortar sites, weapons caches, and the like.

Then we left around 1500 and got back about 2000. We stayed covert coming back too, until we were in an orchard and a farmer and his child walked out of his house right at us. We talked with him, and he invited us in for bread, tea, and dinner. It was good talking with him. He was very helpful.

At that point, we began moving back quickly for Al Saqlawiyah, hustling hard for the base. We still had ten kilometers to cover to make it back. We were wearing flaks, helmets, camera equipment, R&S gear, chow, and water. By the time we got back in the wire, we'd drank all our water.

At that time, we did not have the side body armor plates. Less body armor then. My flak was lighter. I couldn't imagine doing it with side plates, now. Doc carried seven mags plus his 9-millimeter mags. I carried nine mags and two 9-millimeter mags. Due to the fact that we were a three-man team, we carried a fair bit of extra ammo on those missions.

Both of those missions were the most challenging. The other times I was out, I was in the sniper communications center or augmenting the teams. I was with the sniper communications center about 75 percent of the time and working with the teams on missions about 25 percent of the time.

This combat deployment was my first. I learned a lot about how the Marine Corps employs infantry companies in combat. A positive thing was being close to the platoon, a better bond. Even with the communications Marines, they were very helpful to us.

I could see our frustration in Ronin, the frustration of our scout/snipers, because of a lack of intelligence. They weren't getting the information they needed.

It feels pretty good to turn our gear in and I've met some friends from 1/25 who I haven't seen in a while. Corporal Jorge Colone from Worcester—he's from my high school. And I went to communications school with Lance Corporal John Wheatley from Massachusetts. He's here with 1/25, also. It's good to see him again.

It's an uplifting feeling, now, like taking a knife out of your back. To think that in a few days that we'll be back stateside, celebrating. And also reminiscing on my fallen comrades. I'm fortunate enough to go home to my family. But there are Marines I came here with that won't see their families again.

Altogether, it was an experience being a communicator and working with a group like this. It's not like working with your average line company; these are scout/snipers. I was able to experience the tactical side of the Marine Corps and really work with the scout/snipers. It's a stepping-stone for me, in terms of my next movement in the Corps. Good to be alive. Roger that, good to be alive. Let's get to that bar in Ireland.

LANCE CORPORAL JIM OWEN,
RONIN CHIEF COMPUTER/PHOTO SPECIALIST AND SCOUT/SNIPER

We came through and took this city, the Marines and the Army did, in Second Fallujah, Al Fajr, in November 2004. But now we are still losing people in this city. The *erhabi* still come back in, because of the Fallujah Police supporting *erhabi*.

A huge mistake was not to destroy the massive weapons caches left behind by Saddam's army. The politicians and the higher-ups in the military don't really understand what is happening on the ground here. Or they don't want to admit that they do know, which is also likely true. Also, Nathaniel Fick [a former Marine officer and author of the memoir *One Bullet Away* who wrote a widely read column arguing that the opinions of soldiers on the ground should have no bearing on strategy] is basically saying that we don't need to listen to the opinions on this war coming from junior troops.

He is wrong. Terribly wrong. For a former Marine officer to say that about enlisted men is way out of line. He uses an example of junior troops during the Normandy invasion thinking that what they were doing was stupid, but the end result was capturing Berlin.

But here we seized Baghdad and Mosul in April 2003 but never won the war, in the first place—it's apples and oranges, historically. What's more, we're in a for-real guerrilla war here that he has seen nothing of—he left Iraq in the early summer 2003. We see what's actually going down on the ground.

This is a very different war, in the first place, than the European theater of World War II. There were definite front lines and rear areas, for instance, in Europe in World War II. This is in no way a conventional war.

How can Fick even think to compare this to World War II, on the ground? Has he actually read history? On the ground, this is a very, very different war than WWII. We are in a guerrilla war here, and we are not fighting to win the guerrilla war.

The Marine Corps talks about the strategic corporal and how junior troops can affect operations at a strategic level, that's fine. But what we see and do in combat, as strategic corporals, doesn't matter? That's a contradiction in terms.

History says that in a guerrilla war, you must listen to small-unit leaders, at all levels, from scout/sniper team leader and fire team leader on up, if you want to fight and win. If you want to fight effectively, from jump street. We really need to listen to our junior troops here, more than ever.

Look at Philip Caputo. In *A Rumor of War*, he came to the conclusion as a young Marine platoon commander in 1965 who listened to his junior troops, that the Vietnam War was pointless. But it took senior political and military leaders ten years to realize that. And more importantly, 58,000 American dead. And 2 million Vietnamese dead.

I just want to get the point across that in this kind of conflict, what we junior troops do matters. Our opinions matter. We see, every day, on the street and in the villages, what the Iraqi Army is doing. What the Fallujah Police are doing. What the Iraqis think, what they do, what they say. No one else sees that but us, around the clock.

So how's a general who spends 90 percent of his time in meetings at Camp Fallujah, and other camps, how's he going to know how good the Iraqi Security Forces are if he doesn't listen to his junior troops? If our opinions don't matter, who else is going to know?

We are on the tip of the spear in this war, and it is a guerrilla war. Small-unit leadership, fire team leadership, scout/sniper team leadership, and special ops leadership historically win or lose guerrilla wars.

Common sense and history dictate that you must listen to your junior troops if you want to win a guerrilla war. Fallujah, in microcosm, shows how we are failing in the Iraq War, in western Iraq and the Sunni Triangle.

I'm glad that everybody came through OK in our platoon. Unfortunately, it wasn't the same in the rest of the battalion. But I'm glad that everybody made it through OK. Ronin survived, and we're very grateful that we survived. I've been in three years and four months, and I've got eight months left in the Corps.

HM3 JOSHUA JAMES GUTIERREZ, PLATOON CORPSMAN, U.S. NAVY
Once I get back to Texas, in August 2006, I'll finish school. I'll have a B.S. in Criminal Justice. Hell, yes. I'm getting out. I'd like to start off lower-level in law enforcement, like county police or sheriff's department. Then I'd like to go into the U.S. Marshals or Alcohol, Tobacco and Firearms (ATF), something in federal law enforcement.

Zwirblia spoke truth on the three-day missions, sure. The three-day missions were tough. There were areas of interest near the river and the train tracks. Both our Ronin teams out

RONIN

there were tied up in another mission, so we decided to go and check these places out.

The first time we did it, we went out with a squad and dropped off from them about four klicks from our planned hide site. I fell into a canal and got a concussion. We extracted.

Two days later, we went back out on the same mission, just us three. We knocked out three of our objectives in a period of twenty-four hours. We couldn't get good visibility on the Euphrates. It was really far. Overall, it was twenty klicks, back and forth. Right, all we had was three M16A4s, plus our sidearms.

Definitely, the scout/snipers came and talked to me a lot about their frustrations with the battalion. Part of it was the missions that they were getting. Part of it was our chain of command, all the way up to the S-2, S-3, and the battalion commander.

I think that everybody above us had different ideas, very different ideas, of what they wanted the platoon to do. The platoon is trained to go out and take down terrorists. But they're also trained in reconnaissance and surveillance and counter-sniper operations—all core missions for Marine scout/snipers.

What the battalion wanted us to do, and what Ronin wanted to do, were definitely two different things. Overall, the platoon got very frustrated at their missions. Nothing worked out in our favor.

1st Recon didn't use us to the best of our ability. They've got their own missions that they run, and we've got different missions.

What 1st Recon wanted was no one stepping on their toes. Yes, they violated a classic principle in war: Listen to the man in the field, listen to the man who knows the turf, who knows the lay of the land. Exactly. They had not been on that terrain, and they wouldn't listen to us, who'd been on that terrain. I remember you telling us that, that night in December when 1st Recon's company commander told you, "I own 2/6 scout/snipers now."

That guy, he wouldn't even listen to us, and none of his men had walked the streets of Fallujah before that day. I don't want to say that they were cocky, but they didn't really want our help too much.

The African proverb is accurate, that is correct. Timeless. You don't send the whole village to kill one lion. Right, we didn't send our best lion hunters. They constrained us, and put our teams on OPs, while they went out and took houses. The whole mission was like that for one month.

Us static, behind concrete and barbed wire in OPs. 1st Recon just kept us on a very short leash. But 1st Recon didn't capture or kill one terrorist sniper. We hung tough, as a platoon, as Ronin. We endured.

Going to war with guys like this, Marine scout/snipers, who are tight-knit, gives you a bond that people who don't come over here, who don't see this, will never have. They don't have that kind of bond.

Twenty years down the road, I can give Areballo a call or Jay a call, and we'll still be friends. It opens your eyes to how life is. I think that this deployment has made my mind up about getting out of the Navy. I love my job and I love my country, but I hear it in my wife's voice, every time we talk, how straining it is on her. I'd rather be there for my wife now and start a family.

"I've heard this from many Marines: 'I joined the Marine Corps to defend my country. And right now in Fallujah, we're not defending our country, we're defending the insurgency.' . . . We are on a road to failure."

CORPORAL STEPHEN LUTZE,
RONIN4 LIGHT MACHINE GUNNER AND SCOUT/SNIPER,
MARCH 25, 2006

Three weeks before we flew from Kuwait to Ireland and on to America, Corporal Lutze spoke for many scout/snipers and Marines in a blistering, no holds-barred hour-long conversation, fueled by strong, hot, black coffee as small-arms fire cracked fifty meters away from us in Fallujah on March 25, 2006.

Lutze, who'd reenlisted in-country, spoke in the scout/snipers' hooch in the mortared and rocketed Marine command center in the heart of Fallujah, just south of Fran and east of the Euphrates.

Rats crawled at night, screeching, and the faded yellow and white painted plaster walls reeked of urine in piss bottles. Marines risked death slipping out to the portable toilets, for mortars and rockets had hit Fox Company 2/6 and the command center on a regular basis that March, so we'd piss in bottles and leave them outside the rooms until the stench was unbearable. Then one of us would bag them all up and sprint out to the trash cans, toss them in, and sprint back, all the while praying the Lord's Prayer and Hail Marys and a few Buddhist prayers. Two and a half years earlier, with U.S. Army paratrooper scout/sniper Sergeant Joseph

LeBleu of the 82nd Airborne, I'd walked that same compound in broad daylight without fear of being mortared, rocketed, or killed by terrorist snipers.

Looking at Fallujah: it's a goatfuck. Ba'athists run the show here. They want the dictatorship back. Our leadership, top to bottom, has their heads in the sand, with the exception of Major Dan Sullivan, who I would follow to hell and back.

The people of Fallujah do not show any gratitude for us fighting the insurgents and terrorists here. Our elected officials, and our generals in the Marine Corps, instead of showing interest in fighting the insurgency, they show more interest in winning hearts and minds and training the Iraqi Police, so the Iraqi Police can fight the insurgency. But the IPs *are* the insurgency. The IPs are the threat here; they are the enemy.

Most definitely, Marine command has armed our enemy. The decisions of our generals to keep giving the Fallujah Police more money has armed our enemy.

The IPs not only support terrorists and insurgents, they show their lack of caring at every turn. For instance, they sleep on posts all the time. We've caught them sleeping on post all the time. We've actually caught that on videotape. We videotaped that for proof. Also, they always like to joke around on post, eat, watch DVDs, smoke, not wear their flaks and helmets—it's all a game to the IPs.

At least 35 percent of the Fallujah Police are known, for-real terrorists and insurgents. And at least another 35 percent are borderline terrorists and insurgents. That's Fallujah, where we've invested tons of money in the Fallujah Police, in the IPs, in weapons, gear, vehicles, uniforms—and for what? For arming our enemy.

I think that our generals and our higher officials are not aggressive at fighting the insurgency. Their thinking is that by actually fighting the insurgency, that we will create more insurgents, so they believe that by trying to win hearts and minds, we will defeat the insurgency.

But the Kurds, who believe that by actually fighting and killing insurgents and terrorists, you crush the enemy's will to resist, are winning their guerrilla war in Northern Iraq. And the Kurds are fighting the same enemy we are, but with a radically different strategy—and it is a winning strategy.

We are on a failed road. In Fallujah, in western Iraq, we are on a road to doom and defeat. Bush has failed. He has utterly and completely failed to fight and win the guerrilla war here, and Bush has armed our enemies here. Marine command in western Iraq over the last two years has failed.

We are now accountable for more Al Qaeda cells being in Fallujah than ever before. The lack of aggressiveness and martial spirit, of boldness and daring from Marine command, has helped the terrorists and insurgents regain the terrain here. Ronin attaches to Marine infantry patrols. On patrol, always, I see middle-aged men, young men, teenagers, and children yelling at us in a hateful manner. Cursing us and telling us to leave.

We only control the hundred meters in front of the point man, the patrol itself, and the hundred meters in back of our tail-end Charlie. That's all we control in Fallujah. It's obvious that Marine command does not want us to go after high-value terrorist targets.

The Ahmed Sirhan incident in September is the best example of that, and there are many others. The fact that Marine command has invested so much in sheikhs and imams who support terrorists—in the case of Sheikh Khalid, who *are* terrorists—speaks directly to our failure to win here.

They don't want us to kill these terrorists, because if we kill a sheikh here or an imam there, command thinks that will create a larger insurgency. But when in war does *not killing your enemy* win you a war? Never.

The insurgents and terrorists here are getting exactly what they want.

We cannot change the minds of Sunni Arabs in Fallujah and western Iraq. I haven't seen it get better here. I've only seen it get worse, in the six months that I've been here in combat in Fallujah and Al Saqlawiyah.

There's only two options: Leave Fallujah and admit that we've failed. Or go through Fallujah again and take it. Be more strict.

Take the IPs away, do not allow the Iraqi Police safe haven anywhere in Fallujah and western Iraq, declare martial law, and bring 10,000 Kurdish peshmerga badged as Iraqi Army into Fallujah. The Kurds would then police Fallujah indefinitely. Arabs fear the Kurds. The Kurds can handle this; we can't—we don't have the political balls to take down Al Qaeda in western Iraq. The Kurds have the balls, and more importantly, they have the brains.

Bring 40,000 Kurdish peshmerga into western Iraq and end it. Link them up with Iraqi Army and U.S. Army Special Forces.

If the Shiites, and Kurds, and Sunnis were to unite as one nation, for real, the Sunni Arabs would still conduct terrorist activities against the Shia and the Kurds. The Sunni Arabs do not want a piece of the pie, they want the whole pie, the bakery, every wheat field the flour came from, and all the oil and gas running each engine of every delivery truck.

But the Kurds have crushed the insurgency throughout Iraqi Kurdistan; they will crush the insurgency in western Iraq. The Kurds know how to fight and win at guerrilla war. This is a guerrilla war; you do the math.

If we let the Kurds police Fallujah, it will take a few years, but at least it will start changing for the better. Because we can't continue doing what we're doing now: negotiating with the enemy. Bush has been arming and negotiating with the enemy for three years in western Iraq, and Bush has failed. Our entire national leadership has failed us, as Americans, and as Marines.

If they don't want to finish the job and clear Fallujah again, then the Kurdish solution is the best solution. It would be a helluva lot more effective than what we are doing now. What we are doing now is continuing to go down a road of failure.

I've heard this from many Marines: "I joined the Marine Corps to defend my country. And right now in Fallujah, we're not defending our country, we're defending the insurgency."

I'm not going to sugar-coat the situation here. It is what it is, and we are on a road to failure. We are defending the insurgency, not doing what we should be doing: killing the insurgents and terrorists and winning the war.

We've seen the big picture, the small picture, and the medium-sized picture. We know that we've been denied key intelligence on the enemy, and we know that we've been denied authority to kill our enemy here.

We know just how badly the big-picture strategy is failing here, because we've lived that strategy night and day. The Big Blue Arrow is a Big Tragic Disaster, perpetrated by Bush, who does not know how to fight, how to win, and especially, how to read and how to listen.

Let me state for the record that I will never forget the courtesy, valor, and honor of Staff Sergeant Travis Twiggs. Twiggs is the core of the Marine Corps: hard-core warrior, professional, listens to his men and has faith in his men, and is simply one of the best small-unit leaders in the world.

"You can't take a sheet of music, all written in London or Munich or New York or Washington or Paris, and hand it to a Bedouin musician in the sands of western Iraq and say, 'Now play that music, and love that music.' Money won't change that, either."

ISHMAEL AND JOSHUA,
CLANDESTINE FIELD OFFICERS

Call him Ishmael. He was born on an island and raised near the sea. English was the language by the water. He heard some French in his youth from young women whom he still remembers fondly after two decades and change of clandestine actions in the Near East, Europe, and Central Asia.

Forty-eight in the winter of the sniper, Ishmael was coming to the end of three years in Iraq. He carried a Sig Sauer P226 9-millimeter—a real nail-puncher, as American Special Forces like to say of that sidearm. He also carried a customized HK MP-5, with grips made to fit his hands, and a gangster grip that slips sideways like the old Sten submachine guns of World War II vintage. "Why can't the Yanks figure that out, lad? Strange old world," he said, slipping his HK under a brown leather jacket in Fallujah.

A colleague of his from across the Atlantic, dressed like a construction foreman in jeans and boots, handed us smokes. Call him Joshua. Fifty-one, his hair and goatee all salt and pepper, he wore dark aviator shades and a green and loam *khaffiyah* scarf around his neck.

He carried a 12-gauge sawed-off shotgun, with customized teak pistol grip, rigged under his jacket, and a Browning Hi Power

9-millimeter sidearm, with a thirteen-round clip, in a shoulder holster over a black cotton sweater. Ten more full clips for his Browning were sewn into the inside of a khaki canvas rancher's jacket, of
the sort worn by horse breeders in the American West.

In the winter of the sniper, these two clandestine field officers,
both with more than twenty years in the field in the Mediter-
ranean, the Near East, and Central Asia, spoke frankly of the Iraq
War and a strategy to end it.

Ishmael: We didn't win in Oman with fighter jets and
artillery cannons booming in the bloody night, bombs on call.
That creates more enemies, the last thing you need in any
war, especially a guerrilla war. It is impossible to get the Americans to listen, though—no offense, Joshua . . .

Joshua: None taken.

Ishmael: Do you know the expression, you can't fit the
music on the street to the music on the sheet? And you can't
force the music on the sheet to the music on the street.
Bloody good. I know that Joshua knows it well.

In our trade, you must tell exactly what the field has
revealed. You can't lie about what is bloody well going on
right in front of your nose.

You can't take a sheet of music, all written in London or
Munich or New York or Washington or Paris, and hand it to a
Bedouin musician in the sands of western Iraq and say, "Now
play that music, and love that music." Money won't change
that, either.

Why? Why ought he play that sheet of music? He's already
listening to the music on the street, so to speak. The music on
the street is the music of his culture. That's the melody he
grew up with, that's the melody he knows, maybe that's all he
knows, and that's the melody he will live by.

You can't fit the music on the street to the music on the
sheet. And likewise, you can't force the music on the sheet to
the music on the street. You've got to listen to the music on
the street first, improvise, adapt to it, learn from it, and use it
to your advantage.

Joshua: It's a lost cause, trying to convince Sunni Arabs to play the music on the sheet that Bush wrote in Washington, that Rice wants engraved on the soul of the Near East. The music on the sheet that we are forcing on Iraq. Look at the Sunni Arabs—have they ever for one minute since April 9, 2003, shown any remorse whatsoever for the triggers they pulled on Shia and Kurdish children here? The Sunnis applauded Saddam then, and they applaud him now. Correct, the mapmakers drew up this country, not the people. You've said it yourself, time and again: "Iraq is a map, not a country." Accurate. There is no just cause for the Kurds to be bound at the hip to the Sunnis, nor the Shia. Five thousand years of distinct, very different cultures live here.

The music on the sheet was written stateside. The music on the streets over here, as Ishmael says, is played in a whole different key, in the first place. The Sunni Arab sheikhs and imams, like corrupt South Vietnamese generals in my father's time, will smile and tell us what they think we want to hear. Then pay off Al Qaeda on the side and salt away what's left offshore. Money is all headed in the wrong direction here.

Ishmael: The saddest thing is that we *can* take down Al Qaeda here. We can fight and win here with much cleverer, far less expensive, and far more *effective* methods. But the Yanks refuse to think outside the box.

Get the Marines out of western Iraq. You can't win a counterterrorist campaign, that is at the heart of a guerrilla war, with line infantry, reconstruction aid, concrete and barbed wire, artillery and fighter jets.

Look at the terrorist snipers, exhibit A, winter of the sniper. Give me ten men fluent in Arabic who know Fallujan dialect and who all look Arabic, know the streets and deserts, and I'll find those snipers for you before the next pigeon shits on a mosque. I'll track those snipers and bury them.

What good is one Marine battalion, or ten Marine battalions, in Fallujah? You're guarding reconstruction aid, mate, not fighting a guerrilla war. Problem is, your enemy is fighting a guerrilla war, and he's not playing by the chords on Bush's sheet of music.

Joshua: Everything Bush is doing here is according to a failed plan. The plan never took into account the history, culture, and terrain, in the first place. The plan has busted. The emperor wears no clothes. The plan failed by the end of August 2003; no one listened to us then, or now.

U.S. military commanders, especially the Marines here, refuse to stop backing Sunni Arab sheikhs and imams that we know are in bed with Al Qaeda. There's no such thing as a little pregnant. Al Qaeda owns every mosque in western Iraq. When you own the mosques in any Muslim culture, you own the street, the markets, and everything on them.

Al Qaeda knows what it wants. Osama Bin Laden knows what he wants. Bush, Cheney, and their whole crew know what they want—money—and can't see past the Sunni Arabs and their money.

Al Qaeda doesn't give a hoot in hell about money, they just want to kill us. Al Qaeda wants to see us burn, they want to piss on our ashes, and they want to dance in the smoking rubble of the Lady in the Harbor.

The Kurds understand that, and we don't. Not as a people, not as a culture. Americans just want to click the remote and make the guerrilla war in Iraq disappear. You can't take down Al Qaeda if you're shaking their hand in Fallujah and appointing them to the Fallujah City Council—that's criminal, what Bush has done. And that old saw you hear from officers, "Well, it's above my pay grade": bullshit. It's not above my pay grade.

Nothing has changed, fundamentally, in how we're fighting—and more to the point, not fighting—Al Qaeda. Less than 300 clandestine field officers active in the field against Al Qaeda, right now. March 2006. That's in the entire world. Osama Bin Laden has well over 50,000 terrorist operatives, all covert, all active, all over the world as we speak. And all Al Qaeda has to do is go 100 percent with all human communication, no electronic transmissions of any kind, to easily defeat 99.9 percent of our intelligence-gathering capability. Turn off the cell phones, turn off the computers, and communicate face-to-face and by handwritten messages. Burn the messages after they're delivered. Satellites can't track you if they can't see you, also. One Al Qaeda terrorist under a load of loose straw in the back of a pickup truck, with holes cut into the frame for a sniper rifle, OK, he can roll up, get off at least one shot, and roll out, and not one piece of American technical intelligence saw him—not aerial surveillance, not satellites, nothing.

Now, if you've got significantly increased human intelligence assets on the ground, you've at least got a chance at taking him down—at listening in, in his language, to his plans, in the first place, at eyeballing his every move, 24/7. Satellites can't do that, but human eyes and ears can.

Al Qaeda brought the widow maker to our doorstep on September 11th, killed our people in cold blood, burned down a large part of the Pentagon, and what did Bush do? Build more layers of bureaucracy and put more people behind computers, stateside. Bush has ignored the consummate failure in human intelligence that led directly to September 11th. And you can't take down Al Qaeda with grunts, not in western Iraq or anywhere else. Remove all U.S. military from western Iraq, fight the counterterrorist fight with clandestine assets, and sign a permanent security agreement with the only friends we've got here: the Kurds. Permanent U.S. bases in Dahuk, Erbil, and Suleiymaniyah. Two U.S. Army divisions, one heavy, armored, along with U.S. Air Force assets and total linkup with Kurdish peshmerga and Kurdish counterterrorists.

Ishmael: That's the heart of the heart of this war, but the Yanks won't fight it, and they won't listen on how to fight and win a guerrilla war in the Near East. And for fuck's sake, we did that in Oman—we fought and won a guerrilla war against Arabs for twelve years with less than 200 SAS, '64 to '76. And we recruited Arabs, of the Al Dhofari tribes, to fight and win that war! It's not doctorate-level physics. It's guerrilla war, not rocket science. But you've got to know the languages, culture, and the terrain.

Bombs don't translate well in any culture. Every artillery shell that lies unexploded in Iraq right now that the Coalition has fired is a gift to the insurgency.

Joshua: Point well-taken. Agreed. You won in Oman, no doubt, largely because you concentrated on just that: fighting and winning a guerrilla war. You spoke the languages, read the turf, and knew the culture and history. And you never hesitated to focus on fighting the fight, smart and hard.

Ishmael: Well said, and that last point, on focus, is key. Key to victory in any guerrilla war. We were focused on taking down our enemy, killing our enemy, not on money—not on which contract should go to which corrupt sheikh who we know is in bed with the enemy.

Joshua: Exactly. Let's toast to taking down Ahmed Sirhan, when the Marines finally trust their scout/snipers. Hell, I'd buy you all a drink, but we're in a Muslim country. Tell Ronin survival is victory. Tell Bush that God takes care of fools and drunks, but He doesn't take care of goddamned fools. Payback is coming.

IN MEMORIAM

Sergeant Mark P. Adams, age twenty-five, Morrisville, North Carolina. Weapons 2/6. Killed in action by a roadside bomb on October 15, 2005, in Al Saqlawiyah, western Iraq.

Corporal Jared J. Kremm, age twenty-four, Huppaque, New York. 1st Platoon, Golf 2/6. Killed in action by mortar fire on October 27, 2005, in Al Saqlawiyah, western Iraq.

Corporal Robert Eckfield Jr., age twenty-three, Cleveland, Ohio. 1st Platoon, Golf 2/6. Killed in action by mortar fire on October 27, 2005, in Al Saqlawiyah, western Iraq.

Corporal Joshua D. Snyder, age twenty, Hampstead, Maryland. Echo 2/6. Killed by terrorist sniper fire on November 30, 2005, in Fallujah, western Iraq.

Corporal William G. Taylor, age twenty-six, Macon, Georgia. Weapons 2/6. Killed by terrorist sniper fire on November 30, 2005, in Fallujah, western Iraq.

Private First Class George A. Lutze II, age twenty-five, Virginia Beach, Virginia. U.S. Army. Killed in action by terrorist sniper fire on December 29, 2005, in Fallujah, western Iraq.

Corporal Albert P. Gettings, age twenty-seven, New Castle, Pennsylvania. Fox 2/6. Killed in action by terrorist sniper fire on January 5, 2006, in Fallujah, western Iraq.

Lance Corporal Ryan S. McCurdy, age twenty, Baton Rouge, Louisiana. Fox 2/6. Killed in action by terrorist sniper fire on January 5, 2006 in Fallujah, western Iraq.

Lance Corporal Kyle W. Brown, age twenty-two, Newport News, Virginia. Fox 2/6. Killed in action by terrorist sniper fire on January 7, 2006, in Fallujah, western Iraq.

Corporal Felipe C. Barbosa, age twenty-one, High Point, North Carolina. H&S 2/6. Died in non-hostile vehicle accident on January 28, 2006, in Fallujah, western Iraq.

Lance Corporal Bunny Long, age twenty-two. Modesto, California. Killed in action by suicide truck bomb on March 10, 2006, in Fallujah, western Iraq.

GLOSSARY

Aiken, Lieutenant Colonel Scott: Aiken, from Tennessee, was commanding officer of 2nd Battalion, 6th Marines, 2nd Marine Division, which he led into combat in Iraq in mid-September 2005.

Al Fajr: Arab term for the second battle of Fallujah, November 2004.

Barrett: The Barrett .50-caliber sniper's rifle. Very heavy, accurate, and powerful. No substitute for it when it comes to range. A Canadian sniper in Afghanistan has the farthest recorded kill in combat—2,450 meters, a mile and a half—with a .50-caliber sniper rifle.

Command-detonated: Setting off a charge by hand by running a wire to the explosive. You see what you destroy.

CT: Counterterrorism. The art and craft of taking down terrorist leaders and cells.

Custer: Lieutenant Colonel George Armstrong Custer, commander, 7th Cavalry. Custer refused to listen to his scouts at the Little Bighorn in the Dakota Territory on June 25, 1876. He ignored their firsthand reports of Sioux and Cheyenne warriors in the thousands. Later that day, Crazy Horse and many other braves and warriors, under the command of Sitting Bull, massacred Custer and 210 U.S. Army cavalrymen.

Delta Force: U.S. Army Special Forces Operational Detachment Delta, Combat Applications Group (SFOD-D, CAG). Modeled on the British Army Special Air Service Brigade (SAS). Founded in 1977 by Colonel Charles Beckwith, U.S. Army Special Forces. With U.S. Navy SEALs, tasked with military counterterrorism.

Erhabi: Arab term for terrorist. Iraqi Arabs unsympathetic to Al Qaeda, Black Flags Brigades, and other *erhabi* in Iraq do not use separate terms in Arabic for terrorist and insurgent—unlike Coalition intelligence and the U.S. military. The Iraqi Army, Kurdish *peshmerga*, and Kurdish counterterrorists—like Sunni Arab Iraqis—also make no distinction between Al Qaeda and other *erhabi* in Iraq.

Eyes-On, Eyeball, Scope: All terms that signify looking at something directly and are related to human intelligence—intelligence gained from human sources.

Field Intelligence: Intelligence gained in the field from both human and technical sources, primarily human, and interpreted in the field. Marine scout/snipers have a core mission to gather field intelligence at all times in combat.

.50-cal: Browning M2 .50-caliber heavy machine gun, nicknamed the Ma Deuce. Essentially the same heavy machine gun that the U.S. Army and Marine Corps have used to good effect in combat since World War II. Mounted on tanks, humvees, and guard posts.

Forty: Marine scout/sniper slang for the M40A3 7.62x51-millimeter long-barreled bolt-action sniper rifle, accurate out to 1,000 yards (915 meters). Exceptional sniper rifle, and generally regarded as one of the top five sniper rifles in the world.

Golf 2/6: Golf Company, 2nd Battalion, 6th Marine Regiment.

IA, IAs: Iraqi Army soldiers.

IED: Improvised explosive device, also known as a roadside bomb. Often dug into sides of roads, but also simply placed in mud or under trash near sidewalks in Iraq, thrown out of taxis, or placed in carcasses of dead animals. Remote-detonated by cell phone or other electronic means or command-detonated.

In the black: Put it in the black means to shoot a bullseye.

IP, IPs: The Iraqi Police. IPs discussed in this book are from Al Saqlawiyah Police Station and the Fallujah Police.

Iraqi Kurdistan: Autonomous region of Northern Iraq, defined geographically by the Gara and Zagros mountain ranges, settled by the Kurds for more than 6,000 years. The Kurds of Iraq, led by Mala Mustafa Barzani, declared revolution on September 11, 1961, to forge a nation. On October 15, 2005, 90 percent of the Kurds voted in favor of Kurdish independence. (See Peter Galbraith's magnificent book, *The End of Iraq.*)

LeBleu, Long Rifle: Sgt. Joseph LeBleu, Brooklyn, combat veteran, former U.S. Army Ranger and 82nd Airborne paratrooper scout, who still holds the farthest kill of any sniper in Fallujah: 1,100 meters, firing an SR-25.

M4: U.S. Army assault rifle. Also fires 5.56-millimeter. The M4 has a telescopic butt stock, is lightweight and reliable, and pops up quickly in your shoulder. Superior to the M16A4 in every way but stopping power (both rifles fire a varmint round, 5.56). U.S. Army rifle teams at Fort Benning have fired bullseyes with the M4 at 800 meters.

M203, or .203: The M203 grenade launcher/assault rifle, which fires both 40-millimeter grenades and 5.56-millimeter ammunition. First fielded in the Vietnam War. The M203 is the most versatile small-arms weapon fielded by the U.S. military.

M240G 7.62x51-millimeter medium machine gun: The workhorse of Marine infantry, a fairly heavy machine gun for light infantry but with an excellent reputation for not breaking down in combat. Mounted on gun trucks and also carried on foot patrols by Marine infantrymen. Referred to as a machine gun.

M16A4: M16A4 5.56-millimeter assault rifle. The Marine Corps assault rifle, also called "the musket." Long-barreled, awkward, heavy, and very poorly suited for urban combat.

OP: Observation post.

QRF: Quick reaction force.

RCT-8: Regimental Combat Team 8, 2nd Marine Division, in command of Fallujah from late January 2005 to late January 2006. Headquartered at Camp Fallujah.

Remote-detonate: Setting off an explosive remotely by electronic means such as a cell phone. You don't have to see what you are destroying.

Roadside bomb: Another name for an IED.

Ronin: Japanese term for "samurais without masters." Platoon name and radio call sign for Marine scout/snipers of 2nd Battalion 6th Marine Regiment, 2nd Marine Division, in Fallujah and western Iraq, September 2005–April 2006. 2/6 Marine scout/snipers named themselves Ronin in July 2005, before entering Iraq.

RPG: Rocket-propelled grenade.

SAW M249 5.56-millimeter light machine gun: squad automatic weapon (SAW) for U.S. Marine infantry and U.S. Army infantry. Referred to as a light machine gun.

SR-25: The SR-25 7.62x51-millimeter (NATO round) semi-automatic sniper rifle, favored by U.S. Navy SEALs and also carried by U.S. Army Rangers, U.S. Army Special Forces, and U.S. Army infantry scouts. Combat effective range is classified.

Stalking: The art and craft of tracking your enemy without being detected, on any terrain. Stalking is one of the primary skills of a Marine scout/sniper.

Sullivan, Major Dan: Sullivan of Huntington, Long Island, was the 2nd Battalion, 6th Marines, executive officer in Iraq, since promoted to lieutenant colonel and on duty at the Joint Chiefs of Staff, Pentagon. Deeply respected by Ronin scout/snipers and 2/6 Marine infantrymen.

Terp: Interpreter.

2/6: 2nd Battalion, 6th Marine Regiment, 2nd Marine Division. Combat tour in Fallujah and western Iraq: September 2005–April 2006. Last units of 2/6 left Fallujah on April 11, 2006, with Ronin.

BIBLIOGRAPHY

Aeschylus. *The Orestia.* Robert Fagles, translator. New York: Viking, 1975.

Beowulf. Kevin Crossley-Holland, translator. London: UP Oxford, 1999.

Galbraith, Peter. *The End of Iraq.* New York: Simon and Schuster, 2006.

Gunaratna, Rohan. *Inside Al Qaeda.* New York: Berkley, 2003.

Hemingway, Ernest. *True at First Light.* London: William Heinemann, 1999.

Henderson, Charles. *Marine Sniper.* New York: Berkley, 1988.

Jeapes, Tony, Major General. *S.A.S. Secret War: Operation Storm in the Middle East.* London: Greenhill Books, 2005.

Lewis, Bernard. *The Assassins.* New York: Basic Books, 2003.

McCourt, Frank. *Angela's Ashes.* New York: Touchstone, 1999.

Saigyo. *Poems of a Mountain Home.* Burton Watson, translator. New York: UP Columbia, 1991.

Shakespeare, William. *Henry V.* London: Penguin, 1994.

Tucker, Mike. *The Long Patrol.* Bangkok: Asia Books, 2003.

———. *Hell Is Over.* Guilford, CT: Lyons Press, 2004.

———. *Among Warriors in Iraq.* Guilford, CT: Lyons Press, 2005.

Tzu, Sun. *The Art of War.* Edited and with foreword by James Clavell. New York: Delta, 1988.

ACKNOWLEDGMENTS

With gratitude and thanks to: Ronin scout/snipers; Staff Sergeant Travis Twiggs, combat tracker and Marine infantryman, 1st Platoon Sergeant, Golf 2/6; Lieutenant Colonel Daniel Sullivan, Joint Chiefs of Staff, Pentagon; Captain Martin Keogh, U.S. Marine Corps, infantry, Black Label gun truck platoon commander, Weapons Company 2/6; Black Label gun truck Marine infantrymen and their company commander, Major Thomas Ziegler; Major Kirk Windmueller, U.S. Army Special Forces; "Sev" and "Honcho," U.S. Army 10th Group Special Forces commandos; Kurdish counterterrorist commandos and commanders, Dahuk, Iraqi Kurdistan, and Mosul, Northern Iraq; Western intelligence services' clandestine field agents, Near East, Central Asia, and Far East; Western intelligence services' station chiefs, Near East; Headquarters Marine Corps Public Affairs Office, Pentagon; Dr. Anthony Eksterowicz, PhD, professor of political science, James Madison University, Harrisonburg, Virginia; and Joe LeBleu, former U.S. Army Ranger and sniper team leader.

INDEX

LeBleu, Joseph, 154, 190
Long, Lance Corporal, 146–47, 158
  suicide truck bomb attack and,
    149–51
Loper, Mike, 176–77
  tours of duty experiences, 177–79
Lutze, Stephen, xii, xxii, xxvi, 21, 22,
    24–25, 154, 161, 163, 164, 174
  on Iraqi Police, 115
  on Ronin4's October 5th mission,
    26–32
  tour of duty experiences, 190–94

Matter, John, xxv, 55, 56, 78, 122, 123,
    152
  on failure to take down Sirhan and
    Black Flags Brigades, 59–67
Matthews, James, 38–43, 46
  on Al Saqlawiyah Police Station
    assault, 40–43
  on death of Adams, 42–43
Milstid, Daniel, xii, xxii, xxv, 11, 24,
    55
  on failure to take down Sirhan and
    Black Flags Brigades, 65, 66
minarets, 52
Mohammed, Lieutenant, 135, 136–37
  on Fallujah Police, 137–44
Morley-Mower, Geoffrey, 3
mosques, 39, 98–108
  Al Qaeda in, 52–54
  Jama Al Raqueeb, 102–3, 104
  Jama Badawi, 105–6
  Jama Furqan, 103–4
  Jama Ma'adhiya, 101, 105
  Marines forbidden to enter, 48
Muhammad (interpreter), 65
  on Al Qaeda in mosques, 52–54
Muller, Michael, vi, xxviii, 73, 98–100,
    107, 112, 123, 133, 152
  on mosques, 100–6
Murphy, Timothy, xxviii, 49–50, 73,
    98, 99–100, 102, 112, 123, 133,
    152
  on mosques, 104–8

Novi, Justin, xii, 2, 21, 22, 23, 24, 117,
    174
  on Marines refusal to use Ronin,
    122–26
  on Ronin 4's October 5th mission,
    26–32
  tours of duty experiences, xix–xxx

Owen, James, xii, xxii, xxv, 180,
    181–82
  tour of duty experiences, 185–87

Palmer, Kyle, xii, 10, 76
Parker, Bobby Gene, xi, xxv, 161, 162
  Ronin 1 experiences, 167–70
Parra, Efraim, xi, xx, xxi, xxiii, xxiv,
    21, 145, 161, 162, 163, 168, 174,
    176
  on Keogh, 109
  Ronin1 experiences, 164–67

Ronin
  chronological significant actions of,
    xiii–xvii
  Marines refusal to use, 117, 119–27
  naming of, 1, 2
  teams, xi–xii
Ronin1, 161
  Getscher on experiences of, 174–75
  Hillestad on experiences of, 171–73
  Parker on experiences of, 167–70
  Parra on experiences of, 164–67
Ronin4
  interview with men of, after Octo-
    ber 5th mission, 26–32
  October 5th mission, 22–23
rules of engagement, 20

Sattar, Abdul, Sheikh, 100, 101, 102,
    104
Sebastian, Brian, 7
September 11th, Vergara on, 87–88
Shankhah, Sa'ad Ismail, Sheikh, 105
Shark's Fin, 23
Sirhan, Ahmed, 146, 171, 192
  failure to capture or kill, 4–5,
    12–17, 55–67